AUTISM IN THE SCHOOL-AGED CHILD

D1609079

Expanding Behavioral Strategies and Promoting Success

By Carol Schmidt, RN, BSN
and Beth Heybyrne, MA

Autism in the School-Aged Child
Published by Autism Family Press
2366 South Milwaukee Street
Denver, CO 80210

Information provided in this book is not intended to serve as a substitute for medical evaluation, diagnosis, or intervention with respect to any condition along the autism spectrum. The authors provide no guarantees of outcome based on the implementation of the strategies presented in this book. The information herein is presented in the belief that principles and strategies that have been helpful to some particular individuals will also be helpful to other similar individuals. The authors shall not be held responsible or liable for any undesired outcome as a result of the use of this book.

Copyright©2004 Carol Schmidt and Beth Heybyrne

All rights reserved. No part of this book may be reproduced in any form or by any means without the prior written permission of the publisher, with the exception of pages designated for reproduction or distribution. These pages may be reproduced by parents for use with their own child, or by professionals for use with their clients, but not for distribution to a group of professionals or parents, a school district, school, or clinic. All reproduced materials are intended to be used in conjuction with the book, Autism in the School-Aged Child and not in isolation.

ISBN Number: 0-9674969-3-4

Library of Congress: Control Number: 2004092374

Website: www.autisminschool.com

Printed in the United States of America

2004—First Edition

To God our Father, whose ways are perfect-even in autism.

To Jesus Christ, who gives sight to the blind-even the mindblind.

To the Holy One, who gives wisdom and understanding.

And to Carter, who makes my joy complete.

Carol Schmidt

To Carter, who has taught me how to see the spaces between the words.

Beth Heybyrne

Authors' Note

The information in this book is a compilation of observations made over a period of six years in a variety of settings including, but not limited to: preschool, early childhood education, kindergarten through third grade, extracurricular activities, vacation settings, and home. The strategies developed in this book are applications of behavioral theory and practice, which were preceded by early and intensive behavioral intervention. The authors believe that the principles and strategies set forth in this book may be beneficial to many parents and educators who work with children who have autism. Although some existing research and therapies for autism are addressed and referenced in this book, it is beyond the scope of this particular book to discuss them in depth. The reader is referred to other sources with respect to the theory and practice of behavioral intervention. In addition, the majority of the information presented in this book is the result of direct observation, evaluation, and intervention involving single subject research. This information is offered in the hopes that what has been helpful for one family may also be helpful for others. It is presented as a contribution to the parent and educational community of those who are committed to fulfilling the potential of each unique individual affected by autism. Any application of the information in this book should be made with discretion, keeping in mind the considerable variation within the spectrum of autism as a diagnosis, and the unique nature of individuals affected by it. The authors provide no guarantees of outcome based on the implementation of the strategies presented in this book.

About the Authors:

Carol Schmidt, RN, BSN, received her Bachelor Degree in Nursing from the University of Wisconsin. She is the mother of two children, ages 7 and 9, the older of which is affected by autism. She gained knowledge and experience in Applied Behavioral Analysis through her son's early and intensive intervention. She has been involved in all aspects of his education including discrete trial training, curriculum development, educational planning, evaluation, and intervention. She has assisted numerous families in the application of behavioral theory and practice in both the home and school settings. She has collaborated with educators, both those in general and special education, to develop and implement successful strategies for children with autism in the classroom. Her emphasis on consistent and systematic behavioral intervention across life settings, with continuity between school and home, has been highly successful. She resides in Denver, Colorado with her husband Rob and their two children.

Beth Heybyrne, BA, MA, received her Bachelor Degree in Elementary Education from Plattsburgh State University, and her Master's Degree in Special Education from the University of Colorado. She gained expertise in the principles and practice of Applied Behavioral Analysis through her experiences as a behavioral therapist and classroom paraprofessional. Her experiences include discrete trial training, curriculum development, and educational planning in both the home and school setting for a variety of children with autism. She teaches special education at the elementary school level. She resides in Evergreen, Colorado.

AUTISM IN THE SCHOOL-AGED CHILD:
Expanding Behavioral Strategies and Promoting Success

How to Use this Book:

School:

Home:

Acknowledgements

We are deeply indebted to our families and friends, who believed in us and have encouraged our efforts to make this book a reality. To my husband, Rob, whose love and friendship carried me through the darkest time of my life. To my daughter, Haley, my treasure, whose sparkling eyes and incandescent smile bring beauty to our world. To Carter, who is precious in the sight of God and an unspeakable gift to us.

We thank Rob Nelson for his gifted graphics that breathed life into our words. We thank Victoria and Gary Beck for their inspiration, exemplary example, and direction for this project. We thank the teaching staff at University Park Elementary School for their partnership in educating a very special child. We thank Dr. Annette Groen, for her expertise in Applied Behavioral Analysis that was instrumental in our efforts to overcome the effects of autism.

Carol Schmidt

To my Matt,
Thank you for your knowing words and endless encouragement.

Beth Heybyrne

HOW TO USE THIS BOOK

The strategies presented in this book are based on the theory and practice of Applied Behavioral Analysis (ABA). Although ABA is by no means the only intervention in the treatment of autism, it is the premise for the information presented in this book. The need for predictable experiences, structure, and uniformity are life-long in nature, and the behavioral approach has much to offer those who are involved in the education of persons with autism. This book is designed to assist parents and educators in the continued process of applying behavioral principles within the more natural environments of school and home. Each chapter is organized in a similar fashion, with examples and reproducible summaries for easy reference. Examples are intended to cultivate useful ideas, whether they are implemented as stated or adapted to meet the individual's needs. Example checklists are provided for the school, home, and extracurricular setting and can be adapted for use with children in preschool through 2nd grade. Use with older children may require adaptation of existing examples.

Overview of Applied Behavioral Analysis

Identify target behavior

Reward desired behavior

Achieve mastery

Institute cost response

Limit number of targets

Prompt for success

Overview of Applied Behavioral Analysis

Applied Behavioral Analysis (ABA) refers to the systematic application of behavioral intervention using discrete trial training. Behaviors are isolated and individually addressed, with complex behaviors broken down into components that are each mastered and then chained together. Techniques of prompting, shaping, chaining, and positive reinforcement are highly specific and clearly defined. Initially, intervention is one-on-one in a controlled environment, free of distractions. Data collection allows for immediate identification of progress as well as problems. The immediate goal is to gain mastery of a specific target behavior, which is defined as 90-100% correct response, unprompted, on three consecutive occasions, or with two different therapists. Data collection also identifies acquisition rates, which, if below 70% correct response, indicates that the targeted behavior should be modified to ensure success. In other words, the child is struggling with a task or concept and will most likely benefit from a slightly different approach. The emphasis on success ensures that the child is producing behaviors that can be rewarded. This is essential since the premise is that *behavior that is rewarded will be repeated.* Without something to reward, there will not be progression. Reinforcement is selected and altered based on its ability to motivate the child to produce on-task behavior. Evaluation of the child's skill acquisition is constant and dynamic, enabling both strengths and weaknesses to be addressed.

It is beyond the scope of this book to discuss behavioral methodology in detail. However, the following highlights represent the foundational principles of the interventions presented in this book:

Reward desirable behavior. Behavior that is rewarded will be repeated. The interventions in this book are based on a system of positive reinforcement. Specific behaviors are identified and targeted, followed by immediate reinforcement with a highly desirable item. Immediate reinforcement is systematically delayed until the behavior can be produced with delayed gratification. The child learns to repeat the

target behavior because behavior that is rewarded will be repeated. Early research in behavioral analysis and intervention with children with autism employed aversives (punishment) for unwanted behavior. This approach has fallen out of favor and, when used, is reserved for self-abusive or destructive behavior. Research has determined that positive reinforcement for desired target behaviors is highly effective in the education of children with autism. Intervention is most effective in producing lasting gains if it is administered in a systematic, consistent, and intensive fashion while the child is young. Once initial skills are acquired and the child is "learning how to learn," progress may be enhanced by the addition of a cost response. A cost response is a negative reinforcement rather than an aversive; it is the loss rather than gain of a desired item, producing a positive change in behaviors. For example, if the child earns five minutes of computer time for reading his book quietly, he may also lose five minutes of computer time for not reading his book quietly. Clearly, this differs from being punished for failing to complete the task. In the same respect, adults who do not show up for work usually do not get paid.

Do not, directly or indirectly, reward undesirable behavior. Few people would directly reward an undesirable behavior. However, careful observation should be made to ensure that unwanted behavior is not inadvertently rewarded. The classic example of this occurs frequently with typical children: the child is given a directive, such as "Put your coat on." Having no interest in putting his coat on, he responds by acting out, complaining, or tantruming. The uncomfortable parent, wanting to stop the negative behavior, gives in to the child and changes the required behavior, such as, "Fine, you'll probably freeze, but you don't have to wear a coat if you don't want to." Thus, the child learns that by acting out, complaining, or tantruming that he will get what he wants; his behavior is rewarded and most likely will be repeated. Certainly, some situations are much subtler, and may require multiple observers or methods of evaluation to determine whether inadvertent reinforcement is occurring. Problems in acquisition or mastery (defined in this book as unprompted task completion on three consecutive occasions) of a behavior may be the result of inadvertent reinforcement, which, once identified, can be remedied.

Clearly identify and define target behavior. Discrete behaviors must be identified and quantified, for the child, the parents, and the educators. Each task must be broken down into component behaviors that can be individually targeted for acquisition and mastery. Global behaviors and tasks can thus be accomplished through the incremental mastery of their component parts. For example, the morning entrance routine at school can be addressed by individually teaching each part:

"Get ready for school" means
1) Hang up your coat
2) Take everything out of your backpack.
3) Check the job board.
4) It's time for quiet reading, find your book of the week
5) Sit at your desk to read."

After each component is mastered, the child can be required to complete the entrance routine in its entirety. Complex tasks and behaviors become manageable when broken down and clearly delineated. Task delineation should be presented in writing and include a description of the instruction, the expected response of the child, as well as how and how often reinforcement will occur. For example:

Target: child will raise his hand one time during morning group time to make a correction in the morning message.

Response: child raises his hand at least once, and offers an appropriate, albeit not necessarily correct, suggestion such as "That sentence needs a question mark because it starts with the word 'Who'." Answers must be on topic.

Reinforcement: the teacher gives the child a (+) card to put in his pocket, which is worth 5 minutes of playtime after school. The child understands that the teacher will give the (+) at the end of group time.

Set aside reinforcers for exclusive use. A reinforcer can be anything that will motivate the child to repeat the target behavior. Traditionally, reinforcers have been classified into two categories, primary and secondary. Primary reinforcers are tangible items such as favorite foods, drinks, toys, or tokens that can be exchanged for highly desirable items or activities. Secondary reinforcers are often relational in nature, such as praise, hugs, tickles, or interactive games. Reinforcement must be powerful enough (and meaningful enough) to ensure that the child acts upon the target; thus, reinforcement cannot be freely available to the child. Parents and educators must observe what objects or activities evoke a positive or enthusiastic response from the child, and then set them apart for use during teaching sessions.

Reward achievement of target behavior with positive reinforcement. The child must clearly understand the association between his response to the target instruction and the resultant reward. Reinforcement of any kind should always be accompanied by praise that is behavior specific, for example, "Good work raising your hand for the correction."

Achieve mastery before withholding rewards or using negative reinforcement (cost response). Desired behavior is first acquired and maintained exclusively by the use of positive reinforcement. Over time, some (but not all) children may require the use of a cost response for several reasons:

1. Mastered elements lose immediate or all reinforcement over time. New targets are added and prioritized such that behaviors that the child now accomplishes independently are no longer reinforced, but are nonetheless still required.

2. Mastered elements may not be intrinsically reinforcing; thus, motivation to continue doing them is low.

3. Children with autism, like all children, vary in personality. They exhibit varying degrees of social awareness and understanding. While typical children may maintain certain behaviors because they want to please a parent or teacher, the child with autism most likely will not. Motivation is often artificial in nature but meaningful to the child. When a situation changes and reinforcement is faded out, alternative means of motivation may become necessary. A cost response is the loss of a privilege, token or other form of reward that the child has earned. A cost response should not be administered without fair warning. The goal is

a positive change in behavior, which, if accomplished simply by the threat of a loss, is accomplished nonetheless. If the child does not heed the warning, following through with the cost response is essential. For example:

"Quiet reading is mastered. You no longer get a (+) for that. Second graders are expected to read quietly until the timer goes off. If you aren't reading, you will lose a (+)."

Keep the number of targets small. Achieve mastery of each individual target. Once each component behavior is mastered, consolidate them into their larger target. For example, "Pack your lunch," "Put your homework in your back pack," and "Brush your teeth after breakfast" can become "Get ready for school." Continue to introduce new targets while still requiring that previous targets be completed independently and consistently. Without limiting the child to a definitive number of targets, it is generally recommended to have no more than three targets at a time. However, activity specific targets during the course of a school day may be as many as 10 to 12. In this case, there is only one target behavior required at a time, but the behavior varies with the activity. For example, during morning group time, the child may be required to raise his hand once to answer a question. During quiet reading time, he may be required to read one book of his choice for the entire time, re-reading if time permits. He may be required to complete his classroom "job" independently once mastery is achieved, and so on. In the home setting, target behaviors may be limited to three items such as following a morning schedule independently, checking a homework folder for work yet to be completed, and acting calmly out at bedtime.

Prompt for success. Without success, there is nothing to reward. Evaluation of a target is ongoing and dynamic. The child's response must determine what follows. If the rate of acquisition drops below 70% over several trials, the target must be changed to promote success. If the child acquires the behavior with ease it should be advanced quickly to the next target behavior. Prompts must be systematically faded out to prevent prompt dependency. Only the least necessary prompt to achieve the behavior should be used. The behavioral plan should include systematic fading of prompts.

The purpose of this book is to build on the strong foundation of discrete trial training, expanding the higher-functioning child's ability to learn in "real-world" settings. It is understood that each child is unique and as such, intervention must be individualized. The established principles of behavioral intervention are often discarded as the child matures because discrete trials are more difficult to establish in the natural setting of school or home. In addition, the environment now contains variables previously controlled in the one-on-one setting. Rather than abandon the principles that have produced success, parents and educators should recognize that children with autism have a very unique style of learning that must be considered in a variety of settings. Offering support and accommodations without modifications is essential to fulfilling the child's potential in a multitude of life situations, as well as to the development of independence. There may be confusion regarding the use of the terms modifications and accomodations as they have been used interchangeably to refer to both supports that modify the task as well as alterations in required outcome. For the purposes of this book, accommodation refers to strategies designed to support individual learning needs to promote success. Modification refers to altered, and therefore reduced, expectations or required outcomes.

- Get Ready for School
- Finish Homework
- Check Weather Forecast before leaving

Expanding Behavioral Strategies

The expansion of the behavioral technique to natural environments, whether at home or at school, will not occur without effort. Classically, children with autism do not generalize their skills to new settings or new routines without some supportive intervention. Application of behavioral principles and techniques should include the following:

Environmental prompts. The classroom environment, routines, and teacher's individual style should be observed to determine existing elements that can be utilized for prompts. For example, a written schedule posted for the benefit of all the children is a natural visual prompt that the child with autism can use to determine appropriate on-task behaviors, start and finish times, or activity sequence. Or, if the teacher uses a certain approach with all the children, such as "My attendance chart shows that Sara is not here today. Please come and correct that," then the child with autism can be instructed to respond to this same directive. Existing prompts should be examined for their usefulness prior to the addition of prompts or supports designed solely for the child with autism. That is not to say that additional supports are to be avoided, but simply that an existing prompt that elicits the desired behavior is a natural and effortless choice. Conversely, there may be existing cues that fail to adequately prompt the child. Once existing supports are put into use, additional supports are incorporated based on the child's individual needs.

Fade Prompts. Continued prompt dependency occurs easily when prompts are not quickly and systematically faded out. Failure to incorporate prompt fading into the acquisition plan often results in slow acquisition or inability to achieve mastery. The prompt dependent child learns quickly how little he can do to satisfy the behavioral requirement, knowing that if he waits long enough, someone will do it for him. Visual prompts are easier to fade than verbal prompts, as the child is better equipped to internalize a routine that is presented in a visual format. For example, a detailed instruction for independent desk work may initially look like this:

Find out what to do:
Listen to the teacher's instructions.

Look at the instructions on the board.

Look at what the other kids are doing.

Ask if you still don't know what to do.

Do it by yourself.

Raise your hand when you're done.
The teacher will give you your (+).

The child can work independently with a cue card on his desk. Once he has demonstrated mastery, the cue card can be reduced to its key elements:

Find out: Listen, Look, Ask Last
Do it.
Raise hand.

Finally, the cue card can be eliminated. If initial mastery drifts, an indirect verbal prompt such as "What are you supposed to be doing?" or "How can you find out what to do?" may be all that is necessary to regain the behavior. A cost response is also a useful technique for ensuring continued on-task behavior, or for extinguishing undesirable behavior.

Intrinsic Rewards. In the same manner that existing prompts are examined before introducing artificial ones, so too intrinsic rewards should be identified and utilized before introducing artificial reinforcement. For example, if the teacher allows the children to play a board game when their deskwork is completed, the child with autism who enjoys board games may be intrinsically motivated to finish his work. The parents and educators must be familiar with the types of activities that naturally motivate the child to work. Once the environment has been examined, additional means of reinforcement can be incorporated as needed to encourage on-task behavior. Chapter 2 addresses the concept and implementation of a token economy in detail.

Maintain mastered behavior. Behaviors that the child has demonstrated on a consistent basis must be internalized into his routine. He must assume responsibility for maintaining them, and the parent or educator must hold him accountable through negative reinforcement (cost response).

Advancement of target behaviors. As the child succeeds, behaviors will be mastered and new targets will be continually introduced. The list of behaviors on acquisition is thus dynamic, rather than static, frequently upgraded in response to the child's demonstration of mastery. The child should always be aware of the current targets, which are clearly delineated tasks, each with its corresponding, acceptable response and subsequent reinforcement. *The child knows at all times what he is supposed to do and what he will earn when he does it.* Parents and educators should evaluate targets both on a daily basis and over time, to determine the rate of acquisition and thus evaluate the child's success with each target.

1. Is the child's response below the desired 70% success rate? In this case, the target should be evaluated.

2. Does the child clearly understand the required task? If the answer is "no", then the child should be given instructions in an alternative fashion or provided with support. For example, written directions on a worksheet may be overwhelming in length, or confusing due to unfamiliar vocabulary. "Translating" the directions or breaking them down into several simple steps may be all that is necessary for the child to proceed. If it is apparent that the child understands the required task, yet still cannot respond at 70% or higher, then the reinforcement must be examined for adequacy. The unmotivated child is unlikely to demonstrate acquisition or mastery. If the reinforcement is powerful enough, yet the child is still struggling below the 70% response rate, then the target should be modified to produce success.

Reducing the behavior to its component elements, introducing visual supports, or diminishing the requirement will most likely boost the acquisition rate above 70%.

3. Is the percentage of correct responses increasing or decreasing over time ? If the percentage is increasing, allow the child time to progress. Encourage progress with both primary and secondary reinforcement. If the percentage is decreasing, evaluate the reinforcement and increase it accordingly. Target behaviors can be systematically presented using a Target Behavior Checklist, development and implementation of which is addressed in Chapter 1.

Acquisition of global rather than activity-specific skills. Initially, skills acquired in the school setting result from activity-specific targets. In this method, isolated skills are associated with certain activities in which they naturally occur. For example, hand-raising participation is a naturally occurring element of a group discussion time, so it makes sense to utilize this activity for acquisition of hand-raising skills. However, over time the child must adapt this skill to the global classroom environment, adding discrimination elements so that he raises his hand in response to a question rather than simply at a designated time. Global skills build on the foundation of a variety of activity-specific skills, which are then generalized to a variety of settings. Generalization of skills are crucial to a child's long-term success in the classroom.

Promoting Successful Communication

Studies indicate that there are two main factors that influence the best outcome of a person with autism as they enter adulthood: the early development of expressive language, and a non-verbal IQ of 70 or higher (Howlin, p. 26). This book is designed to build on the foundation of early intervention by expanding language and promoting independence through specific target behaviors. Strategies for expanding language development are integrated throughout this book based on promoting success in specific areas such as classroom participation (Ch. 6), socialization (Ch. 7), and sibling interactions (Ch. 18).

Verbal vs. Nonverbal Child. Although the techniques and examples in this book are intended for use with verbal children, the principles can be applied to non-verbal children as well. Clearly, the modifications and supports necessary for the non-verbal child will vary from those of the verbal child. Thoughtful consideration should be made regarding the classroom placement of the non-verbal child so that he is given the best opportunity to succeed.

Comprehension deficits. Children with autism who have developed expressive language may demonstrate comprehension levels inconsistent with their vocabulary. This becomes problematic when it is presumed that they understand fully what is said to them or by them, resulting in an overestimation of their competence. Difficulties with abstract language such as descriptive language, prediction, explanations, and inference are common elements of the challenges inherent in language use for the person with autism (Maurice, p. 316).

Problems with delivery of language. Poor understanding of social rules and the impact communication has on others is at the core of language delivery problems. Literalness, bluntness, repetitive speech, and odd semantic patterns are common among even the highest functioning individuals. Problems with intonation and delivery such as stilted, mechanical, or poorly modulated speech may give the mistaken impression of lower intelligence in a child of adequate cognition (Howlin, p.31-40). Any of these speech anomalies can be annoying at best and intolerable at worst. Furthermore, the lack of reciprocity with conversational language only adds to the social isolation that so commonly exists among the socially impaired. Specific strategies for improving socialization can be found in Ch. 7.

Subtle Language Deficits. The child with autism may demonstrate a variety of subtle language deficits that may set him apart from his typically functioning peers. Often, conversational skills are weak and contextual cues are missed. A child may struggle with initiating, maintaining, or extending a conversation. He may contribute odd, off-topic remarks. He may insist on using names rather than pronouns, to the extent that the conversation sounds emotionally disconnected. He may fail to reciprocate conversation, preferring the comfort of isolated topics and narrow interests. Any or all of these characteristics can contribute to compromised social skills, rejection, and ridicule.

These subtle language deficits will clearly set the child apart as he attempts to participate in the classroom. Parents and educators may be at a loss as to how to manage such anomalies. Specific strategies are addressed in Ch. 6.

Elements of language acquisition are addressed specifically as they relate to the issues of participation and socialization, wherever these arise in the remainder of the book. Of particular concern is the perseverative nature of verbalizations that can contribute to inattention. As the child with autism grows, collections of objects may be replaced with collections of facts and information (Howlin, p.99). These "verbal obsessions" may become more involved with age and may serve many purposes from elimination of boredom to anxiety management. Nonetheless, these verbal behaviors are particularly problematic, as they are much more difficult to monitor, modify, or extinguish. Identifying the antecedent, that is the function of the behavior, is helpful in determining a management plan. In general, gradual changes are more effective than an all-out ban on the behavior, which may result instead in an escalation rather than an extinction. It is imperative that these behaviors be identified and attended to early in life, before they become entrenched and unmanageable later. In addition to these negative communication styles, children with autism often have difficulty with word retrieval, pronouns, and semantics. General strategies for improving communication include:

1. Increase the child's understanding of appropriate speech. For example, "Your friends like it when you ask them about *their* interests, not just yours. "What do you think Tommy likes to talk about?"
2. Decrease the use of inappropriate speech. For example, "It's weird to keep repeating the same thing over and over. Children may not want to play with you when you do that."
3. Decrease anxiety to minimize verbal obsessions. For example, "I know that you feel nervous when you have to wait in line. There are only three more people ahead of us so we will be done soon. It's not OK to talk to everyone here about prime numbers. You can talk about the movie you are going to see or just wait quietly."
4. Reduce the attention gained for inappropriate speech. For example, "It's nice that the other kids call you the "globe master," but not everyone likes geography as much as you do. Before we go to Joey's party, I want you to make a list of three other things you can talk about."
5. Set limits on when, where, how often, and with whom verbal obsessions may occur. For example, "You may talk about trains only when we are at home, and only at dinner."
6. Teach alternative skills. For example, "I'm a little tired of hearing about animals. Let's play 20 Questions instead."

Although language development is not specifically addressed in this book, the more appropriate and socially functional language that the child with autism gains, the better off he will be in the social arena, vocationally, and as an independent adult. As parents and educators work cooperatively to maximize the potential of the child with autism, they can be encouraged that their efforts today will reap benefits both for the immediate setting, and for the long-term. With autism, the future is now.

CHAPTER 1

TARGET BEHAVIOR CHECKLISTS
The tool and the technique
Introduction

Success in the classroom environment can be achieved by using a target behavior checklist. This beneficial tool provides structure, routine, and predictability across various educational settings. Initially, the checklist will be activity based, focusing on specific tasks or behaviors within designated contexts. Continued success can be achieved by advancing to a skill-based checklist in which targets are global rather than activity specific. Skills such as information seeking and self-regulation are useful in all educational settings. Eventually, the child can internalize and generalize the principles, thus progressing toward independence.

Domain

1. School
2. Home
3. Extracurricular Activities

Approach

Activity-based checklist

An activity-based checklist is the starting point for a behavioral intervention plan and provides the following:

Individualization. Each checklist is designed specifically for a particular child, incorporating details from his or her own classroom routine, schedule, and expectations. Specific targets are identified for each activity, allowing for on-task behavior throughout the course of the school day. Instructions on how to develop a checklist are provided in the following section.

Immediate reinforcement in the classroom. The schedule for reinforcement is written into the checklist, with priority targets receiving the highest level of reinforcement. Every target behavior that produces a desired response is rewarded. This is best accomplished using a token economy, which represents earned rewards with delayed gratification, rather than immediate, primary reinforcement.

However, reinforcement must be powerful enough to elicit a correct response; some children will require immediate, highly desirable, and tangible reinforcement. High priority should be placed on developing delayed gratification so that primary reinforcers can be quickly faded out of the classroom setting. Token economies are ideal in this setting and are discussed in detail in Chapter 2. An example of immediate reinforcement in the classroom would be, "You did great raising your hand to participate in group time. You earned a (+) for that."

Clearly delineated target behaviors. Specific requirements such as a description of the behavior, frequency of occurrence, and the setting in which it occurs all help to define the target behavior.

In addition, when and how to prompt are noted to maintain consistent intervention when multiple educators are involved. This is the fine art of identifying and creating discrete trials within the natural environment; this is a significant challenge when compared to the controlled setting of one-on-one intervention. The following examples are representative of common age-appropriate targets, clearly stated for the benefit of both the child and the instructor:

- Preschool: "Say 'Here' when your name is called."
- Kindergarten: "Take one sheet of paper. Then pass the paper to the next person."
- 1st grade: "Check the job board and do your job for the day."
- 2nd grade: "Read at your desk quietly until the timer goes off."
- 3rd grade: "Everyday after lunch, complete any work in your unfinished work folder."
- 4th grade: "Every Thursday, put your homework in the basket by the teacher's desk."

Specific behavioral expectations. The child must understand what is expected of him in order to succeed. The checklist presents these expectations in written form for the accomplished reader, or in a pictorial fashion for the non-reader. The child should know what he needs to do, how often he needs to do it, what happens when he does it, and what happens when he doesn't do it. Do not assume that the child will instinctively discern any or all of these components; each must be explained and evaluated for recall and comprehension. Visual cue cards are useful in assisting the child to remember details of these expectations.

Efficient data collection. The checklist format is conducive to documentation as each required behavior is listed and can simply be noted as (+) or (-), or some similar designated symbol for accomplishing/failing the task. In similar fashion, frequency and types of prompts can be quickly noted with a P for prompt or NP for No prompt. A brief narrative can be included for pertinent details that fall outside of the abbreviated notations. Statistical information is readily available, such as % of correct responses, which in turn allow for immediate evaluation of acquisition rate and mastery. Mastered items can be noted with an M and reinforcement faded out. Mastered items are chained together and consolidated until the activity itself, rather than isolated components, becomes the target. See the examples at the end of this chapter.

Short and long term perspective. In the short term, individual tasks are targeted for mastery. Because each target is isolated, evaluation of success or difficulty in acquisition is clearly identified. The progression of targets should also be readily apparent, when the long-term goal of independence is kept in mind. Over time, these initial tasks are combined into mastered activities, which are then advanced to a skill-based checklist. For example, an independent reading task at the beginning of the school year may require several individual targets:

Independent Reading:
1. Pick a new book.
2. Read until the timer goes off.
3. Write 3 sentences in your journal.

By the end of the year, individual components that have been mastered are now combined into one activity: Independent Reading.

Assistance in planning for the school year. It is understandably challenging to foresee the future, yet educators and parents are frequently asked to plan ahead for an entire school year. Funding, services, and classroom placement may be dependent on just such a broad perspective. The Individual Education Plan (IEP) is, by nature, a yearlong planning tool, incorporating the child's current abilities with plans to achieve specific goals by the end of one school year. Activity-based checklists present clear and concise goals with systematic progression that assists in this educational planning process. For example:

- Beginning of the school year: Sally will acquire information seeking strategies such as "Find out what to do."
- End of the school year: Sally will demonstrate independence in utilizing mastered information seeking strategies.

Clear identification of mastery. The benefits of the checklist can be clearly seen by looking at a

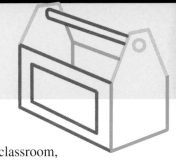

Key:
(P) aide prompt
(TP) teacher prompt
(KP) kid prompt
(M) mastered
(0) no prompt, unsuccessful
(1) no prompt, 1 success

(2) no prompt, 2 successes
(3) no prompt, 3 successes
now mastered
Yellow highlighted items are
current targets that earn tokens.
Mastered items no longer earn
tokens.

scenario in which it is *not* in use. The target behaviors are poorly identified, if at all. Without clearly defined, written targets, expectations vary widely between educators and the child with autism. Inconsistencies in addressing behaviors are confusing and overwhelming to the child, resulting in a variety of negative responses ranging from non-compliance to tantruming. Further comprehension deficits or off-task behavior may be misinterpreted as "naughty" or "bad" behavior. Misinterpretation leads to inappropriate management; the child may be punished rather than supported in his efforts to make sense out of the chaos that he perceives. On the other hand, a checklist represents a systematic method of introducing, acquiring, and mastering individual behaviors. Each time a target is accomplished unprompted, it is recorded on the checklist. Three consecutive, unprompted successes propel the target into the "mastered" classification. The checklist is then revised to indicate that this mastered behavior is now required, reinforcement is faded out, and a new target is promoted to take its place.

The following is an example of a partial checklist:

1st Grade Checklist

> **Get ready for school:**
> (P) Talk to or play with friend before school.
> (M) Line up when the bell rings.
> (2) Say "Hi" to your teacher.
> **Lunch Count:**
> (1) Mark your name for "hot" or "cold" lunch.
> **Morning Lesson:**
> (P) Read the morning message with your class.
> (1) Raise your hand to answer a question.

Identification of deficits in comprehension and cognition. Not every target addressed will be easily acquired and promptly mastered. When a child struggles through multiple revisions of the target behavior, it may indicate deficits in comprehension or cognition. Supplemental instruction outside of the classroom may be necessary to elevate the child's understanding of concepts that elude him. In these situations, careful evaluation should be made with regard to the home environment and/or outside resources so that the classroom instruction is not halted in order to attend to specific issues affecting one child. If on-task behavior can be maintained in the classroom, and the child puts forth reasonable effort, comprehension can be better enhanced in a controlled

environment outside of the classroom, such as after school tutoring or discrete trial training. For example:

> Initial target: "Write the name of the main character on your report." (The child continually needs prompting, indicating a need to revise the target).
> Revised target: "Who is the story about?" (The child still cannot achieve unprompted success).
> Revised target with prompt: "A *who* question is answered with a *person*. Who is the person in the story?"

The child has demonstrated a weakness or inability in *question discrimination*, and the target should be further revised or eliminated until question discrimination is mastered.

Facilitation of socialization. The child with autism will likely not engage in social interaction unless it is required of him. In addition, even the most elementary social skills may be lacking without specific instruction. The checklist allows complex social interactions to be broken down into component behaviors that can be individually targeted for mastery. Initially, the child can gain success by fulfilling an activity specific social target such as "sharing your crayons during art." This situation can easily be created if it does not naturally occur. Once the child has demonstrated mastery, generalization occurs when the target is expanded to variable settings and stimuli; thus, "sharing your crayons" becomes "sharing your supplies" and "during art" becomes "anytime you are at your desk." Socialization strategies are described in depth in Chapter 7.

Skill-based checklist

A skill-based checklist builds on established skills acquired through use of an activity-based checklist and provides the following:

Participation elements. Once the child with autism has mastered the routine activities of the classroom, the checklist will shift to global skills that promote and require active participation rather than mere passive attendance. In the same manner as the activity-based checklist presented clearly defined targets, the skill-based checklist presents generalized, social, and educational skills in clearly defined targets.

The difference is that most of the useful skills in the classroom setting are not confined to specific activities, but are found in variable settings and situations. The child with autism will benefit from a systematic approach that brings meaningful structure to abstract and complex behaviors. For example, appropriate hand-raising, responding to a question and/or contributing information in a group setting is intuitive for the typical child who understands the social dynamics and unspoken rules of interaction. In contrast, the child with autism finds nothing meaningful in this unpredictable and constantly changing setting. Therefore, he has no intrinsic motivation to participate. Individual components of this complex task such as "when to raise your hand" (in response to a question), "when to put your hand down" (when someone is called on), and "what to say if you get called on" (on-topic response) can be individually targeted, mastered, and then combined into successful "participation" in the group setting. Development of participation is addressed in detail in Chapter 6.

Classroom routines are utilized. A skill-based checklist is a progression of the previously mastered activity based checklist. Therefore, it is assumed that previously mastered routines will be maintained through the cost response system that motivates the child himself to take responsibility for these items. The approach for dealing with mastered behaviors that are not maintained is addressed on page 16.

Independent work skills. Independence requires that previously learned skills be generalized across various settings. Independent work skills result when the child learns routines, information-seeking skills, a work ethic, and then takes responsibility for mastered activities. Because reinforcement is incorporated into the checklist, the child is motivated to apply himself to activities that he is capable of, and for which he has been successful. The systematic nature of the checklist enables the educator or parent to identify what skills have been mastered, which can then be independently required of the child. Without the insistence on independence, the child will tend to drift into prompt dependency, sitting idle, knowing that if he waits long enough, someone will step in and prompt him.

Information seeking skills. Through the checklist, isolated activities can be targeted for information seeking skills, which can then be generalized. Ultimately, for the child with autism to succeed in the classroom, he must be taught to use information-seeking skills, and then apply them across settings, taking responsibility for "finding out what to do." Without a systematic approach, the child will gravitate toward prompt dependency, waiting for the teacher or aide to tell him what to do, rather than receiving reinforcement (for achieving the goal of information seeking) or a cost response (for failure to meet the goal).

Addresses comprehension issues. Deficits in comprehension are readily identified when on task behavior is acquired and mastered systematically. If the child is clearly "on-task", meaning that he knows what is expected of him and is putting forth reasonable effort, yet the end result varies from the required standard, then comprehension may be lacking. It is important for educators and parents to work together so that comprehension can be addressed individually without excessive disruption to the classroom at large. It may be most beneficial for the child to complete the task in the classroom setting to the best of his ability, and then repeat the task with instruction in a controlled setting, such as at home or after school with a tutor. Or, it may bring to the teacher's attention a situation in which visual support for the entire class may be an easy solution, providing the necessary concrete information for the child with autism and the typical child as well, without undo attention or disruption afforded to one child.

Expansion of the social requirement.
Introduction of social skills in specific settings begins with the activity-based checklist. To reiterate, the child with autism is unlikely to engage in social interaction unless there is something to be gained. Most typical children are intrinsically motivated by

social interaction; it is valuable and rewarding without artificial motivation. However, socializing with peers often lacks meaning for the child with autism, and thus artificial motivation in the form of reinforcement is initially necessary for the child to succeed. Many social interactions will become intrinsically rewarding as the child gains mastery and confidence in his interactions, at which point artificial reinforcement can be faded out. The skill-based checklist can then expand on the concept of "being social" by requiring that the child use previously mastered skills in natural settings, such as recess or partner activities. It is essential for the child with autism to understand that socialization is required. Parents and educators seeking long term function and gains, as well as adult independence for the child with autism must appreciate and anticipate the unavoidable social interactions that he must face. Unless the child learns early on that "being social" is required, rather than optional, he may choose to have nothing to do with it. Such an approach to life is dysfunctional at best, and places him in a position of on-going dependence. The concept of "being social" is continually addressed and expanded, always advancing from rote application to dynamic interaction.

The checklist allows for direct reinforcement of skills that may otherwise be avoided. The child clearly understands what he is rewarded for in the social arena, which otherwise may be meaningless or beyond his understanding. In the same way that concrete skills can be acquired through isolation, acquisition and mastery of individual target behaviors, abstract and complex social skills also can be acquired. Both verbal and non-verbal targets are addressed, and should include verbal response and initiation, play participation and initiation, as well as the meaningful relevance of social targets (i.e. why it is important that you face the person you are talking to, etc.). It is important for both educators and parents to recognize that socialization is more than simply existing in the presence of other children, whether in the classroom or on the playground; it must include meaningful exchanges and interactions with peers. Socialization is more than polite compliance. Socialization is discussed in detail in Chapter 7.

Implementing the School Checklist
Creating the checklist

Identify reinforcers that will positively affect

behavior in the classroom setting. Initially, the child may require the use of immediate and tangible reinforcement. Reinforcement must be sufficient to result in acquisition of target behavior, as well as repetition and subsequent mastery. In very early (preschool) settings, the child with autism can receive artificial reinforcement without drawing undue attention; however, as the child advances, such techniques become more noticeable to typical peers, and will eventually distinguish the child. Emphasis should be placed on developing delayed gratification and implementing a token economy in the school setting. Token economies are described in detail in Chapter 2.

Set aside reinforcers for school use only.
Reinforcement is only powerful when used exclusively for the desired behaviors. A child that can earn an hour of computer time by exhibiting good behavior at home will probably not be motivated to work for it at school. Certainly, reinforcement for desired behavior at home is recommended; however, reinforcement must be distinguished between school and home so that motivation exists in both settings. Continuity across settings in terms of predictable structure and behavioral application is the premise of this book.

Compose an exhaustive activity based list.
Specify all routine behaviors within the activity (see Examples). All scheduled and predictable elements in the child's daily routine should be noted. Initial target behaviors can be identified, as well as future targets, providing perspective and assistance in long-term planning.

Identify mastered behaviors, if any. Activities, skills, or routines that the child has demonstrated independence with on three or more consecutive occasions may be classified as mastered. Mastered items are expected and required of the child, to be done consistently and without prompts. They are not directly reinforced, except, of course, with verbal praise. Mastered items can provide a foundation to build on; natural expansion can occur by adding a new element or requirement. This new item is the target behavior, which may or may not need to be acquired in isolation. For example, the child that has mastered the school entrance routine of hanging up his coat and taking everything out of his back pack, can progress to checking the job board. Thus, the checklist notation "Get ready for school" now includes all three behaviors and is only successful when all three are done. Quick acquisition may be achieved in this fashion, in which mastered behaviors are chained with a target. Of course, many situations will require that the target behavior be mastered individually, in isolation, before combining with previously mastered behaviors. Mastered items are not targeted unless they are missed on 3 occasions. The technique for addressing previously mastered behaviors that have drifted is discussed in the following section.

Isolate target behaviors in each activity. Initially, one target behavior per activity may be all that the child can handle without being confused or overwhelmed. Clearly define, for both the child and the educator, what is required to successfully achieve the target.

List the immediate rewards as well as the end of the day rewards. If using a token economy, all rewards will be delayed. Clearly delineate the cost response, where applicable. The rationale and technique for implementing a cost response is also discussed in the following section.

Include rules and consequences for negative behaviors. Whereas a cost response applies when a child does not meet the target, consequences apply when negative behavior, such as tantruming, is exhibited. The child should be instructed regarding behavior that is and is not allowed in the classroom. For example, he may need to be explicitly taught that it is "OK to feel sad when you lose a (+), but it's not OK to scream when you lose a (+)." A specific strategy should be implemented when the child displays negative behavior. This strategy should be delineated in writing for both the teacher and the child. If the child responds to disciplinary techniques that the

teacher uses for typical children, then this would be the preferred approach. If not, then the approach should be modified so that it is effective for the child with autism, meaning that negative behavior decreases or is eliminated.

Using the checklist

Prompt enough to achieve success. Target behaviors must be achieved so that there is something to reward. There are a variety of opinions among autism educators regarding the best approach for prompting. Applied Behavioral Analysis advocates the use of "least to most" prompting; this approach emphasizes using only enough prompting to achieve the desired behavior. In this way the child is encouraged to utilize his potential, and is only prompted when it is necessary to succeed. The Verbal Behavior technique advocates "most to least" prompting; in this approach, the child is encouraged to succeed quickly and consistently, albeit with prompts, so that there is always something to reward. Prompt dependency can occur using either technique, and should be properly addressed when it does occur. Without debating the pro's and cons of these techniques, it should be noted that prompting must be individualized and systematically faded out. When selecting a prompt, the child's abilities and learning style should be considered so that the prompt is appropriate for him, promoting success without denying him the opportunity to produce his best effort. Prolonged use of prompts, without evaluation and revision, will create prompt dependency regardless of which technique is used.

Reinforced success will be repeated. This is the foundational principle for all behavioral intervention, both in the discrete trial setting and the expanded environment of natural settings. Failure to provide reinforcement may result in diminished acquisition rates, as well as weak stimulus control (the child's learned association between a given instruction and his required response). The child who is rewarded for on-target behavior learns that his response to a given stimulus has the power to elicit something of value to him. Thus, he is motivated to repeat that response. This principle, although at times presented in an artificial fashion, merely expands on similar reward based behavior within our society such as payment for services rendered, or a promotion based on achievement. Reluctance to implement a reward system is an unfortunate and misguided approach to the reality we know as autism, and may prevent the child with autism from reaching his full potential.

Fade out prompts by diminishing systematically. A variety of prompts may be used, depending on the nature of the target behavior and the learning style of the child:

1. Physical: hand over hand or other physical prompt. This is generally considered to be an enormous prompt and should be used only when necessary. For example, a child who is introduced to the use of scissors for the first time may require a hand over hand prompt.

2. Direct verbal: telling the child what to do; "You need to cut it." This is an explicit prompt and generally can be used to fade out a hand over hand prompt. On many occasions, it will be the initial prompt. The distinction must be made between an instruction and a prompt: if the teacher tells the entire class, "You need to cut it", this is an instruction. If, however, other methods of communication have been used, such as a demonstration of the activity, then the additional and individual verbal direction, given specifically to the child with autism, is a prompt. The point of reference should always be the typical child. Are the majority of them completing the task independently by recalling the demonstration and referencing the model? In this case, even the repetition of the original instruction is considered a prompt. However, if many of the typical children need additional instruction to accomplish the task, then the child with autism may be included and independence or on-task behavior should be evaluated accordingly.

3. Direct written: written prompts are generally preferred over verbal as they contribute to greater independence. The child who is given cue cards outlining step by step instructions can then be required to follow them independently, eliminating the need for constant verbal prompts which can quickly lead to prompt dependency. Lesser written prompts such as key words, lists, or picture cues can be used, depending on the task. One approach is to keep a small dry erase board on the child's desk; the teacher, aide or child can then note key words that will guide him in the task. This is especially useful for novel activities in which the child may not be able to use other strategies to determine on-task behavior.

4. Peer prompt: in this situation you are making use of the child's peers by either instructing the child with autism to ask a classmate or instructing a typical child to prompt in your place. This is particularly useful because peer prompts occur naturally; children typically assist their peers and gain self-esteem and a sense of responsibility when assigned such a task. Careful selection of capable and cooperative peers is essential to ensure appropriate modeling of desired behaviors.

5. Indirect prompt: this type of prompt includes questions or elements within the environment (such as observational learning) that promote independence; "Use your strategies to find out what to do." "What are the other kids doing?" Often, the use of indirect prompts signifies that the child is one step away from independence. As with all prompts, indirect prompts must be faded out. It is relatively easy for a child to become prompt dependent with the use of indirect prompts, often because the educator is unaware that such directives are truly prompts. Although the child may readily complete a task when asked, "What are you supposed to be doing?" he may fail when this prompt is removed. Careful observation should be made and a plan established to fade the prompt and expect independence.

6. Rehearsal prompt: this is a prompt given prior to an activity as a "reminder". For example, as the child is entering the classroom, he may be reminded to check the board for information. Rehearsal prompts should only be used for a short period of time and it is best if they are quickly replace by another form of prompt such as a written cue. Rehearsal prompts require relatively little on the part of the child and are used to establish immediate success so that reinforcement can be given and the pattern for repetition established.

Achieve mastery. Mastery is achieved when the behavior occurs 90-100% on two occasions, with two different instructors, or on three successive occasions. Percentages are helpful when evaluating performance in a discrete trial fashion; in other words, if the target behavior is to "put your finished work in the basket when you are done" and the child completes the task independently on three out of five occasions, the rate of 60% falls below the level of mastery. Prompts should be utilized to keep the rate of acquisition above 70%, then systematically faded. Mastery is not achieved until the task is completed 90-100% unprompted. Complex activities that often occur in natural settings make discrete trial application difficult or impractical. Task variability is often high, so that, for example, the deskwork that was required yesterday may be completely different today. Thus, on-task behavior may be the same ("find out what to do and do it by yourself"), but the context ("write a story about clouds" vs. "write a paragraph about the student assembly") may be entirely different. Whether to use percentages or successive occasions as the qualification for mastery is incidental, as long as it is clearly identified and consistently implemented.

Promote mastered items. Mastered activities are now expected and required to be performed independently and unprompted. Reinforcement is faded and eventually eliminated. These items should be kept on the checklist until the child incorporates them into his routine and demonstrates maintenance. As the target behaviors advance, and new tasks demand attention, it is not uncommon for a mastered behavior to drop back in frequency. The method for handling maintenance of mastered behavior is as follows:

1. **Confirm mastery.** Be sure that the behavior was truly mastered using the mathematical approach listed above.
2. **Confirm maintenance failure.** Three consecutive instances in which the mastered behavior is dropped (not performed unprompted) constitutes maintenance failure.
3. **Evaluate antecedent.** The child may be unmotivated to perform the mastered behavior now that he is no longer receiving direct

reinforcement for it. In this situation, instituting a cost response is recommended. Cost responses are explained in the following section. The child may be confused regarding changes in target behaviors, may not understand the meaning of "mastered" (i.e. "Mastered means you can do it by yourself now"), or may simply forget. In these situations it is recommended that the mastered behavior be prompted until mastery is restored. However, continued prompting indicates that the behavior is not mastered and should be returned to acquisition.

Introduce a new target behavior to replace the newly mastered item. The checklist should represent continual progression of skills, incrementally introducing new targets for acquisition while maintaining previously mastered ones. Whenever a new target is introduced, the child should be briefed on what is now expected of him. The behavior should be clearly defined, in writing, so that the child, parents, and educators know what he must do to succeed, and what support or accommodations are necessary to facilitate that success. In addition, the child should be informed of what he will receive as a specific reinforcement for accomplishing the task. This explanation must include the fact that he will not receive reinforcement if he does not meet the established criteria. It may be helpful to explain to the child with autism "why things have changed" since he may be resistant or upset. The new target must be made meaningful to him. When all individual routines/behaviors within a given activity are mastered, then the entire activity can become a single target by consolidating these mastered components.

Limit number of targets. It is essential to recognize the need to "let some things go" since it is impossible and counter-productive to target all behaviors at once. Prompt the child through items that will later become targets. Too many targets will dilute the reinforcement and be overwhelming for the child. It is better to target just a few items and quickly gain mastery.

The checklist must be active, not static.
Constant, daily evaluation is crucial to the implementation of the checklist. Evaluate the use of prompts; prolonged prompts dictate a restructuring of the target behavior, breaking it down further to facilitate success. Maintain forward momentum by setting the child up for success. Plan for transfer of stimulus control to the teacher: don't assume it will occur naturally. Items that are mastered then become the teacher's domain; he/she is then responsible to require and reinforce it. Plan for generalization by expanding the target to similar settings.

Clearly define cost response(s). A cost response is specific negative reinforcement designed to motivate the child in situations in which positive reinforcement is weak or ineffective. Negative reinforcement differs from aversives or "punishment." Negative reinforcement is the loss or withholding of previously earned rewards. In a token economy, the child may have to give up one of his tokens as a cost response. Some children can be influenced simply by delaying desired reward activities; for example, a child who is eager to enjoy his earned play time immediately after school may have to wait until after dinner as a cost response. Generally, a cost response is not incorporated until a target is mastered because most acquisition occurs with positive reinforcement. However, some children may need a cost response to motivate them to achieve on-task behavior or to maintain mastered behaviors. Initially it will probably be quite artificial, but to be effective it must be powerful enough to motivate the child to change his behavior. The loss of a hard earned token may or may not motivate the child and must be evaluated for effectiveness on an individual basis. Once an effective cost response has been identified and implemented, long range planning to progress to more natural consequences, such as what other children receive in a similar situation, should be considered. A cost response during school hours vs. after school hours should be carefully evaluated for effectiveness vs. disruption. A cost response administered after school is ideal, if the child can maintain the association between the target behavior and the cost response over time. However, if he cannot, then the time delay may render the cost response ineffective. The goal of the cost response is to change the child's behavior so that

The checklist must be **active**, not static.

the target behavior is acquired. Thus, an effective cost response is one that changes the child's behavior in a positive fashion, which should be readily apparent. A more immediate cost response may be necessary for the child who cannot maintain the cause and effect association over time. If this is the case, and the cost response must be administered within the classroom setting, its effectiveness must be balanced with the child's tolerance of negative reinforcement; if the child reacts to the cost response with an emotional outburst, he may disrupt the entire classroom, making negative reinforcement challenging for everyone involved. Frustration tolerance is clearly beneficial in the school environment and is addressed in detail in Chapter 11.

Diminish checklist over time. The initial exhaustive and detailed list is eventually condensed to an index card with general topics and activities and is finally faded out completely. The long-term goal is that the child with autism acquires skills that afford him independence in the classroom, as well as life skills into adulthood. Immediate reinforcement is replaced with delayed reinforcement, and finally faded out and replaced by intrinsic motivation. The transition from an artificial system of reinforcement to a more natural "work at school, play at home" approach should be planned for and introduced only when the child has gained adequate independence and self-regulation. When the child begins to take pride in his accomplishments and exhibits little anxiety over lost rewards, he may be ready to try a less rigid reward system. For example, the checklist can be replaced with a "daily report card" on which the teacher records information, but rewards are less directly related to performance. Rather than earning a check or a (+), now the child receives a letter (such as "G" for good, "P" for needs practice, "R" for re-do) to indicate attention, effort, and task completion. Explanations are given that if you "do your work at school, you get to play when you get home," and "if you chose to not do your work at school, you will have to do it when you get home. That means less time to play." A specific example of a daily report card can be found at the end of this chapter, and details on transitioning from artificial to natural reward systems can be found in Chapter 8.

Implementing the Home Checklist
Creating the checklist

Create continuity across domains.

The successful child with autism enjoys continuity between school and home. Expectations are clearly defined, and rewards obtained when those expectations are met. What makes sense to him at school is also incorporated into his life at home. To the child with autism, rules, boundaries, rewards, and consequences bring order and comfort to an otherwise disorderly and uncomfortable world. When clear behavioral expectations are left behind at school, long term gains are compromised and home life may be frustrating for the entire family. The parent(s) may resist such an artificial approach, but undoubtedly will enjoy the benefits of their efforts to maintain predictability and structure within their home.

Identify reinforcers for use in the home setting. They should be different from those that are designated for school use. Family oriented activities such as outings, games, or special meals may be creatively used for reinforcement of home target behaviors. A child's favorite dinner or dessert may motivate the child to complete his homework after school; a favorite outing such as a movie, bowling, swimming, etc. may be offered when mastery has been demonstrated. This is not to suggest that all family activities cease or that the family as a whole becomes enslaved to the checklist; rather, specific favorites may simply be reserved as rewards while others are

The successful child with autism enjoys continuity between school and home.

incorporated into the family's routine. Typical siblings can participate by having their own goals and rewards. Sticker charts or other visual methods of applauding accomplishments need not be designated only for the child with autism.

Separate the reinforcers. In order to be effective, reinforcement must be set aside for exclusive use, and cannot be freely accessible to the child. Often it is challenging to identify multiple activities or items that the child with autism shows an interest in, let alone finds motivating enough to work for. Continuous observation must be made to ensure that reinforcers remain powerful and effective for the child. Rotation and change to keep them "fresh" is essential. In addition, there is a difference between what the child may consider interesting or entertaining vs. what he considers rewarding and for which he will work. Parents must be in the habit of noticing novel toys, games, or activities which engage the child's interest, and which can be tried as reinforcers.

Identify target behaviors. Identify elements within home routines and activities that can be isolated, acquired, and reinforced. Complex routines such as mealtime can be broken down into their components, which are targeted and mastered individually. Examples of routines that can benefit from the use of a home checklist include morning routines ("getting ready for school"), mealtimes, after school activities, after dinner activities, hygiene, dressing, bedtime, and chores, to name a few. Eating issues are specifically addressed in Chapter 12, and sleep issues in Chapter 13. Examples of a home checklist can be found at the end of this chapter.

Limit target behaviors. Remember not to overwhelm the child with too many targets at once. Some items must simply wait until the child gains mastery with priority targets. If, for example, family mealtime is nearly impossible due to disruptions, tantrums, escape behaviors, or any number of negative behaviors, this may be the first priority. Rather than trying to ineffectively deal with a child who does not sit still, leaves the table, prefers to play rather than eat, or tantrums when something different shows up on his plate, a systematic, one target at a time approach is recommended. A child must stay at the table and sit still before any other issues are addressed. Making this a target behavior with specific, highly desirable reinforcement is much more likely to accomplish the desired behavior than constantly reiterating, "Stay at the table. Sit down and eat your dinner," and so forth.

Clearly define behavioral requirements. On task behavior is more likely to occur when the expectations are clear and direct. The child must know what is required of him. The visual learner will benefit from written or pictoral instructions, rather than auditory instructions alone. Written instructions also ensure that multiple caregivers adhere to the same standards of expected behavior. Variations in adult perceptions of what is considered successful will quickly confuse the child and delay acquisition.

Supplement reinforcers with visuals.
Implementing visuals such as a chart or Velcro board to display achievement helps to show progress and can be used for accumulated rewards, such as a child's favorite outing, once mastery is demonstrated.

Using the Home Checklist

Prompt enough for success. Without success there is nothing to reinforce. The principles listed above, regarding implementation of a school checklist, also apply in the home setting.

Monitor prompts. Excessive prompting creates prompt dependence and prevents mastery. Heavy or consistent prompting requires restructuring of the target into multiple tasks. In the home setting, in which a parent attempting to implement a checklist is also preoccupied and distracted by other responsibilities, it is easy for prompting to continue unchecked. Careful attention to the acquisition rate, (how long it takes for him to learn it)will help to identify prompt dependency and the subsequent need

to restructure the target for quick and progressive success.

Keep the checklist active not static. When targets are structured for success, acquisition and mastery should occur quickly, and targets are then advanced accordingly. The child should not be "stuck" on a target, but continually building upon the foundation of mastery gained. For example, once the entire mealtime routine is comfortably mastered, then a social component can be added, since most people talk when gathered for a meal.

Plan for generalization. Parents should not assume that the child with autism will naturally generalize acquired behaviors across settings, but must utilize a plan to foster and reward generalization. Reinforcement for generalized behaviors should be faded once the behavior is established and maintained. Rationale should be given whenever reinforcement is eliminated; the child that understands is more likely to comply. Simply stating, "That's great that you hang up your coat at home just like you do at school. What a big kid you are! Now we'll work on teaching you to pack your lunch" will help the child to transition to a new target.

Implementing the Extracurricular Activities Checklist
Creating the checklist

A target behavior checklist is also useful for activities such as sports, lessons, playing with peers, and community outings. Creating a checklist for extracurricular activities is essentially the same as it is for school or home. Specific target behaviors are identified and isolated, prompted and reinforced sufficiently for acquisition, and mastered.

Inform instructors and peer participants that there is an intervention plan to ensure the child's success. Adults should be aware that the child has expectations and guidelines to help him participate to the full extent of his ability. The question of whether or not to identify the child's diagnosis is entirely up to the discretion of the parents. There are advantages and disadvantages to either approach. Too much information may result in over-compensation on the part of well meaning adults; too little information may result in frustration for the child, parents, instructors, and other participants. Each child and situation must be evaluated individually, but the following general principles are useful:

1. Assure the instructor that you will provide the resources and personnel necessary to accomplish your goals, without requiring expertise or undue attention on his part.
2. Encourage the instructor to treat the child in the same way as he would any other child.
3. Inform the instructor that your child learns in a different way than his peers do, and that you are confident that he will succeed if allowed support in the learning process.
4. If the child can be sufficiently motivated merely by using a checklist card that defines the expected behavior, simply inform the instructor on the use of the checklist card.
5. If the child needs minimal support, and the instructor is cooperative and willing to work with the child, success may be achieved by clearly explaining what the child must do to earn his reward.
6. If more support is necessary, or the above efforts are unsuccessful, the parent should consider providing one-on-one assistance for the child in the form of an aide.

Using the Extracurricular Activities Checklist

The principles of implementation are generally the same as for the school and home checklists. However, the following additional factors should be considered:

Frequency of behaviors should be addressed. Behaviors that occur in a repeated fashion, as in sporting activities, should include a frequency component. The child needs to know if he will be reinforced for every occurrence, and if not, how often.

Rehearsal prompts are useful for activities that occur infrequently, such as once or twice a week. The child may not recall the targets if not reviewed prior to the activity.

Example Checklists

The following examples can be reproduced or modified for use in the classroom. The checklist can be advanced according to the following guidelines and notations:

Highlight current targets. Extensive initial checklists should have the current targets highlighted or otherwise noted, with future targets listed. It should be clear to the child and educator which behaviors will be reinforced and which are listed only to give perspective on the long term direction (that is, behaviors which will become targets in the future as mastery of other targets occurs.) These future targets appear on the checklist but are not prompted or reinforced yet. By listing them, the child can be made aware of what is to come as he progresses. In addition, the child can be prepared by saying, " Soon you will have to (identify specific future target)."

Indicate prompts. The use of prompts to gain success should be identified on the checklist with (P) for aide prompt, (TP) for teacher prompt, or (KP) for kid prompt.

After three consecutive, prompted successes, prompts are faded out. The target behavior is reinforced when successful, now without prompts. Indicate this on the checklist with (0), (1), (2), or (3), as the number of unprompted, consecutive successes.

Identify mastery. After three consecutive, unprompted successes, the target is considered mastered. Indicate this on the checklist with (M). Inform the child that the target behavior is now "mastered, that means you can do it" and will no longer be rewarded. Explain to him that "now you will have to (do something new) to earn your token," but that he is still expected to complete the mastered target: "but, of course, you still have to (maintain mastered behavior)."

Consolidate targets. Individually mastered behaviors are consolidated into global targets. Once all of the components of an activity are individually targeted and mastered, the activity itself can be required in its entirety. For example, "Get Ready for School" replaces "Hang up your coat," "Hang up your backpack," "Mark the lunch chart," "Answer the question of the day," and "Sit on the rug."

Introduce new targets. Behaviors that have been 'on hold' can now be bumped up to priority status, replacing the previous targets that have been mastered. This maintains an active checklist.

Maintain mastered elements. Behaviors or activities that have been recently mastered should remain on the checklist for a short time until the child has incorporated them into his routine. Mastered targets must be maintained. Once consistently maintained, they can be dropped from the list or consolidated into a single activity.

Preschool Checklist
(half day, beginning)

Get ready for school:
(P) Line up with your class
(P) Walk in line with your class
(M) Hang up your coat and backpack
Message board:
(2) Read the message or look at the
    picture message
(1) Find your name card
(P) Answer the question by putting
    your name card in the right place
    on the chart
Rug time:
(M) Find your spot on the rug
(TP) Sit with quiet hands and quiet
    mouth
Attendance:
(P) Raise your hand and say "Here" when
    your name is called
Calendar:
(TP) Look at the calendar with your class
(0) Say the date out loud with your class
Weather:
(P) Raise your hand to mark the weather
    chart
Jobs:
(TP) Look at the job board
(P) Follow the job rules
Songs:
(TP) Sing with your class
(2) Do what the teacher does (follow the
motions)
Story time:
(3) Sit with quiet hands and quiet mouth
(P) Look at the book every time the page
    turns
(2) Remember your favorite part to tell
    the teacher

Key:
(P) aide prompt
(TP) teacher prompt
(KP) kid prompt
(M) mastered
(0) no prompt, unsuccessful
(1) no prompt, 1 success
(2) no prompt, 2 successes
(3) no prompt, 3 successes
    now mastered

Yellow highlighted items are current
targets that earn tokens.

Mastered items no longer earn tokens.

Recess:
(M) Stay with your class on the
    playground
(M) Line up when the bell rings
(1) Walk in line with your class
Group time:
(KP) Sit at the table with the "Raccoons"
(M) Share the supplies
(2) Do what the other kids are doing
(P) Ask for help if you need it
Centers:
(M) Stay at your center
(KP) Share the toys at the center
(3) Follow the center rules
Dismiss:
(KP) Line up when your group is called
(2) Get everything out of your mailbox
(P) Put it in your backpack

Preschool Checklist (half day, end)

Get ready for school: This is mastered, you can do it.
Message Board: This is mastered, you can do it.
Rug Time:
Raise your hand to answer a question.
Share your story when your name is called.
Attendance: This is mastered, you can do it.
Calendar: Participate with your class.
Weather:
Raise your hand to mark the weather chart.
Pick the clothing you would wear for the weather and mark it on the board.
Jobs: Look at the job board and do your job by yourself.
Songs: This is mastered, you can do it.
Storytime:
Look at the book.
Remember what you liked best about the book.
Ask a friend, "What did you like about the book?"
Recess:
Answer "Yes" when someone asks you to play.
Play with your friends for 5 minutes.
Group time:
Sit with your group.
Pass the paper along when it comes to you.
Ask a friend to share supplies: "Can I use that when you are finished?"
Centers:
Say "Yes" when a friend asks you to play at your center.
Dismiss: This is mastered, you can do it.

Kindergarten Checklist (full day, beginning)

Get ready for school:
Say "Hi" to your teacher or to a friend
Hang up your backpack and coat
Lunch count: mark your name by "Hot lunch" or "Cold lunch"
Check the board to find which center to go to
Learning Centers:
Stay at your activity
Follow the center rules
Talk to someone at your center
Large Motor Activities:
Follow group instructions
Do what the other kids are doing
Group Time:
Calendar: count with your class
Raise your hand to participate in the morning message
Put your hand down when someone is called on
Group Work Time:
Follow group instructions
Talk to a friend about your project: "Look at what I made."
Outside Play:
Ask someone to play with you on the playground
Music:
Sing with your class
Do what your teacher does (follow the motions)
Lunch:
Ask a friend to sit with you
Rest and Read Aloud:
Sit quietly with your head down
Tell your teacher one thing about the story
Story Time:
Look at the book every time the page turns
Listen and remember who the story was about
Afternoon Group:
Follow group instructions
Work with your partner
Free Choice Centers:
Stay at your activity
Talk to someone at your center
Share the toys at your center
Dismiss:
When your group is called, get your coat and backpack
Line up at the door

Kindergarten Checklist (full day, end)

Get ready for school: This is mastered.
Learning Centers:
Tell a friend about what you are making.
Ask a friend about what they are making.
Large Motor Activities: This is mastered.
Group Time:
Raise your hand every time you can answer a question.
Raise your hand to make a comment.
Group Work Time: Work with your partner.
Outside Play:
Ask a friend to play soccer with you.
Play for 5 minutes. Then you can go to the playground.
Music: This is mastered.
Lunch:
Ask a friend about their favorite things.
Tell your friend about your favorite things.
Quiet Reading: Fill in your book report sheet telling who and what the story was about.
Storytime:
Look at the book for the whole story.
Tell the teacher 3 things about the story.
Afternoon Group:
Listen to the teacher so you know what to do.
Look at what the other kids are doing so you know what to do.
Ask the teacher or a friend if you still don't know what to do.
Free Choice Centers: Play with a friend for 5 minutes of your center time.
Dismiss: This is mastered.

1st Grade Checklist (beginning)

Get ready for school:
Talk to or play with a friend before school
Line up when the bell rings
Say "Hi" to your teacher
Lunch count:
Mark your name for "hot" or "cold" lunch
Homework:
Put your homework in the basket
Morning Lesson:
Read the morning message with your class
Raise your hand to answer a question
Jobs:
Check the job board
Do your job
Ask for help if you don't know what to do
Independent desk work:
Find out what to do:
      Listen to the teacher
      Look at the board
      Look at what the other kids are doing
      Ask last
Do it by yourself
Reading:
Pick a new book from your book bucket
Read it quietly
Fill in your worksheet
Writing:
Get your supplies
Write your name on the top
Follow the writing lesson plan
Lunch:
Sit next to a friend
Practice 3 turns in a conversation
Math:
Raise your hand if you know the answer
Follow group instructions
Specials:
Follow group instructions
Do what the other kids are doing
Ask for help if you don't know what to do
Partner Reading:
Listen when it is your partner's turn to read
Read slow and loud when it is your turn
Dismiss:
Check your mailbox
Put everything in your backpack
Say "Good-bye" to your teacher or a friend

1st Grade Checklist (end)

Mastered means I can do it. I don't get a (+) but I will get a (-) if I don't do it.

Mastered:

Get ready for school
Lunch count
Homework
Job
Dismiss

I earn my +'s for:

Participation
Find out what to do
Do it by myself
Being Social

Morning Lesson: participate=raise my hand and answer a question.
Independent deskwork: find out what to do: listen, look, ask last.
Reading: follow the list in your reading journal.
Writing: find out what to do: listen, look, ask last.
Math: participate=raise my hand and answer a question.
Specials: follow your cards for art, gym, music, and library.
Partner Reading: participate=listen and talk with your partner about the story.

2nd Grade Checklist (beginning)

Get ready for school:
Do the lunch chart
Job
Independent Reading:
Pick a new book
Read until the teacher tells you "reading is over."
Write 3 sentences about the story: Who, What, and Where
Group time:
Participate: Raise your hand every time you know the answer
Independent Desk Work:
Find out what to do: Listen, Look, Ask last
Do it independently
Lunch:
Talk to your friends
Play with your friends at lunch recess
Math:
Participate: raise your hand every time you know the answer.
Find out what to do and do it
Social Studies/Science:
Find out what to do and do it
Journal Writing:
Write the date
Write 5 sentences about something that happened today
Specials:
Follow group instructions
Ask a friend if you don't know what to do

2nd grade checklist (end)

Mastered means I can do it. I don't get a (+) but I will get a (-) if I don't do it.

Mastered:

> Lunch chart
> Job
> Independent Reading
> Journal Writing
> Social before school and at lunch

I earn my +'s for:

> **Participation:** every time I know the answer.
> **Find out:** use my strategies.
> **Do it:** keep busy. You can't earn a + if you just sit there.
> **Social:** talk to your partner when you are working together.

3rd Grade Daily Report Card

- Science
- Social Studies
- Math
- Working with a partner
- Spelling
- Reading
- Writing
- Penmanship

70% or higher	G = Good Work, you can play.
50=69%	P = Practice, after you play
less than 50%	R = Re-do, before you play

Home Checklist

Getting Ready for School (beginning)
Get Dressed for School

1. Check the thermometer to find out the temperature.
2. Wear the right clothes for the weather. If it is 60 degrees or warmer you can wear shorts. Otherwise wear long pants.
3. Wear shorts or pants with pockets.
4. Wear a shirt that goes with your pants. Ask me if you are not sure.

Pack your Lunch

1. Put a block of blue ice in your lunch bag.
2. Make your sandwich. Use the "How to Make a Sandwich" instructions.
3. Get a container and put your sandwich in it.
4. Get a plastic bag and put 5 carrots in it.
5. Put your milk money in your pocket. Milk costs 35 cents.
6. Put your lunch bag in your back pack.
7. Clean up everything you use. Put food back where you found it.

Breakfast

1. Set up your place at the table.
2. Get a glass and pour your juice.
3. Get a small dish of fruit.
4. Take your vitamin.
5. Tell me what you want for breakfast.
6. Clean up your place at the table.
7. Brush your teeth.

Make your bed and clean up your room
Follow the task sheet by your bed.

Homework

1. Check to see if you have any homework to do in your folder.
2. If you are finished with your homework, choose a book to read.
3. Show me your work when you are done.
4. You may play on the computer from 8:30 to 8:45 if you do your work.

Go to School at 8:45.

1. Wear a sweatshirt if it is 45 degrees or warmer. Wear a coat, hat, and gloves if it is colder than 45 degrees.
2. Look outside to choose the right shoes or boots.
3. Take your back pack.

Getting Ready for School (end)

Get Dressed for School
Pack your Lunch: sandwich, vegetable, milk money
Breakfast: juice, fruit, vitamin
Brush teeth, make bed
Homework: finish what's in folder, then read a book for the book log
Computer time: 5 minutes for each homework activity
Be Ready for School at 8:45: return library books on Monday, turn in homework on Thursday

Extracurricular Activities:

Sports Camp Checklist

1. Stay with your group. Your group is called the Rockets. Haley is also in your group.
2. Participate = do what the other kids are doing
3. Tell your instructor if you don't want to do something. If the water is too cold for swimming, you can play cards instead.

Today's schedule:

8:30-9:00 Open gym. You can shoot baskets. You can earn a double (+) if you ask someone to play with you.
9:00-10:00 Gymnastics
10:00-11:00 Ice skating
11:00-12:00 Floor hockey
12:00-12:30 Lunch
12:30-1:00 Outside play
1:00-2:00 Swimming (or cards)
2:00-3:00 Climbing wall
3:00-4:00 Soccer
4:00 Go home

You can earn a (+) for each activity that you participate in. Each (+) is worth 5 minutes of free play when you get home.

SCORE!

You can earn 5 minutes of computer time for each (+).
You need to get 70% or higher to get a (+).
90% or higher is double (+)!

If you goof around you will not get a (+). Playing on the keyboard is goofing around.

Sunday School

You can earn a (+) for each activity at church.
    Story time: the story was about _____
    Music: sing along
    Arts and crafts: look at what your friends are doing
    Scripture memory verse: this week's verse is 1 John 4:10.
    Games: play along, watch your friends to know what to do.

Ski Lessons

You can earn a (+) for each run when:
    You control your speed.
    You make at least 20 turns.
You need to stay with your group. Your instructor's name is _____.
Your lesson is from 1:00 to 3:30. Then you can go home and have your play time.

T-ball

You can earn a (+) each time you participate:
- Talk to your friends. Answer when they talk to you.
- Wait your turn at bat. Swing hard! You will get a check for each ball you hit. 5 checks = (+)
- Run the bases: to first base when you hit the ball, then to the next base when someone else hits the ball.
- Try to catch the ball with your glove. Throw it to the first baseman.

Common problems and problem solving strategies:

1. **Too many targets.** When the child is attempting to acquire new skills, he must be able to concentrate on only a few at a time. Too many behaviors on acquisition will result in a child who is overwhelmed, unsuccessful at many tasks, and successful at few.

   Approach: Reduce the number of priority targets. All mastered items should be advanced and reinforcement eliminated. This strengthens the power of reinforcement available for current target behaviors.

2. **Too many rewards accumulated.** This results in a diluted reinforcement schedule; because the child has so many targets, he earns plenty of rewards, and as a result, each earned reward becomes less valuable. Thus, if a child can easily earn 20 +'s a day and each + is worth 5 minutes of play time, he will not be very motivated to work for each one. After all, there is not much difference between 95 minutes and 100 minutes-both are excessive! However, on a more moderate reinforcement schedule, each + is more valuable and readily worked for.

   Approach: Consolidate easy targets to create a single target. Promptly achieve mastery and eliminate reinforcement, making it available for more important targets.

3. **Easy targets.** The child will quickly learn that he gets the same reward for accomplishing an easy target as he does for a more difficult one. He thus has little reason to expend effort on the priority target behaviors.

   Approach: Try to keep the value of each reward equal by requiring equal amounts of effort across tasks. Consider temporarily increasing the value (i.e. double +) for priority items until lesser targets are mastered and advanced.

4. **Target behavior expectations are not clearly delineated.** If the child does not know what is expected of him, he is unlikely to achieve it. If the behavior is vague, the child may demonstrate only a minimal effort, yet insist on receiving his reward. From his perspective, he has completed the task until informed otherwise.

   Approach: Clearly define behavioral expectations. Simplify them and list them in writing. Explain specifically what is required to earn the reward. Whenever possible, quantify the requirement ("Every time," "name 3," "From 11:00 until 11:05," "50% or higher" etc.).

5. **Weak or ineffective reinforcement.** Rewards that have been used for a period of time become "stale" and less desirable. If the reward is not motivating enough that the child will work for it, the system becomes ineffective.

   Approach: Evaluate and change reinforcement. You may only need to "freshen up" the system, not completely renovate it. For example, a few new toys may be all that is needed to make the play time rewarding again. Or you may find that "bonus prizes" or accumulated prizes will motivate the child to succeed. For example, if the child accumulates 40 or more +'s by the end of the week he can earn a favorite outing.

6. **Inadequate success, nothing to reinforce.** Without success, the system fails. There must be something to reward in order for the behavior to be reinforced and repeated. Concern over prompt dependence may result in insufficient prompting to achieve success.

   Approach: Increase prompts to promote success. This common problem is easily corrected in a mathematical fashion. Prompts are given until success is demonstrated on three consecutive occasions with prompts; then prompts are faded until success is demonstrated on three consecutive occasions without prompts. If the child demonstrates initial progress followed by regression, reintroduce the prompts.

7. **Changing up more than one variable at a time.** This may be perceived by the child as unfair, confusing, or both. For example, if the child has mastered a situation in which 50% success is required to earn a token, such as a reading comprehension worksheet, then advancing the target to 75% while also increasing the difficulty of the questions asked would be problematic.

   Approach: Change only one element at a time. In the same fashion as a discrete trial, advance only one element of the behavior at a time to ensure accurate evaluation.

8. **Stagnant checklist.** Slow acquisition rates may indicate prompt dependency. If the child knows his inactivity or apathy will ultimately result in a prompt, he is trained to simply wait. Since behaviors on acquisition are rewarded even when prompted, his reward is guaranteed.

   Approach: Evaluate and fade prompts. How long has this prompt been used? Is this the least prompt sufficient to produce the desired behavior, or can less be used? Who is doing the most work, the child or the educator? The educator must be vigilant in fading prompts while still promoting success. In some, but certainly not all situations, temporarily increasing reinforcement can be used when the child performs the target behavior independently rather than prompted. Thus, reinforcement may look like this: "You earned double +'s because you wrote your story all by yourself!" It is important to reinforce independence but also important to fade heavy reinforcement quickly.

The Tool and the Technique

Chapter Summary

Activity-based checklist:
- Allows for individualization
- Offers immediate reinforcement
- Clearly delineates target behaviors
- Isolates mastered elements
- Identifies comprehension deficits
- Facilitates socialization

Skill-based checklist:
- Incorporates participation
- Promotes independence
- Develops information-seeking skills
- Fosters long-term success
- Expands socialization

CHAPTER 2

TOKEN ECONOMY
Reinforcement that works
Introduction

The child that can delay gratification will operate in the school setting better than if reinforcement must be immediate. A token economy is a system in which the child receives delayed reinforcement represented by immediate token distribution. The token must represent something of value to the child. If he does not work for it, he probably does not consider it valuable enough and the reinforcement should be changed. Tokens are the "money" that the child uses to "buy" his rewards and can be presented in any number of forms. Objects such as pennies, stickers, or small cards with a star or (+) can serve as tokens. Tokens are then exchanged at a later time for the predetermined reward. Token distribution should be as unobtrusive as possible to avoid drawing undue attention to the child within the classroom setting.

Domain

1. Immediate reinforcement
2. Short-term delayed reinforcement
3. Long-term delayed reinforcement
4. Accumulated reinforcement

Approach

Immediate reinforcement occurs when a token or a reward is given immediately after the target behavior is obtained. The purpose of token distribution is to substitute for immediate reinforcement. By offering a token in place of a reward, the child learns to delay gratification while still associating reinforcement with on-task behavior. The need for immediate reward diminishes as the child learns the value of the token to provide something he desires at a later time. For example, the child who is highly motivated by candy cannot receive chocolates for every task in the classroom setting without creating some problems among his peers. It is far better to offer him a token, such as a star on his checklist, which he receives for accomplishing the target, and which he can then trade for chocolates after school. Token distribution is always accompanied by verbal reinforcement specific to the task. This concurrent administration of a token with specific praise for how it was earned helps to strengthen the association between on task behavior and reinforcement, thus contributing to repeated target behavior. Immediate reinforcement may be necessary for the child who has limited ability to delay gratification, or it may be used to add emphasis to a high priority target. Nevertheless, immediate reinforcement with items other than tokens can be obtrusive in the school environment and will distinguish the child from his peers. Tokens should replace immediate reinforcement as quickly as possible.

Short-term delayed reinforcement, for the purposes of this book, occurs when reinforcement is offered discretely within the school setting but not immediately after the target behavior is demonstrated. This may occur in one of two ways: as a short time delay in receiving tokens, such as at the end of the activity; or as a desirable activity or item presented within the classroom rather than after school. When the child cannot delay gratification for the entire day, intermediate reinforcement is a reasonable approach. If the administration of tokens is delayed, the child may become anxious during the waiting period. This anxiety may be significantly decreased by verbal reassurance that the token was indeed earned, and will be given at the end of the activity. Some children may initially need very specific reassurance such as a definitive time, "at 11:30"; however, it is best to fade this quickly so that the inevitable variations in schedule do not contribute to anxiety when the child must wait beyond the time indicated. Allowing the child to mark his tokens on a card at his desk may also help to alleviate anxiety associated with intermediate reinforcement. If the child can delay gratification for a short period, but not until after school, then reinforcement within the context of the school environment is the next step. Specific times or opportunities should be designated for receiving rewards, such as between activities, at recess, or during lunch break. Newly introduced or highly challenging targets may need the added incentive of a special reward during the school day to provide sufficient motivation for success. For example, the child may be motivated by tokens or pennies in his pocket that he can *feel* but which remain unseen and do not draw undue attention to him.

Long-term delayed reinforcement, for the purposes of this book, occurs when reinforcement is offered after school. The child redeems the tokens he has earned during the school day for predetermined rewards. This is what the child has been working for, whether it is accumulated play time, computer time, or other desired privileges. The ultimate goal of the token economy in the classroom setting is that, through positive reinforcement, a target behavior is acquired during

school and reinforcement delayed until after school. Usually, a systematic progression of delayed gratification is necessary to maintain the association between a given behavior and the subsequent reward received several hours later.

Accumulated reinforcement occurs when a larger or more valuable prize is earned after multiple repetitions of a target behavior are achieved. Weekend outings, evening activities, or special purchases can be used to motivate on-task behavior over a longer period, such as a full week at school. Accumulated rewards require that gratification be delayed for several days or even a week. This type of reinforcement should be in addition to daily reinforcement and not a substitute for it.

Examples:

Immediate reinforcement. The target behavior is to "raise your hand at group time." The child is given a small slip of paper with a (+) on it immediately after raising his hand, which he can keep in his pocket. Verbal reinforcement is given concurrently, "Good job raising your hand at group time." (If it is a classroom aide who is distributing tokens, praise should be given quietly and discretely; if it is the teacher who is in charge of the token economy, it is natural for her to give praise to any child who participates so there is no need for such discretion). Initially, the child should be told, "You earned a (+) for that" as he is given the token to strengthen the association between achievement and reward.

Short-term reinforcement. A child may not be able to delay gratification until after school; he may be more motivated if the school day is broken up into manageable time periods. For example, success has been demonstrated using two different lunch bags, one that the child considers "desirable" and one that he considers "less desirable." If a series of target behaviors are met prior to lunch, as indicated by the child earning 5 or more tokens, he is allowed to choose the "desirable" lunch bag, composed of his favorite turkey sandwich, potato chips, and a cookie. If the target was not met (less than 5 tokens earned), he must choose the "less desirable" lunch bag, which is adequately nourishing but not rewarding. Of course, the use of food as a reinforcement in no way denies the child, it simply utilizes the privilege of choice, requiring on-task behavior to earn that privilege. Furthermore, opportunities for the child to make choices can be offered in a number of classroom settings unrelated to the target behaviors, thus allowing the child a sense of control. A child may earn tokens that allow him to add a favorite activity to recess such as bringing a favorite toy to school (all within reasonable parameters; no toys that isolate the child or allow self-stimulating behaviors should be used). "Hot potato," "Simon Says" and other games that the child enjoys can be used as intermediate rewards. Choosing certain centers or playground activities can also be reasonable intermediate rewards.

Long-term reinforcement. Tokens can be earned and "redeemed" for prizes after school. A (+) can be worth five minutes of rewarding play with favorite toys, videos, or on the computer. If the child earns ten or more (+)'s, a bonus can be given such as a desirable snack, favorite beverage, or special dinner food. A visual chart identifying what the target behaviors are and how each (+) was earned can help reinforce school accomplishments. A short discussion immediately after school centered around a chart or Velcro board can help the child to see concretely what he did during the school day to earn his rewards. A visual representation of the playtime earned can be displayed using a pair of "clock signs," such as merchants use to indicate "Will Return" time. Display these clocks next to the child's chart and label one for "Start Time" and the other "End Time," so that he can readily see the rewards that his efforts at school have earned him. This system can help make the abstract more concrete and build self-regulation; the child can learn the responsibility of playing only within the allotted time frame, as well as offering motivation for future accomplishments. For example, the child can see from his chart that he could have earned more playtime if he had raised his hand and participated during math group, thus adding motivation for the next school day.

Fading out the token economy need not be a monumental task. As the child progresses within the school setting, the transition from a concrete, artificial system of reinforcement to a more natural system of work and play can be made. It is best attempted during an extended break from school, and presented in a positive manner, such as "Congratulations! You earned a promotion!" Clearly delineated expectations and continuity of structure should be maintained to alleviate any anxiety associated with the change. For example, the following information can be displayed on a poster:

Congratulations! You earned a promotion! Soon you will be in 3rd grade, and now you don't have to earn your playtime anymore.

_____

Kids who are in third grade work hard at school, and play when they get home.

_____

Kids who are in third grade know that they must do their work at school. If they don't, they will have to do it at home and they won't have as much time to play.

_____

Playtime is a privilege you can keep if you make good choices, and you can lose if you make bad choices.

_____

If you are cooperative you will keep your play privileges. Cooperative means doing what you are asked without complaining.

_____

If you are flexible you will keep your play privileges. Flexible means you play different games, not just the same thing over and over.

Accumulated reinforcement. The more motivation for target behaviors, the more the child will achieve. A "weekend prize" such as a trip to a restaurant or a favorite outing can be earned by accumulating a designated number of tokens. A "star" can be earned for each day that the child earns ten or more tokens. Five stars at the end of the week earns the bonus prize. By accumulating a designated number of tokens during each school day, consistency across behaviors, or overall on-task behavior, is rewarded. By consistently demonstrating one particular priority target, such as handraising at group time, consistency within a behavior is rewarded. Adding an accumulated reinforcement to the existing token economy will often promote rapid acquisition and mastery.

It is essential that the system be set up to ensure the child's ongoing success. Constant failure to achieve the desired rewards will frustrate the child. The system must be constantly evaluated and altered to achieve high motivation and high rates of success while still challenging the child to progress. The key to a successful behavioral plan is to isolate targets, prompt for success, reinforce for guaranteed repetition, and then advance the target upon mastery. A strong token economy will ensure optimal success when used in conjunction with the isolation of clearly identified target behaviors, sufficient prompting for acquisition, reinforcement adequate to reproduce desirable behaviors, systematic mastery of targets, and continual target advancement.

Chapter Summary

- Tokens can promote development of delayed gratification
- Immediate reinforcement: given after target achieved
- Short-term delayed reinforcement: given at the end of activity
- Long-term delayed reinforcement: given after school
- Accumulated reinforcement: given at end of week

CHAPTER 3

CHOOSING THE RIGHT SETTING

The teacher and the classroom
Introduction

The child with autism requires certain environmental supports and should be matched with a teacher exhibiting certain qualities to ensure an optimal learning experience. Choosing an appropriate classroom and teacher are initial and important steps toward the child's success. Once an appropriate setting has been identified, specific instructions regarding the behavioral approach, adequate information regarding the affects of autism on learning style, and individual characteristics of the child can be discussed. See Chapter 4 for specific information on "coaching the teacher."

Domain

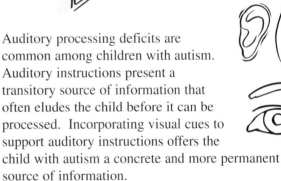

1. Teacher qualities
2. Classroom requirements
3. What to avoid

Approach

Teacher qualities

Consistent follow-through on instructions.
This refers to the expectation that a given instruction be met with an appropriate effort or response. Follow-through should also include a strategy for non-compliance. It is a great disservice to any child when a given instruction can either be followed or ignored; but for the child with autism, inconsistent or absent follow-through is problematic, and will prevent or delay acquisition of target behaviors. If an instruction is given and the child with autism is non-responsive, the teacher has two options: to ignore the lack of response and move on, or to persist until a response is obtained. Failure to follow through on the instruction will quickly produce prompt dependency, or worse, a learned response of non-compliance. The child who is already comfortable with non-compliance will be reinforced to continue in it. The teacher should be observed for follow-through on instructions given in both a visual and auditory fashion, in the context of a typical teaching environment.

Pairs visual and auditory instructions. Many children benefit from multiple learning styles.

Auditory processing deficits are common among children with autism. Auditory instructions present a transitory source of information that often eludes the child before it can be processed. Incorporating visual cues to support auditory instructions offers the child with autism a concrete and more permanent source of information.
Examples include:
1. Writes step-by-step instructions on the board for the entire class while giving verbal instructions.
2. Uses models, diagrams, and graphs to support verbal explanations.
3. Displays charts that support independent work and which provide ongoing instruction after verbal instructions are completed.

Not adversely influenced by a diagnostic label.
"Autism" is a word that provokes a multiplicity of impressions, both accurate and inaccurate. In recent years, an increased incidence of autism has resulted in widespread publicity and anecdotal accounts that contribute to a wide range of ideas about what autism is and how it manifests itself. In addition, prior

experiences with low functioning children with autism can directly influence a teacher's expectations. It is important to ascertain the teacher's preconceived ideas regarding autism so that low expectations, excessive prompting, and unnecessary modifications for the child can be prevented.

Teachable. A teacher who is inflexible, unwilling, or resistant to implementation of a behavioral approach in the classroom will hinder the child's ability to succeed. It is imperative that the teacher not feel threatened by suggestions that the aide or parent offers, and equally imperative that those suggestions be presented in a non-threatening fashion. Both the teacher and the typical children will welcome many aspects of the behavioral approach, since structure and predictability are useful educational strategies. How to coach the teacher is presented in detail in Chapter 4. The first step is to identify a teacher who is willing to receive and implement instruction according to the educational plan that best serves the child with autism.

Discerns and addresses distractions. The teacher must recognize instances when negative behaviors, which are allowed for typical children, become problematic for the child with autism. A teacher must use the behaviors of typical children as a reference point when evaluating the behaviors of the child with autism. However, she must also recognize that what is a harmless diversion or temporary distraction for a typical child may be self-absorbing or self-stimulating for the child with autism. She must be willing to address any behavior that prevents the child from focusing, attending, and complying.

Gives concise verbal instructions. Long explanations may be impossible for the child with autism to comprehend. Although the use of enriching language should not be discouraged, a concise summary at the end of a lengthy instruction is encouraged so that it is clear to the child with autism what is expected of him. As was mentioned previously, supplementing auditory instructions with visual cues, such as a list of key words, is extremely helpful and more permanent than a transitory verbal instruction. In addition, utilization of recall such as, "What are you supposed to do?" is useful to determine whether or not the child understands the instruction. Comprehension must exist before the child can act on the instruction. For example, "Today we are going to do a math activity using a variety of board games. Everyone will need their math notebook, a pencil, and three markers. We will choose partners and then go ahead and pick one of the games from the box at the back of the room. Then when everyone is ready we

will meet at the rug to go over the assignment." This is a lengthy, multi-step instruction. A more concise version, presented in both an auditory and visual fashion would be:
1. Choose a partner.
2. Choose a game.
3. Get your supplies.
4. Come to the rug.

Firm disciplinarian. The teacher must be able to keep the child's long-term interests in mind. Lifelong function into adulthood begins with solid instruction during childhood. Academics are generally "black and white" and can be systematically taught through behavioral intervention; but self-regulation, responsibility, and rules that govern morals and social interactions are abstract, complex, and variable. Maintaining as much predictability as possible in these situations, including consistent follow-through on consequences, will greatly benefit the child with autism. Conversely, modification of expectations, or leniency because of the child's condition, will confuse him and hinder his progress. Rules, expectations, rewards, and consequences must be clear, consistent, and predictable.

Classroom requirements

Structured. The classroom under consideration should be highly predictable in schedule and routines. The children, in general, know what they are supposed to be doing. As much as possible, variations in routines are announced in advance and transitions are planned.

Rich in visuals. Observe the classroom for charts, labels, schedules, and other visual sources of information. Is the chalkboard or dry erase board prominent and easy to read? Are routine activities, such as reading and writing activities, presented in a visual format? Can a visual learner find out what to do by utilizing existing environmental supports and cues?

Organized. Observe the classroom for organization; does everything have its place? Are storage and supply areas clearly labeled? Are individual work areas free from clutter? Does the classroom set-up promote the children's independence or does its disorganization promote dependence?

Small class size or student-to-teacher ratio. Class size and student-to-teacher ratio are often predetermined by the school district. As much as possible, the parent of the child with autism should seek a small class size with a low student to teacher ratio.

Distractions are kept to a minimum. The child with autism must learn to function in the existing environment without simply eliminating all distractions; however, until self-regulation is gained, some elimination of distractions will probably be necessary. The classroom under consideration should be quiet and controlled, not loud and rambunctious. Are there excessive or unnecessary visuals that distract the child with autism? Are items of interest, such as numbers or maps, displayed where they may interfere with attention during group activities or deskwork? If so, can they be moved? Can the noise level be controlled by closing windows or doors? Are there fans in the room during warm weather? How are the desks or work areas positioned? Evaluation of the classroom environment should take into consideration the individual characteristics of the child, including sensory issues such as a hyperactive or acute auditory, visual, tactile, or olfactory state.

Clearly defined, consistently enforced discipline policy. Discipline should be enforced among all children in the classroom to ensure the optimal learning environment. The classroom and teacher should be observed for adherence to the school's discipline policies. Whenever possible, these same disciplinary policies should apply to the child with autism. Supplemental approaches to discipline are described in detail in Chapter 10.

What to avoid

Incongruent teaching philosophies. A teacher who is resistant to or who refuses to accept a behavioral approach will be difficult to work with. Attempting to conform the child with autism to a typical learning style is also ill advised. In addition, a teacher that denies the nature or extent of disability ("he'll grow out of it") will contribute little to the child's success. Although most teachers will benefit from specific instruction and coaching to assist them in their approach to the child with autism, it is not appropriate to expect a teacher to change her teaching philosophy. Success is more likely to occur with a teacher who fundamentally agrees with the premises of behaviorism.

Accommodating style. The teacher who alters her teaching style by lowering standards for the child with autism violates the basic premise that the child must learn to adapt to the realm of typical peers, rather than expecting the world at large to adapt to him. It is imperative that the teacher understand the difference between modification and accommodation.

Views special education as the only viable treatment option. The teacher who presupposes that the child with autism can only succeed within the confines of a special education setting will expect little of the child, and severely limit his potential. The teacher may have developed this perspective through a previous negative experience or through inadequate knowledge of autism in general. If the teacher can be persuaded through improved knowledge and assurance that all necessary support will be provided, a positive climate for success may be created; if not, however, then other teaching options should be considered.

Examples

Teacher qualities

Follow through. The teacher says "Everyone find their spot on the rug." If the child does not respond, the teacher repeats the general instruction; if no response again, then the general instruction is made specific: "(Name), find your spot on the rug." Every instruction must eventually produce a response.

Pairs visual and auditory instructions. The teacher writes on the board the key components of verbal instructions.

Not adversely affected by the diagnostic label. The teacher does not presume failure or lower the standards based on the diagnosis of autism. She does not talk down or heavily prompt. For example, if the general instruction of "Everyone find your spot on the rug" is followed by a physical prompt and/or "John, you need to come and sit here" without the opportunity for the child to act on the general group instruction, the standards are lowered.

Teachable. The aide is able to give positive input regarding weak areas of teaching style. For example, "Some of the kids, including John, seem like they don't know what to do next. Maybe a list on the board would help."

"John really needs some motivation to complete his desk work. Do you think we could schedule center time after writer's workshop instead of before?"

Discerns and addresses distractions. "John, looking at the calendar is distracting you from your work. You need to finish by 11:00 or give me back a (+)."

Concise verbal instructions. "First we will finish our math workbooks. When you are done you may pick a book to read at your desk."

Strong disciplinarian. "John, it is not OK to just sit and look around the room when you should be working. You will have to miss out on recess and finish your work then."

Classroom requirements

Structured. Since unpredictable and varying schedules may cause frustration, clearly posted daily schedules are useful. In kindergarten, a detailed time schedule may be appropriate:

9:00-9:15	Get ready for class: hang up backpack, sit on the rug
9:15-9:30	Songs
9:30-10:00	Morning message and Storytime
10:00-10:30	Morning Centers
10:30-11:00	Recess and Snack
11:00-11:30	Theme lesson
11:30-11:45	Clean up and wash hands
11:45-12:30	Lunch and Outside Play
12:30-12:50	Read aloud book
12:50-1:30	Afternoon Centers
1:30-2:00	Art
2:00-2:30	Songs and Dance
2:30-2:50	Recess
2:50-3:00	Clean up and Dismiss

In 1st grade, a more general schedule may be appropriate:

9:00-9:30	Business
9:30-10:00	Group Time
10:00-11:30	Literacy Workshop
11:30-12:30	Lunch and Recess
12:30-1:00	Read Aloud
1:00-1:30	Math
1:30-2:00	Science or Social Studies
2:00-2:30	Reading
2:30-3:00	Gym

As the student progresses in grade level, the schedule should become more general in nature. As long as the time frames are clearly delineated, there remains the opportunity for frustration related to activities that violate those time boundaries. Therefore, it is important to fade out the time parameters. By 2nd or 3rd grade, the schedule may be dropped altogether, replaced by daily routines that are learned and memorized. The child with autism must then rely on observational skills and memory rather than a visual tool.

Rich in visuals. Written instructions for activities are prevalent. When routines or recurrent activities are not presented in written form, the child with autism may need a cue card or small dry erase board at his desk. Daily or frequently occurring activities can be outlined in writing until the routine is committed to memory. For example:

"Writer's Workshop"
1. Think of a topic.
2. Write a list of 3 details.
3. Write a sentence for each detail.

Organized. The classroom is uncluttered and neat. Books and supplies are readily found in labeled bins or bookshelves. Individual desks or work areas are kept neat and organized. Daily or frequently occurring routines, such as attendance or lunch count, are represented by the use of charts, graphs, or "hands on" manipulatives.

Class size or student-teacher ratio. 1: 20 or less is desirable, especially in the lower elementary grades. This may be predetermined by the school district.

Distractions. The child can be positioned with his back to number charts or maps that distract him. If distractions continue and the child lacks self-regulation to succeed in the existing environment, the charts or visuals may need to be removed. If self-regulation exists, then positive reinforcement for on-task behavior or attention should be introduced; for every opportunity that the distraction exists, and the child remains on-task, he is rewarded. So, if "looking at the numbers" is the identified distraction, then whenever the numbers are in view and the child attends to the

teacher in group time (as initially determined by looking at the teacher rather than turning around to look at the numbers), then a token is given along with specific praise, "I like how you paid attention and did not look at the numbers; you earn a (+) for that." Once the child has mastered the attention component, the reinforcement is faded out and a cost response added, so that any violation, (i.e. turning around to look at the numbers) results in the loss of a (+). After the attention component is addressed, a participation element can be added; now, in addition to not looking at the numbers (a negative behavior), the child must also participate in group time by raising his hand (a positive behavior). Once acquisition and mastery occur, the two elements can be combined and generalization of distractions in other settings can be addressed.

Job Decription for the Classroom Aide
1. Keeps in mind the overall goal of creating independence.
2. Makes observations to evaluate progress and problem solve.
3. Understands and implements the behavioral technique.
4. Uses data collection to revise targets that continue to fall below the 70% necessary for acquisition.
5. Advances mastered targets and transfers control to the teacher.
6. Provides appropriate prompting to ensure success.
7. Provides visual supports to promote comprehension and success.
8. Offers reinforcement for on-task behavior and transfers control to the teacher.
9. Communicates with staff and parents regarding progress and problems.
10. Advocates for the child with peers by increasing understanding and acceptance.

Discipline. Specific rules of behavior should be listed with the corresponding rules of discipline. Visual supports can help the child with autism to understand and comply with the established rules of the classroom. For example, a chart with each child's name on it, along with a color-coded card for each child, can be used to represent behavioral expectations and disciplinary measures:

"Green light=good behavior"
"Yellow light=lose 5 minutes of recess"
"Red light=lose all recess"
The behaviors that will result in a color change should be clearly delineated. Disruptive behaviors such as talking out of turn may warrant a change from green to yellow; a second violation would warrant a change from yellow to red, and so forth.

Careful observation and selection of a teacher and classroom setting that suit the unique learning style of the child with autism are foundational to his success. Poor selection of either one, the other, or both, will likely hinder efforts to educate him among typical peers.

Chapter Summary

Teacher Qualities

- Consistent follow through on instructions

- Pairs visual and auditory directions

- Not adversely influenced by diagnostic label

- Teachable

- Discerns and addresses distractions

- Gives concise verbal instructions

- Firm disciplinarian

Classroom Requirements

- Structured

- Rich in visuals

- Organized

- Small teacher-to-student ratio

- Minimal distractions

- Clearly defined, consistently enforced discipline policy

CHAPTER 4

COACHING THE TEACHER
Classroom strategies for success
Introduction

The parent, aide, or educator must work diligently to transfer stimulus control to the teacher. In discrete trial training, "stimulus control" refers to the child's learned association between an instruction (the stimulus) and his response, whereby positive responses are rewarded and the behavior is subsequently repeated. Stimulus control, in this context, refers to the ability to elicit a response from the child based on the same type of association, that is, that target behavior within the classroom is acquired by reinforcement and subsequent repetition. The child will learn to expect the teacher (rather than the aide) to require the target behaviors, reinforce positive responses, and deliver the appropriate cost response. Only when the teacher has established stimulus control can the child function independently in the classroom. This transfer must be calculated and systematically pursued.

Domain

1. Information pertaining to autism
2. Transferring stimulus control
3. Classroom strategies

Approach

Information pertaining to autism

The parent, aide, or educator should present useful information without unnecessary depth that may limit the teacher's expectations for the child. It is an individual decision whether or not to reveal the child's diagnosis, and there are both advantages and disadvantages associated with either choice.

Disadvantages of revealing a diagnosis of autism include:

1. A lowered expectation of ability based on preconceived ideas or previous experience with autism. This unfortunate reality is well known in the world of special needs.
2. Anxiety or fear related to inadequate knowledge. The teacher may be unable to cope with something she knows nothing about. Adequate knowledge is essential before determining if the teacher will be comfortable with the child in her classroom. If she is not, the child's success will be compromised.
3. The application of a meaningless label without clearly delineating the child's ability and disability. Simply stating "autism" without any

> *The parent, aide, or educator should present useful information without unnecessary depth that may limit the teacher's expectations for the child.*

explanation will more often than not elicit a blank stare. It is naïve to assume that even the most highly qualified teachers with advanced degrees and/or extensive experience are automatically knowledgeable regarding the complexities of autism.

Advantages of revealing a diagnosis of autism include:

1. A cooperative relationship between parents and educators is more likely to exist when an honest presentation of the child's ability and disability is laid out from the onset. With this approach, a level of trust is established, ensuring that there

will be open communication and collaboration to manage difficulties and maximize academic potential.

2. A greater effort at understanding the challenges faced by the child with autism is more likely to occur when those involved in his education are adequately informed.

3. A measure of compassion may be afforded the child who finds life chaotic and confusing. This is perhaps the greatest advantage to revealing a child's disability, whether or not it is by means of a diagnostic label.

Disadvantages for *not* revealing a diagnosis of autism include:

1. Negative behavior will most certainly be viewed as non-compliance at best, belligerence at worst. When this occurs, the typical management approach by teaching professionals is discipline, which is unlikely to correct problems in the child with autism and will probably be counterproductive.

2. Without the framework of a known disability, the teacher may be left to piece together a wide range of splintered skills and deficits. Even her best effort may be ineffective in the face of profound social impairment, expressive language difficulties, and auditory processing deficits.

3. Little to no compassion is afforded a child who presents as "difficult." Even the most patient of individuals can be exasperated by the repetitive and dysfunctional traits of the child with autism. Understanding to some degree the challenges he faces can do much to promote a sensitive and caring approach in the classroom.

The advantages for *not* revealing a diagnosis of autism include:

1. The problems associated with preconceived ideas and lowered expectations may be avoided.

2. The stigma associated with a diagnostic label is difficult to remove, even when the child progresses and is well integrated among his peers.

> *It is crucial to provide accurate information about the child's abilities and limitations in a manner that is designed to develop useful and successful strategies. This information should be comprehensive but not exhaustive.*

Regardless of the decision parents make, whether to reveal the diagnosis or not is only part of the issue. In both situations, it is crucial to provide accurate information about the child's abilities and limitations in a manner that is designed to develop useful and successful strategies. This information should be comprehensive but not exhaustive. Information on neurophysiology and genetic predisposition may be interesting but not necessarily relevant to the day to day effort to improve language and comprehension. On the other hand, the high-functioning child with autism may appear quite able to the uninformed. Every effort should be made to assist the teacher in understanding the issues that will either encourage or undermine the child's success in the general education classroom.

Dysfunctional traits. The teacher needs to be aware of the elements within the classroom environment that may distract the child or promote perseverative behaviors. All children are subject to distractions; however, it is important for the teacher to understand the greater appeal that certain items (such as numbers or patterns) have for a child with autism, as well as his limited restraint or ability to self-regulate.

Artificial nature of reinforcement. The teacher may be uncomfortable with the "artificial" nature of the token economy. It should be explained that the child is motivated differently and his need for motivation is much greater than that of his typically functioning peers; without this system of reinforcement he is unlikely to develop intrinsic motivation. It should be noted that heavy reinforcement will be faded to the least amount necessary for success, at which point the "artificial" nature of the reinforcement will be minimal. Ultimately, as the child gains skill, intrinsic reinforcement within the natural context of the classroom can replace the artificial reinforcement. Explain the plan to develop or increase the child's ability to delay gratification, at which point reinforcement is received outside of the classroom.

Specific elements of the child's individual learning style. Children with autism tend to be visual learners, and many also exhibit auditory processing deficits. The teacher should understand that pairing auditory instructions with visual cues is helpful (and may be necessary initially). Any strong sensory aversions should also be mentioned, along with the plan to address them. It is helpful if the teacher selected takes the opportunity to observe the child in his current educational setting.

Independence without modification. Ensure the teacher that you do not want her to alter her teaching style or lower her standards for the child, but rather that the goal is to support the child so that he has the best opportunity to succeed in the typical classroom.

Short-term perspective is enhanced when information regarding the systematic method employed to achieve specific and isolated target behaviors is provided. Ensure the teacher that the approach is positive and success oriented. "Behavior that is reinforced will be repeated" should be continually stressed. Avoid in-depth discussions of methodology that may overwhelm the teacher. Remember, the teacher has an entire class to attend to and needs only specific, manageable instructions that will help the child to succeed without demanding too much of her time and energy. Wherever possible, offer to prepare or provide materials for her. The parent

who presents as a cooperative partner in the educational process is generally appreciated and respected.

Long-term perspective is gained when the long-range goal of complete independence is in view. Assure her that independence is planned for and each target that is mastered puts the child closer to that ultimate goal. Discuss how, initially, the child will be prompted enough to achieve success, but then the prompts will be faded out.

Transferring stimulus control

Children with autism often have difficulty generalizing learned skills across settings and among varied authority figures. It may take them an unusually long time, by typical standards, to recognize an unfamiliar person on a consistent basis. Then the child must learn to attend to and comply with the instructions given by this unfamiliar person, the teacher. Add to that the varied complexity of speech, facial expressions, voice inflection and an environment rich in distractions and the likelihood of succeeding is low. However, with a systematic approach to transferring stimulus control, the child will gradually transition to following the teacher's instructions, diminishing or eliminating the need for a classroom aide. In order for this to occur, the following items need to be addressed:

Teacher follow-through must be monitored and strongly encouraged. Every instruction to the child must have a response. Typically, when the child with autism is slow to respond, or fails to respond, the teacher is unsure how to handle it; she may simply ignore it and move on to another child who is eagerly waiting to answer. Often, the teacher is unaware of inconsistent follow-through until it is brought to her attention, or she may be uncomfortable because she doesn't know how to elicit a response from the child. The aide must diplomatically call attention to the inconsistent follow-through and offer suggestions to help the teacher.

Reinforcement must become the teacher's domain. First, a target behavior is prompted for success. Then prompts are faded out, and mastery is achieved once the child demonstrates the behavior on three consecutive occasions, unprompted. Once mastered, tasks or behaviors are then transferred to the authority of the teacher. Now, rather than the aide providing reinforcement, the teacher rewards successful behavior. As a result, the child transfers the association of rewards earned by desired behavior to now refer to the teacher rather than the aide. The child will now look to the teacher to reward his success.

Mastered items become the teacher's responsibility to reward or consequence. Once the child has demonstrated mastery with the teacher, reinforcement is faded and a cost response is added. By fading reinforcement of mastered behaviors, new targets can be introduced. By adding a cost response, the child is motivated to maintain mastered behaviors in the absence of direct, positive reinforcement.

Classroom Strategies

Accommodations that enable the child to perform without compromising the quality, quantity, or character of the required work must be made. Sequential, written instructions can be used to modify existing tasks while still requiring equal quantity and quality of work. Graphic organizers that offer pictorial representations are useful to many children who are learning to categorize and organize their thoughts and expressions. A few examples are presented at the end of this chapter. Scaffolding, identification of beginning steps and end points, and concise language choices are all helpful to the child with autism, who may appear paralyzed by instructions that lack these necessary parameters. Work assignments that are open-ended may never be attempted.

Visual supports that utilize the child's unique style of learning must be provided. Visual supports may take many forms such as written instructions, picture labels, models or hand gestures. All of these visual supports enhance and clarify auditory communication. Demonstrating an assignment and providing a finished model are useful to many children and are legitimate teaching methods.

Adequate time must be provided for the child to complete his work. "It is important to remember that visual thinking is slower than verbal thinking and the student must be given adequate time to respond to instructions, to requests for information and to given tasks." (Gardner, p. 20). Deficits in language processing or fine motor skills can also delay the completion of assignments or standardized testing and should be taken into account.

Language should be minimized in volume and complexity. It is a common mistake among teachers to multiply misunderstanding with more language rather than to simplify instructions with less language. "When children are not on task it is easy for the teacher to increase the amount of verbalization in attempting to manage them." (Howlin, p.272). The teacher should understand the importance of concise instructions that utilize the least amount of language necessary. Complex vocabulary should be replaced with simple and familiar words that promote on-task behavior rather than confusion and non-compliance. Language choices should also avoid sarcasm and non-literal or abstract meanings that the child with autism invariably will interpret literally. For example, "Your desk looks like a tornado came through" may mean nothing to the child, and any action implied in the statement will be lost. "Your desk is too messy, please clean it up" is more likely to be understood and acted upon.

Word retrieval issues should be eliminated whenever possible. Word retrieval simply means that the child has the cognitive skills needed to produce an answer but lacks the ability to convert his thoughts into expressive language. Auditory instructions can be presented in a way that minimizes word retrieval issues simply by offering choices rather than using an open-ended question. For example, a teacher who usually asks open-ended questions such as "Why did the girl cry?" can instead ask, "Did the girl cry because she was sad or because she got hurt?" This method offers the child with autism an opportunity to display correct or incorrect understanding without the limitation of word retrieval.

Scaffolding refers to a teaching strategy in which complex tasks are broken down into their component parts and addressed individually. This strategy is essential for the child with autism and many other children will also benefit from this teaching approach. Examples of scaffolding appear throughout this book and represent a fundamental aspect of behavioral intervention.

Examples:

Information pertaining to autism. "John is a strong visual learner, and we will help him to gain independence by supplementing auditory instructions with visual cues. John has learned to take notes and he will write down key words that will help him complete his work. John is fascinated with numbers, so we must discourage him from staring at the multiplication charts on the wall; he will be easily distracted by them and may not be able to regain his focus the way that other kids would. I will develop a plan to help him with that. It is important for John to have motivation for things that the other children are naturally eager to do; I know it seems kind of "artificial", but John works very well when he gets a (+) for his achievements. Those (+)'s are meaningful to him because he can "cash" them in after school for things that he wants. It is really important for all of us to help John succeed in the classroom. It is not in his best interest for us to modify things for him; we want to help him learn to operate in 'our world,' not change the world to suit him.'"

Short-term perspective. "For the first week or two of school, we will be working on developing a routine and becoming familiar with the classroom setting. I will develop a checklist that will help us isolate individual tasks that we can start with. I will let you know exactly what we are working on from week to week. Please don't hesitate to ask me questions. First I will help him to follow the routine of coming in at the bell, hanging up his coat and backpack, then sitting on the rug for group time. I will have one or two specific items for each major activity through out the day, such as getting supplies together when he is working at his desk, and putting finished work in the basket."

Long-term perspective. "As time goes on, John will master individual activities within the major groups. Then, instead of being rewarded for each little task (like lining up at the bell, hanging up his coat and backpack, finding his spot on the rug etc.) he will be rewarded for "getting ready for morning group time." After he settles into a routine, we will start working on information seeking skills and participation elements."

Transferring stimulus control. "We will start by requiring him to raise his hand for each opportunity in the morning group time. Then we will require that he raise his hand and answer when he is called on. Lastly, we will turn this task over to you, so that he looks to you for a (+) when he raises his hand and answers appropriately."

Visual supports
Example #1: Supplement auditory instructions with written instructions on the blackboard or other classroom display.

Example #2: Create posters for frequently used patterns such as "The Writing Process." Include the required elements such as
>Rough Draft = first story
>Edit = correct your misspelled words
>Final Draft = copy your writing with the corrections

Adequate time
Example #1: "I want you to do your best work, even if it takes you longer than the 20 minutes we have now. I will give you a (+) if you finish steps 1 and 2. You can earn another (+) for finishing step 3 during Job time. I did not give you a job today."

Example #2: "This is a test so you need to do your best. You will be finished when you have read each question slowly and marked the best answer. It doesn't matter what time it is on the clock. You will get a (+) for each section that is 70% or higher so don't rush."

Controlled language
"It's 'Loose Ends' time for 10 minutes. Use this time to complete any unfinished work that you have in your desk" becomes, "It is time to check your 'Unfinished Work' folder. Finish your 'Math Practice' page first, then go on to your story and finish that."

Word retrieval
Example #1: "Choose a science book for your research project" becomes "Would you like to do your research on planets, mammals, or the human body?"

Example #2: "Are you finished with your reading assignment?" becomes "Did you read all of the chapters and fill in your book report sheet?"

Example #3: "What is your favorite kind of book?" becomes "Which do you like better, books about facts or books that tell a story?"

Example #4: "Who is our mayor?" becomes "Who is our mayor, George Washington or George Montoya?"

Scaffolding
Example #1: Sequential instructions with beginning and end points:
>**Assignment:** "We have been studying about our community. Today we will each write a paragraph about our community and them make a class book."
>**First:** choose a topic from the list on the board.
>**Next:** write a title using this topic.
>**Next:** write down 4 facts you know about that topic.
>**Next:** write a sentence for each of the 4 facts.
>**Last:** copy your sentences to make a paragraph.

Example #2: "Work with your partner to make a timeline of the story" becomes:
1. You will be working with Kaitlyn.
2. First talk about what happened in the story. Kaitlyn can write them down.
3. Then talk about when it happened. Put a number next to each thing on your list. Whatever happened first gets a 1. Whatever happens next gets a 2. Number all of them.
4. Now write them in order on your time line from first to last.

The child with autism will have the optimal success in the typical classroom setting when the teacher understands and participates in the behavioral plan. The parent, aide, or educator should work diligently to transfer stimulus control to the teacher, thus establishing and promoting the child's independence, self-regulation, and sense of accomplishment.

The following page is an example of information that can be presented to the teacher or other professionals involved in the education of the child with autism. It can be modified or reproduced in its current format for this purpose. It should be accompanied by detailed written information regarding the strengths, limitations, and abilities of the particular individual child, and should not serve as a substitute for such information.

General Information about Autism

Autism is a condition that has a variety of presentations, from very low functioning and non-verbal to very high-functioning and capable individuals. The causes of autism are unclear, and many interventions have been implemented with variable success. There is no "test" that identifies autism; it is a diagnosis made by the presence of certain behaviors rather than clinical findings. As a result, the term "autism spectrum" is often used to identify a child or person with certain characteristics. These characteristics may include some or all of the following:

1. **Social impairments.** People with autism often do not understand the subtle social cues that govern interpersonal relationships. As a result, they may appear resistant to social situations, and may seem quite uncomfortable around their peers. Children with autism may avoid other children, preferring adult company because adults may interact with them in a more predictable fashion. They may act out or demonstrate negative behaviors in social situations not because they are trying to be difficult, but because they do not understand what is so natural to the rest of us.

2. **Language difficulties.** Many people affected by autism never develop speech. For those that do, language remains perplexing and challenging. They may require visual supports to help them better understand what they hear. As they grow, language problems such as bluntness, literalness, and flat speech may contribute to further social isolation. It may also make them appear less able or less intelligent. Some individuals display repetitive speech that appears odd and unusual. These speech patterns are often employed to decrease the anxiety associated with social situations. In addition, a child may be hindered by off-topic or irrelevant responses, and the inability to initiate, maintain or extend a conversation.

3. **Reading comprehension deficits.** People with autism may appear to be good readers. Many have well-developed vocabularies. However, it is common for individuals to decode what they read with very little comprehension.

4. **Poor or absent imaginary skills.** Young children may show no interest or ability in pretend play. School-age children may show difficulty with abstract concepts and may need concrete visual supports to help them achieve.

5. **Weak initiative.** Many people with autism do not have the motivation to apply themselves or to reach their potential apart from rewards or positive reinforcement. However, many will work diligently when the task is clearly defined and there is an associated reward system. This may seem "artificial" or "unnatural" to some, but is a proven and often essential method of success for the individual affected by autism.

6. **Difficult or negative behaviors.** A variety of behaviors from simple self-absorption to self-abusive and injurious behavior may be present. It can be disturbing and disruptive to have these occur in the classroom setting. Generally, high-functioning school-age children with autism have eliminated negative behaviors prior to entering school. If not, there will be a detailed plan available to specifically manage these issues. The safety and education of both the child with autism and the typically functioning children are taken into consideration in the placement of this child in the general education classroom. It is more likely that the behavioral issues are less obvious. A child may be easily distracted by sights and sounds that make it challenging to pay attention. He may appear non-compliant because he does not understand what is expected of him. He may not seek out assistance or may not follow instructions without a system of motivation.

The presence of autistic characteristics is not a direct indicator of intellect. Each individual should be assessed and educated according to their ability. Many individuals with autism have unique skills and special interests that demonstrate remarkable intelligence. It is entirely reasonable to expect them to participate and contribute to society, but it is likely that they will need understanding and support to accomplish this goal.

Hopefully, this information will be useful to you in the partnership that successful education requires. Specific details of the individual with autism will be provided, along with strategies to promote success in the classroom. We look forward to working with you in this unique and promising educational experience.

Main Idea and Details

Detail

Main Idea

Detail

Detail

Main Idea and Details

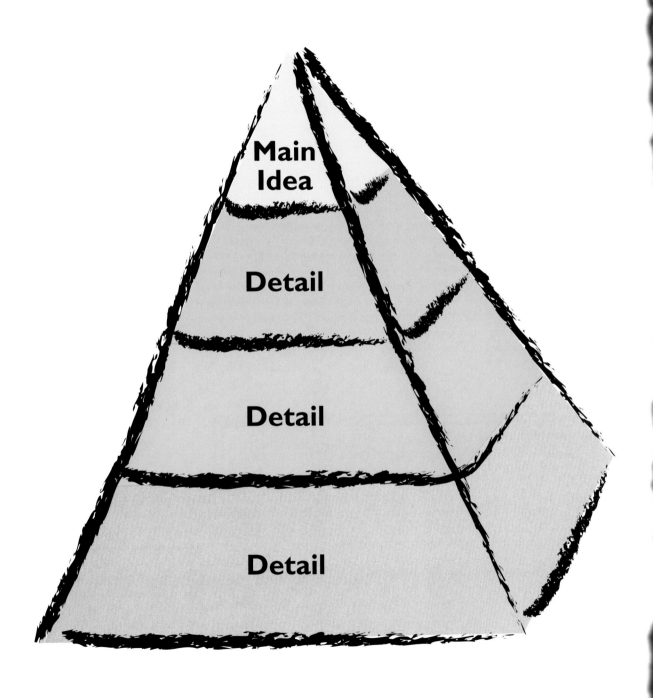

Story Map

Characters (who):

_____

_____

_____

_____

_____

_____

Setting (where):

_____

_____

_____

_____

_____

_____

What happened at the beginning of the story?

_____

_____

_____

What happened in the middle of the story?

_____

_____

_____

What happened at the end of the story?

_____

_____

_____

Beginning, Middle, End

Beginning

Middle

End

Chapter Summary

Transferring Stimulus Control from Aide to Teacher

- Follow through on instructions
- Providing reinforcement
- Maintenance of mastered items

Classroom Strategies

- Provide visual supports
- Allow adequate time
- Minimize language in instructions
- Eliminate word retrieval issues
- Utilize scaffolding for acquisition

CHAPTER 5

IMPROVING ATTENTION
Managing distractions and teaching attention
Introduction

To some degree, distractions are inevitable and often harmless for the typical child. However, for the child with autism, distractions can be compelling and consuming, a path of escape into a world of comfortable predictability. In addition, hypersensitivity to auditory or visual stimuli, comprehension or auditory processing deficits, and decreased or absent social anxiety all contribute to inattention. Gaining his attention is frequently challenging and a typical teaching approach may be inadequate. Simply telling the child to "pay attention" is not likely to accomplish the desired result. The instruction "pay attention" must be isolated into specific tasks in specific situations before it can be generalized across settings. In general, attention and distraction are mutually exclusive. A combined approach of positive reinforcement for self-regulation of distracted behavior along with positive reinforcement of appropriate attention tasks is the key to making gains.

> *For the child with autism, distractions can be compelling and consuming, a path of escape into a world of comfortable predictability.*

Domain

1. Managing distractions
2. Attention teaching tasks
3. Measuring attention

Approach

Managing distractions. Before a child with autism can successfully attend to the desired instructions or activities, he must learn to self-regulate his indulgence in distractions. This is not likely to occur without specific instruction and reinforcement. He must understand that certain behaviors are classified as "distractions" and that "distractions keep you from your work." In addition, if something keeps him from completing the target behavior, it can be viewed as detrimental to his ability to earn rewards. Thus, he is not being "punished" for inattention but rather is experiencing the natural consequence of a behavior that is incompatible with attention. Preoccupation with visual stimuli that the child finds gratifying can be self-stimulating, or may serve as an escape behavior. Self-regulation requires that the responsibility for refusing to engage in distractions is transferred to the child. Using language such as "Who's choice is it?" or "It's not my problem if you

don't get your work done, it's your problem" may be helpful. Managing distractions should include the following:

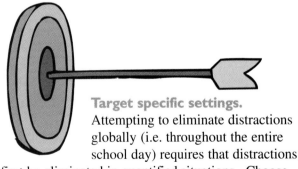

Target specific settings. Attempting to eliminate distractions globally (i.e. throughout the entire school day) requires that distractions first be eliminated in quantified situations. Choose one activity that occurs daily, if possible, and target only that setting until mastery is achieved. It is best to choose an activity that is short in duration to ensure success. Attempting to manage distractions for a five-minute individual reading time is a more realistic starting point than a 45- minute group time. Similarly, there are fewer distractions to address in an individual reading time than there are in a group setting; thus, the type of activity used for an initial target should be selected accordingly to promote success. As is the case of all behaviors that require an ongoing performance, (rather than a one-time accomplishment) it is essential that the parent or educator stay ahead of the child's ability to succeed so that there is a behavior to reward. Thus, if the child can self-regulate a particular distraction for only 30 seconds, the target may be 20 seconds initially and expanded incrementally with success. Mastery should first be achieved within a particular setting, for the entire duration, then expanded to other settings.

Identify sources of distractions. The initial target behavior should be selected based on the short duration of the activity and the limited number of inherent distractions. Whenever possible, existing distractions that can be easily eliminated should be controlled or removed prior to establishing the target. For example, if a multiplication table displayed on the wall can be eliminated as a potential distraction simply by changing the child's desk assignment, this would be a reasonable and sensible alternative to creating an additional target of "Don't look at the numbers. They are a distraction and they are keeping you from your work." Existing distractions that are not readily controlled serve as the target behavior. It is best if the target consists of only one type of distraction such as "numbers." Initial management should directly address the distraction: "You will get a check for every minute that you are looking at the teacher and not at the numbers." It is important to provide an appropriate alternative such as "looking at the teacher" so that the child knows what

he *should* be doing. Reinforcement should focus on the positive behavior rather than simply the absence of negative behavior. So, the child is praised for "looking at the teacher" rather than "not looking at the numbers."

Teach self-regulation. Ultimately, the goal is for the child to manage his own behaviors so that he can be productive in the classroom. Once it is established that distractions are a negative behavior that will diminish rewards or result in consequences, then the next step is to teach the association between distractions and productivity. The child needs to learn that distractions will keep him from getting his work done, and if he doesn't get his work done his rewards are diminished or consequences ensue. Now the target behavior is no longer the simplistic "don't look at the numbers" but rather encompasses self-restraint and on-task behavior. The reward is given for the finished product or for the effort put forth rather than for eliminating a negative behavior.

Attention teaching tasks

Visual. Situations in which visual cues exist or can be incorporated are the best in which to begin attention training. As always, the child should be set up for success. Elements of high interest, such as numbers or patterns, should be used to gain the child's attention so that there is a desired behavior to reward. The child should be informed of the expected behavior that will earn a reward. For example, "You need to look at the equations on the board for math group." When the target behavior is exhibited, the reward (token) is given along with verbal praise specific to the task: "Good *paying attention* to the equations. You earned a + for that." As a result, the child's understanding of "paying attention" is expanded to include "looking at the equations." It is important to assess the child's existing attention span, if any, so that successful attention tasks can be quantified. If the child has an

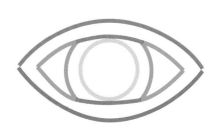

attention span of 30 seconds, success will not be achieved if the requirement is to "pay attention for group time," a 15 minute activity. Initial attention required should be slightly less than what the child is currently capable of. The parent, aide, or educator must always be one step ahead of the child so that he succeeds. Only when he succeeds, can he be rewarded, and only when he is rewarded will the behavior be repeated. So initially, any attention must be quickly applauded and reinforced. With mastery, the quantity of attention increases incrementally, building on existing skill without requiring more than the child can achieve. Similar tasks should be isolated and targeted in other settings. A story that is read aloud to the class contains both an auditory and visual component that may need to be addressed separately. Initially, the attention target may be "Look at the book." Once this minimal level of attending is mastered, the auditory components of comprehension and recall can be targeted. It is important for the child to understand that most people will presume that he is "not paying attention" if he does not exhibit eye contact. However, it is also important for the teacher to understand that the child may be attending well even in the absence of consistent eye contact. Therefore, eye contact should be taught and required of the child with autism so that he meets this common social expectation and avoids what may be considered rude behavior. The teacher, on the other hand, must include additional methods for determining the adequacy of his attention such as comprehension and recall.

Auditory. The child may need supporting visual cues in order to attend to an auditory task. The aide or teacher may note key words for comprehension, recall or instruction for on-task behavior. Multiple step activities can be outlined so that the child can then 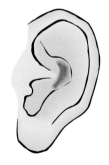 complete them independently. The child can be taught to take notes himself, as long as he is able to keep up with the ongoing instruction. If he spends a lot of energy focusing on the writing task he may be unable to hear the next instruction.

Measuring attention

It cannot be assumed that the child with autism who avoids eye contact is also inattentive. These children often utilize their peripheral visual field to compensate for the aversion to prolonged eye contact. However, it is recommended that eye contact be required in certain situations initially and expanded simply because the world at large associates eye contact and attention. A discrete trial approach can be used, preferably outside of the school setting initially, in which eye contact is the direct target behavior. Isolating this behavior into specific situations such as "Look at me when you are talking" can be reinforced and mastered before expanding to other settings.

Recall. The child's attention can be measured by eliciting detailed information after an instruction has been given, a story read, or an activity completed. Recall tasks teach the child that attention is required, and that he will be rewarded for attending to information and events. Initially, recall should be elicited immediately after the information is given, so that long term memory does not affect the trial. The child should know the target behavior required of him in advance, such as "After the story you need to tell me one thing about it if you want to earn a +." Immediate reinforcement should be given and verbal praise specific, "Good paying attention to the story!" When mastery of immediate recall is achieved, gradual time delay can be incorporated. The child may be required to demonstrate recall at the end of the activity, at the end of the period (morning or afternoon), and then after school. Each progression must be reinforced and eventually reinforcement is faded out. Task progression includes advancing the recall requirement from "one thing about the story" to multiple details, characters, setting, and main idea. Recall can be enhanced by using visual supports generated by the child such as jotting down key words or filling in a worksheet.

Comprehension. Attention can also be measured by eliciting and evaluating comprehension. Instructions for individual activities given in a group setting can be evaluated by asking the child to explain what he is going to do to accomplish the task. This should involve more than just restating the given instruction (recall) and should represent the child's interpretation and understanding of the instruction. Questions such as "What are you going to do?" for recall and "How are you going to do it?" for comprehension may be helpful. Story comprehension can be measured by requiring the child to fill in a short worksheet or index card with questions pertaining to the story. This approach can easily be quantified using a "percent correct" approach. Whenever possible, quantifying a task is beneficial for both the child and the teacher. The child knows exactly what the expectations are and what constitutes a success. The teacher can deliver rewards in an objective fashion. For example, success can be gained initially with 50% correct (or higher, as long as success can be achieved consistently). The comprehension requirement can be advanced by increasing the percentage necessary and/or requiring more detailed or difficult responses.

Examples

Managing distractions.

Observations of the child in the classroom reveal that he is frequently distracted by numbers on the wall, flickering fluorescent lights, hallway noises, and loose strings on his clothing.

Example #1: Numbers on the wall: the child's desk is relocated so that his back is to the number charts. The behavioral target now becomes "not turning around to look at the numbers." If the behavior occurs at a high frequency, the initial approach should be to reward short time intervals in which the behavior is absent, for example 30 seconds. Constant reinforcement is provided by giving checkmarks; each 10 checkmarks equals a (+) or token. Quickly advance to "not looking at the numbers during reading" (or similar activity period) until the entire day is addressed. Thus, the child who demonstrates mastery of an activity period (reading) is then required to complete the activity without violation ("You did a good job not looking at the numbers. You really paid attention to your work"). Positive reinforcement is faded from incremental checkmarks to a single reinforcement for the entire activity ("You earned a (+) for paying attention to your reading"). The requirement is advanced by

lengthening the period of time required from one activity to two, and so on, until the target becomes the entire school day ("You really paid attention today. That's great that you did not look at the numbers all day"). Finally, reinforcement is faded altogether and a cost response becomes the motivation to maintain the acquired behavior; instead of earning a (+) or token for "not looking at the numbers" the child who demonstrates mastery is expected to complete his work without this distraction. To do so now results in negative reinforcement, or the loss of a token ("You did not pay attention during writing. You will lose a (+) because looking at the numbers keeps you from your work"). In addition to addressing the negative behavior ("looking at the numbers"), the child should be redirected to appropriate functional behavior. Thus, "Looking at the numbers keeps you from your work. You need to get your work done" replaces the emphasis on the inappropriate behavior with the appropriate task at hand. Where there is function there is less room for dysfunction.

Example #2: Fluorescent lights. A small desk lamp is placed on or near the child's desk to minimize lighting distractions. The behavioral target is similar to the above example.

Example #3: Hallway noise. The teacher keeps the door closed whenever possible. In addition, the parents help to desensitize the child by having him do his homework with a radio on in the background (talking, not music). Direct and immediate reinforcement at home for working with auditory distractions helps the child to tune out similar distractions at school.

Example #4: Loose strings on clothing (or similar fidgeting behavior). The behavioral target is "quiet hands" as a positive approach or "no picking" as an alternative. The child may initially be told to "Fold your hands during rug time" or a checkmark approach can be used. Again, be sure that the child knows what he is supposed to be doing, not just what he is not to be doing. Thus, "Fold your hands and listen" is a better instruction. In addition, if the child can be given a recall or comprehension requirement to keep him occupied with attending, his focus can be directed away from the distraction.

Example #5: Individual work setting. The child focuses on the wall clock rather than on his desk work. Use the clock to your advantage. If the reading time is 20 minutes, design a reading goal for each 5 minute period. Praise the child for completing the designated task during each interval. Offer an incentive for finishing on time: "You will get a check for each period that you finish on time. If you get all four checks you can sit quietly and use your calculator until 11:00. Then we will start math."

Example #6: Group setting. The child is consumed with his personal space on the carpet, annoyed by the close proximity of his peers, resulting in inattention. The child (or perhaps all of the children) is given an "X" on the carpet that defines his space. He is assured a space that is adequate and where he is not jostled by his peers. The target now becomes "sitting well" or "good carpet manners". The child is redirected to "look at the teacher" and rewarded for attention through recall and comprehension evaluation.

Attention teaching tasks: examples of visual tasks

Progressive instruction and development of attending skills begins with the child's first school experience. Attention in the preschool setting is represented by on-task behaviors in a variety of settings. As the child begins to function within the classroom routine, the transfer of stimulus control to the teacher begins as well.

Example #1: Preschool.

1. Line up: select a designated peer for the child to stand behind. If the child does not recognize or differentiate well between peers, place a sticker on the back of the child that he should line up behind. The child should not be placed at the head of the line where there is no one to follow; nor should he be placed at the rear since there is no one to line up behind him. The child needs to be placed between two peers in order for it to truly be "lining up." The task of lining up is usually in response to an auditory stimulus such as a ringing bell or a command. Using a visual strategy can help the child to comply. Often, the child with autism does not understand how close or how far to position himself around other people. The task of lining up with his peers is a good opportunity to teach what is considered appropriate. The child may gravitate toward the back of the line because he is most comfortable there; he can distance himself as much as he likes. In this case, another child should be designated to line up behind him. Reinforcement should include "Good paying attention to the bell."

2. Calendar: prompt the child to look at the visual when the teacher is discussing the calendar; reinforce with "Good paying attention and looking at the calendar."

3. Job board: identify each job with a picture or symbol; supplement with a written description for each job. For example, "The door holder holds the door open at 10:00 and 11:30."

4. Hand Motions: the preschool age child will learn to sing and follow hand motions that correspond to the song. This promotes observational learning and is an opportunity to reinforce paying attention to the teacher.

5. Story time: prompt the child to look at the book as the teacher reads it and shows the pictures to the class. Reinforce "paying attention to the story."

6. Recess: utilize familiar or mastered games such as "Follow the leader" or "tag." In this way, attending to socialization is introduced.

7. Group time: the preschool child will most likely

have the benefit of a model or demonstration for activities that are explained with verbal instructions. Use the visual as a focal point for the child's attention, "Look at what she made. Now you make it."

8. Centers: post a sign at each center that identifies the "rules" or guidelines for appropriate play. All centers will require that the child "Stay at your activity." Wandering is not allowed. Be sure that the child knows the physical boundaries of each center. Other rules should include what is appropriate for the child to do. For example, the block center may have rules such as "Share the blocks," "Build something," and "Never throw the blocks."

Example #2: Kindergarten

1. Group instruction: this is clearly where attention becomes an issue. The use of models and demonstrations should continue whenever possible. Utilize recall to determine the degree of attending and reinforce verbally, "Great paying attention!"

2. Incorporate recall into the checklist requirement: "You need to tell me what you are going to make to earn a (+)." Supplement auditory instructions with written step-by-step instructions. A cut-and-paste art project lends itself well to a simple cue card:
   Draw 3 circles: small, medium, large.
   Cut
   Glue small on top of medium on top of large.
   Draw face, hat, and stick arms.

Example #3: First grade and up:

1. Find out what to do: introduce information-seeking skills by providing written key word instructions on the classroom board or at the child's desk. Introduce the strategy of "Listen, look, ask."

Listen to the teacher
Look at the board and at what your friends are doing
Ask the teacher or a friend if you still need help

2. Do your work independently: once the child knows what he is to do, he should be given adequate visual supports to allow independent completion.
   Listen: "Make a list of your favorite foods."
   Look: Favorite=like the best
   I know what to do, so I can do it myself.
   Do it by yourself.

3. If recall is adequate but there is no follow through, the child must recognize his need to ask for help.
   Listen: "I'm going to write a story about a time I felt proud."
   Look: my friends are writing.
   I don't know what to do.
   Ask: "I need help. I don't know what you mean."

   Prompt: "Proud means feeling good about something you did or made. Tell me about that. Good, now write 4 sentences about that."

4. Working with a partner: Tape an index card to the child's desk or folder that delineates what is required for "working with a partner."
   I help my partner
       when I make a comment.
       when I ask a question
   My partner helps me.
       I can ask my partner for help.
       I can look at what my partner is doing.
       I need to listen to what my partner says.

5. Participation: "Morning Message" is an example of a group activity in which the teacher has written a message on the board. The teacher asks the class to read it together, and then raise their hands to make a spelling or punctuation correction. To create a situation in which the child "pays attention", the initial target is to "read along." Some children have difficulty participating in unison, in which case, that is a separate target. If the child follows along without reading out loud (based on observed eye contact), this may be considered adequate. However, a recall or comprehension component must be included to determine true attention versus

mere on-task visual compliance. The ideal would be for the child to participate in making a correction as this would clearly indicate adequate attention and comprehension. However, recall without participation, such as asking "What are you supposed to do?" with a response of "Make a correction" could be used. Does the recall indicate that the child understands this directive? Not necessarily. Ultimately, comprehension should be demonstrated by participation.

Attention teaching tasks: examples of auditory tasks

Example #1: Preschool

1. Attendance: use a cue card to prompt the child to say "Here" in response to his name. Fade the use of the card quickly.
2. Unison: many preschool activities incorporate participation through unison. "Say it with the class" requires attention to the task and can be prompted by observational learning ("Do what the other kids are doing").
3. Group time: auditory instructions should be supported with a demonstration or model.

Example #2: Kindergarten

1. Storytelling: listening to peers telling a story may be extremely challenging. Include a recall element on the checklist such as "What did your friend talk about?" and reinforce with both primary (token) and secondary ("Good listening!") reinforcement.

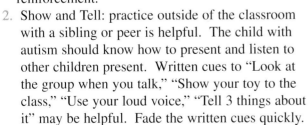

2. Show and Tell: practice outside of the classroom with a sibling or peer is helpful. The child with autism should know how to present and listen to other children present. Written cues to "Look at the group when you talk," "Show your toy to the class," "Use your loud voice," "Tell 3 things about it" may be helpful. Fade the written cues quickly.
3. Participation: expectations of the kindergarten age child should include answering when called on by name. Prompt the child verbally ("Answer") or with a cue card.

Example #3: First grade and up

1. Group instruction. The task is set up for success by starting with short, concise instructions for familiar tasks; "Make a list of your favorite sports. Then write a story about one of them." Recalled details that the child provides can be written into a key-word format: "List sports. Write about one." This written cue card can be used at the child's desk to provide a permanent prompt for the transient, auditory instruction. The child is verbally reinforced for "paying attention."
2. Hand raising and answering: participation within the group setting begins with attention to group dynamics. Visual cues such as a hand held sign (a 'stop' and 'go' sign, red on one side, green on the other) that indicates 'good' and 'bad' opportunities for hand raising can help the child to learn this complex skill. The child should be praised and rewarded for "paying attention" to good hand raising opportunities.
3. Working with a partner: when the instructions are auditory, the teacher can provide the child with written strategies to follow. Tasks within the partnership can be delineated and divided up. Emphasis can be placed on the partner as a source of information, "If you don't know what to do, ask your partner." Praise the child for "paying attention to your partner."

Measuring Attention
Using recall

1. Read-aloud stories. The target becomes recall of one salient detail from the story such as the name of a character or an event that took place. Inform the child prior to the story that "You will have to tell me who the story is about to earn a (+)." The target progresses to an increased number of recall responses such as "who the story was about and what happened." Initial recall targets must be direct rather than interpretive.
2. Group Lesson: add a recall component to the checklist by requiring that the child tell you "What was the lesson about?" or similar information. This would apply to classroom instruction that does not directly lead into a task, for example, discussing the characteristics of clouds.
3. Group Instruction: here the teacher is giving

information necessary to complete a task such as incorporating the lesson into a writing task. The recall element should indicate that the child knows what he is supposed to do.

Using comprehension

If the child can recall auditory instructions given to the class but can not translate them into meaningful steps that enable him to complete the assignment, an intermediate step is needed. A written cue card that expands on the group instructions can bridge the gap in understanding and allow the child to complete the task independently rather than being prompted through it. Thus, "Write a story about a time you felt disappointed" is expanded to:

1. "Disappointed" means when you did not get something you wanted.
2. Think of something you want. Write it here:
3. Now think of a time you did not get it.
4. Write 5 sentences that tell about it. Tell what happened and how you felt.

The child with autism can significantly improve his attention through an approach that minimizes distractions, teaches self-regulation of distracted behaviors, and provides attention teaching tasks within specific situations. Attention skills must be well established before the child can participate in the group dynamics of the classroom.

The child with autism can significantly improve his attention through an approach that minimizes distractions, teaches self-regulation of distracted behaviors, and provides attention teaching tasks within specific situations.

Chapter Summary

Manage distractions according to:
- Specific setting
- Source
- Teaching self-regulation

Teach attention through individual tasks:
- Visual tasks
- Auditory tasks

Measure attention through:
- Recall
- Comprehension

CHAPTER 6

DEVELOPING PARTICIPATION
From observer to participant
Introduction

> The child with autism may view participation as merely a necessary task for which he has no interest apart from artificial reinforcement.

The child with autism in the inclusion setting is expected to participate in the classroom community along with his typical peers. Group participation is complex and abstract to the concrete thinker and must be broken down into its component tasks. Participation is, by nature, a social experience. Typical children usually find motivation and gratification through participation as a result of interaction with other people, as well as a sense of pride and accomplishment. The child with autism may view participation as merely a necessary task for which he has no interest apart from artificial reinforcement. Creating successful participation requires systematic dissection of complex group settings, with isolation and mastery of component skills. Participation elements rarely lend themselves to a discrete trial format. Furthermore, environmental cues may be variable, transient, or absent. For example, the child may understand that he should raise his hand during group time. However, the transient nature of an auditory instruction may elude the child with an auditory processing difficulty. Thus, instructing the child to respond to an environmental cue such as "when the teacher asks a question" will be ineffective. Alternative strategies must be used that encourage on-task behavior based on more permanent cues.

Domain

1. Following commands
2. Imitation of peers
3. Responding
4. Initiating
5. Working with a partner or group

Approach

Following commands

Simple participation begins with the child following the teacher's verbal, group instructions. Simple, one step instructions must be mastered before moving on to multiple step instructions. At the preschool and kindergarten level, individual participation is predominately in response to auditory group instructions. Stimulus control is transferred to the teacher when the child no longer needs to be prompted by the aide to "Do what the teacher says," and so forth. Reinforcement should be accompanied by specific verbal praise. Commonly, the child with autism will respond only to directions given to him by name, "John, clap your hands" rather than to the general group instruction, "Everybody clap your hands." The teacher should be instructed that using his name is a heavy prompt and that it is preferable to repeat the instruction with emphasis, "*Everybody* clap your hands." If the child still fails to respond, then using his name as a prompt is appropriate and must be followed by an unprompted trial. So the trial looks like this:

Teacher: "Everybody clap your hands." **Child:** no response.
Teacher: "Everybody clap your hands." **Child:** no response.
Teacher: "John, clap your hands." **Child:** claps hands
Teacher: "Everybody clap your hands. Great clapping John!"

Once the child demonstrates mastery of a few routines or generalizes his response to "Everybody" instructions, the word "participation" can be introduced when giving secondary reinforcement ("Good clapping! That's good participation!"). The child's understanding of participation as a requirement in the social community cannot begin too early.

Imitation of peers

Another component of early participation is based on observational learning skills. The child with autism should be prompted to look at what the other children are doing and do it. If this skill is weak, it should be practiced at home or in a one-on-one setting such as at recess. This skill will serve the child well in a multitude of lifelong settings. As the child makes gains toward independence, observational learning skills will be incorporated into information-seeking strategies. Prompts can include "Do what Sally is doing" and "Look at what your friends are doing." Oftentimes verbal commands are paired with observational learning so that the child can rely on the stronger skill (observational learning, because it is visual) to assist with the weaker (following commands, because it is auditory).

Responding

Answer when spoken to. The next level of participation involves the child's ability to respond consistently. In the classroom setting, the child can earn reinforcement for participating when the teacher speaks directly to him (as opposed to the group). For example, "John, what are you going to write about?" if followed by an appropriate response, can be rewarded for participation and/or attention. This form of participation represents the easiest for the child with autism since it does not require initiation on his part, nor does it require discernment of environmental cues as is the case in hand-raising.

Participate by appropriate hand raising. This target is far more complex than simply completing a motor task on cue. The child who raises his hand in a group setting must discriminate appropriate hand-raising opportunities. Simply raising his hand when other children do is not enough. For example, if the antecedent is "Raise your hand if you are somebody's sister" the male child who merely imitates an action without processing the auditory component that precedes it invites ridicule. The child who is hindered by an auditory processing deficit or word retrieval issues may find appropriate hand raising an extremely challenging task. In addition to the inability to discriminate *when* it is appropriate to raise his hand, he may not understand the content of auditory material sufficiently and quickly enough to formulate an answer and respond appropriately. Initial success may be achieved by first requiring a recall component that indicates adequate attention and comprehension of the topic presented. Once the child demonstrates understanding, he can be required to make an on-topic comment. Formulating an appropriate comment may be much easier than quickly processing and responding in a question-answer format. A social story that explains the details of *when and why* he should raise his hand can be useful in promoting understanding and motivation. For example:

When should I raise my hand? I should raise my hand when I want to make a comment. I should raise my hand when I know the answer to a question.

Why should I raise my hand? I should raise my hand so that my teacher knows I have an answer. Then she will know to call on me.

When should I not raise my hand? I should not raise my hand when I don't have a comment or an answer.

When should I put my hand down? I should put my hand down when I get called on. I should also put my hand down when someone else gets called on.

Why should I put my hand down? I should put my hand down when someone answers because then the question is done.

The rapid rate at which questions are answered, corollary questions are introduced, and multiple answers are presented further complicates the task. The child with autism may be several questions behind the group by the time he can process the first question, often resulting in answers that, although originally appropriate, no longer apply. For example:

Teacher: "Who can tell me why the boy got in trouble?"

Student: "Because he forgot to do what his Mom asked him to do."

Teacher: "Right. Has that ever happened to you?"

Child with autism: "The boy did not do his chores."

Clearly, the child's answer was on-topic initially, but the delay in processing and presentation prevented him from answering the current question. The teacher who understands the child's impairment will reward his efforts while correcting him and protecting him from ridicule by his peers.

Teacher: "That's right, John, the boy did not do his chores, just like Sara mentioned when she said that he forgot to do what his Mom asked him to do. Thank you for giving us a more detailed answer. Can you think of a time when you forgot to do your chores?"

Child with autism: "Sometimes I forget to put my clean clothes away."

Teacher: "Excellent!"

Difficulties with hand raising often invite ridicule from peers and may present a challenge to the teacher unfamiliar with a systematic approach to skill acquisition. Initial instruction and practice in a controlled environment, such as a small group setting, can allow the child with autism to succeed and acquire

skill before generalizing it to the classroom setting.

Scaffolding should be used to break down the hand-raising target into component tasks that can be individually acquired and mastered. Mastered components can be chained together and combined until the target is achieved and generalized. Heavy reinforcement should be used to ensure that the child is sufficiently motivated to succeed at this difficult target behavior. The teacher's cooperation should be requested so that opportunities for success are created. Accommodations to support the child's efforts include designating a specific time for the child to comment, designing a question specifically for the child, and providing information in advance about the topic to facilitate rehearsal.

Answer in unison. "Say it with the class" can be achieved using prompts inherent within the task ("when everyone else says it") or by making use of the repetitive and predictable nature of the task. Certain daily routines always require group participation and these are the easiest targets to begin with. Once mastery occurs in the predictable events, speaking in unison can be expanded to other areas such as group settings in which the teacher asks a question of the group rather than an individual.

Initiating

This is the highest level of participation and is complex and abstract. There are multiple variables that make it difficult for the child with autism to know what is required of him. Since creative thinking is extremely difficult, the generation of unique ideas requires instruction in "brainstorming" and other techniques that promote abstract thinking skills.

Asking Questions. Teach simple, common questions that the child can use to approach a peer at a designated time such as recess or lunch. List "Ask a friend about (topic)" on the checklist and reinforce each initiation. Advance to include variability in types of questions as the child may easily get stuck. If the child is not directly observed (which he should be initially) then introduce a recall component to ensure task accountability ("What did you ask Sydney about? What did she say?"). Advance to turn-taking so that the child listens and responds to the peer's statement.

Conversation. Verbal initiation advances from asking questions to reciprocal statements (comments) and question-answer combinations. The child must have already mastered 100% responding to peers before engaging in a rolling conversation. The initial conversation target is one turn (each child speaks once), advancing to multiple turns.

Contributing factual information. The child should first learn to differentiate between fact and opinion. Contributing a factual statement during a specified setting such as morning group time can be a starting target for initiation.

Contributing opinion. In a similar fashion, designate opportunities for contributing opinion. For both factual information and opinion, the opportunity to succeed should be created if it is not readily available.

Working with a partner or a group

As the child progresses through the school system, the emphasis on working with other children increases. The child with autism will probably find this difficult because of the social nature of partner and group work. The more that unpredictable settings can be made predictable, and expectations quantified, the easier it will be for the child to succeed.

> *The more that unpredictable settings can be made predictable, and expectations quantified, the easier it will be for the child to succeed.*

Following a partner's lead. It is easier to follow a peer than to lead. Choose a peer who demonstrates mastery of the activity as well as leadership skills. Clearly define each role that leader and follower will assume. Delineate in writing for the child with autism what he is expected to do when "working with a partner."

Leading a partner. Start with simple expressive instructions using mastered activities. For example the child instructs his partner on how to complete a task, or play a game. Choose an initial activity that the child is very comfortable with, skilled at, and highly interested in.

Working with a group. The child should begin by listening to ideas presented by the group and respond to them, such as with "That's a good idea." The target advances to contributing an idea. The child should also learn to ask, "What can I do?" It is not uncommon for the assertive children with leadership skills to dominate, and the task may be completed without the participation of the child with autism. In this case, an adult should intervene by discussing with the group that everyone should have a chance to participate. If problems persist, specific tasks may need to be designated for the child with autism.

Examples:

Example #1: Following commands: simple, one step instructions.
"Line up for recess."
"Wash your hands."
"Put your finished work in the basket."
"Clean up your desk."
Reinforcement should be accompanied by "Good participation."

Example #2: Multiple step instructions.
"After you clean up your desk, line up for recess."
"Before you get your writing supplies be sure to choose a topic for your story."
"First we will write in our journals. Then when you are finished you can pick a book to read quietly."

Example #3: Imitation of peers.
"Look! Do what Haley is doing."
Games such as "Follow the Leader" and "Simon Says" strengthen imitation skills. Imitation skills are then advanced to observational learning opportunities. The child who does not know what to do based on listening or attending can gain the necessary information by observation and imitation: "Do what your friends are doing."

Example #4: Responding.
Child answers "yes", "OK", "sure", "no thanks"; answers something verbally 100% with peers, then 100% with teacher, then with unfamiliar adults, and last with unfamiliar kids. Start with specified opportunities such as 100% with peers "at lunch", then generalize to other situations and fade out prompts and reinforcement.

Example #5: Hand raising cue card.
>**Listen** for a question.
>**Think** of your answer.
>**Raise** your hand.
>**Answer** if you get called on.
>**Put your hand down** when you or someone else answers.

Example #6: Recall.
>Initial target may be recall of main idea, "Today's lesson is about ___." Multiple choice answers can be used to eliminate word retrieval issues.

Example #7: Comment without hand-raising.
>Advance to include a comment made to the teacher at the end of group time, "I'm going to write my story about cheetahs."

Example #8: Comment with hand-raising.
>Comments made at the end are now incorporated within the group time itself. "A cheetah is a mammal."

Example #9: Group hand-raising.
>Additional success with hand raising can be set up using a group request without a verbal response, such as "Raise your hand if you can name a mammal that hunts for it's food. "

Example #10: Individual hand-raising.
>Finally, question and answer format is targeted within the group time. "What animal runs the fastest?" " A cheetah."

Example #11: Answering in unison.
>"Count out loud with the class for the number of days in school." "Sing the Calendar song with the class." Generalize from specific situations to all situations in which classmates are speaking in unison.

Example #12: Initiating by asking questions.
>"Where should I sit?" "When is gym?" "Do we have a spelling test today?"

Example #13: Initiating conversation.
>"Shannon, do you like to go to the zoo?" "Joey, what is your favorite sport?" "What did you do yesterday?"

Example #14: Contributing facts.
>"An invertebrate does not have a backbone." "Broccoli is a vegetable."

Example #15: Contributing Opinion.
>"I think snakes are scary."
>"I don't like going to the dentist."
>"I like hamburgers but I don't like mustard."

Example #16: Working with a partner by following.
>At school, partnering with a peer for classroom jobs: "John and Peter will be our meteorologists this week. Peter will find the forecast and John can record it on the log." At home, simple jobs such as emptying small trash cans: "John, you can help your sister empty the trash. Susie will hold the trash bag and John will dump the trash in."

Example #17: Working with a partner by leading.
>"John, tell Sarah how to play Simon Says." "John, show Peter how to do the mathematician's job."

Example #18: Working with a group.
>Entry level participation in "Building a Castle" could be "John, you get the supplies we need. Here's the list." Or, "You can pick the colors for the flag. What should our flag look like?"

Chapter Summary

Participation through:

- Following commands
- Imitation of peers
- Responding
- Initiating
- Working with a partner

CHAPTER 7

SOCIALIZATION TARGETS AT SCHOOL
Creating opportunities

Introduction

From its initial identification by Leo Kanner (1943) to the present, profound social impairment has been a defining characteristic of autism. Social impairment manifests itself in a variety of ways. Children with autism often avoid their peers, preferring the company of adults. They may find it difficult to understand the unpredictable nature of conversation, fail to read social cues in expressions, and remain oblivious to voice inflection and body language. They are literal and concrete in their thinking and at a loss to understand the ambiguous demands of their social environment. Their compelling need for rules finds little conformity in the chaotic world of subtleties. As a result, relationships are utilitarian, uncomfortable, and often avoided. Unlike their typical peers, socialization is not intrinsically rewarding or desirable and as such will not just "happen." Socialization must be taught, planned for, generalized, and heavily reinforced.

A desire for sameness seems to be a plea for order amid social chaos

Domain

1. Determining expectations
2. Designing a plan
3. Addressing language concerns
4. Teaching useful social skills

Approach

Determining expectations

Parents and educators should work together to set reasonable social targets. Expectations that are too difficult in the social arena will produce failure rather than success. In addition, a long-term perspective based on research findings should be considered in determining the social requirements of the school age child with autism. Current research on adults with autism offers a sobering and realistic view of persistent social difficulties even among those individuals who are otherwise educated and employed (Howlin, p. 87). Unfortunately, even intensive social instruction may still yield only limited results. Furthermore, since socialization is often more utilitarian than enjoyable, it is important to consider what skills would be most useful both for the present and into adulthood. For example, the child that shows no interest in pretend play may benefit more from developing ball skills that allow him to join in games at recess. Skills that are general rather than specific, such as the ability to seek assistance, initiate and respond to greetings, display good manners, and operate in the public realm of purchasing goods and services should receive priority in the strategies that are developed and implemented. Although enormous amounts of time and energy may be expended in an effort to improve social skills, ultimately expectations should include modifying the demands of the social environment. "Whatever strategies are employed to improve social functioning, it is important to recognize that the fundamental deficits are likely to remain throughout life." (Howlin, p. 87). Certainly, low expectations can limit an individual's potential and should be avoided. Reasonable, useful, and attainable social skills should be the focus of any intervention plan.

Designing a plan

Social targets should be required on the target behavior checklist. It should never be presumed that socialization will simply occur due to environmental influences. The child with autism is unlikely to attempt socialization without the motivation of a token economy. Furthermore, even in the presence of motivation, the child may not have the skills to be successful. It can not be overemphasized that profound social impairment is a characteristic of autism by definition, and thus an area of concerted effort in the education of children with autism. However, expectations and efforts should not be abandoned or discouraged in light of current research findings as each individual is unique and their potential is unknown until properly explored. No outcome is ever guaranteed except in the case in which no attempt is made to alter it.

The social plan should be individualized according to the child's current level of understanding and function. Strategies designed for implementation in the school setting may need to be rehearsed or otherwise addressed at home to support and complement efforts at school. As always, success must be attainable and targets created with this in mind. Failure will lead to frustration and further lack

of motivation in the child who may find no inherent return for his investment.

Addressing Language Concerns

Understanding and implementing useful language remains a significant challenge even among those considered high functioning. Speech is a transient mode of communication, existing only for a brief moment and requiring a rapid rate of processing. "Tasks that require the sequential processing of transient information constitute an area of weakness in autism." (Quill, p. 267). Thus, auditory communication may "evaporate" well before the child can process it, let alone act upon it. Visual supports can convert transient, auditory messages into more readily available information, allowing time and opportunity for the child to interpret and respond. Visual strategies take advantage of the child's strengths rather than requiring the use of auditory skills that are weak or absent. Visual supports increase understanding, resulting in an increase in compliance, making them a useful strategy for a variety of tasks and situations.

Expansion of social language should always include tasks to increase understanding so that language becomes meaningful, perhaps even intrinsically rewarding, rather than merely utilitarian. Quill notes that:

> "…premature emphasis on expressive requirements, without regard to helping children with autism understand the events and situations that give rise to them, places those children at risk for the development of isolated, out-of-context skills that will be of minimal benefit to them." (p. 147-148).

Even with understanding, however, socialization targets may be extremely challenging for the child with autism. It is helpful to distinguish between non-verbal and verbal social targets, using non-verbal tasks to provide initial success in the social arena.

For example:

Non-verbal social targets

1. Parallel activities, such as jumping rope or swinging.

2. Joining existing activities, such as basketball or tag.

3. Manners, such as waiting his turn in line or maintaining appropriate interpersonal space.

Verbal social targets

1. Greetings, such as saying, "Hi, how are you today?"
2. Responding, such as answering on-topic when spoken to.
3. Initiating, such as "Will you play hopscotch with me?"
4. Conversing, such as maintaining a conversation of 3 turns, or other quantified targets.
5. Seeking information or assistance, such as, "I don't know what to do. Can you please help me?" and so on.

Expansion of social language should always include tasks to increase understanding so that language becomes meaningful, perhaps even intrinsically rewarding, rather than merely utilitarian.

Social targets should be balanced by both verbal and non-verbal tasks. Since non-verbal target behaviors are more likely to be successful and desirable to someone who struggles with language, these may be used to promote success when verbal targets become too difficult. With acquisition and success, more verbal targets can be added or advanced.

The Teach Me Language (Freeman and Dake) manual is an excellent resource for improving language in children with autism and related disorders. Complex aspects of language are presented in a concrete, visual, and systematic fashion that is easy to implement.

To Order Teach Me Language, telephone SKF Books, Inc., at **(604) 534-6956**

Teaching useful social skills

Manners should first be addressed at home and continued within the public realm. Common language use such as "Please," "Thank you," "You're welcome," "Excuse me," and "I'm sorry," should be required and maintained. In addition, the child should fully understand and be expected to use language rather than physical action to meet his needs. Pushing, shoving, hitting, and so on are unacceptable methods of dealing with peers. Interrupting should also be addressed. This may present unforeseen challenges when the child does not readily notice when others are speaking. The "mindblindness" characteristic of autism may be a contributing factor since the child may be uninterested in what others think, feel, or say. Nevertheless, speaking out of turn should be addressed both at home and in public.

Public behavior includes standing in line, waiting your turn, raising your hand, and so on. Every effort should be made to help the child understand and follow the "rules" of socially acceptable behavior in public. Even when understanding is lacking, children with autism prefer rules that govern behavior. Compliance with social norms will serve them well, helping them to avoid unnecessary negative attention that results from inappropriate behavior or ignorance.

Peer interactions

within the school environment can begin in comfortable settings such as at lunch or recess. Social requirements should be clearly delineated and include an obvious end point, especially when language is required. For example, requiring the child to "Talk to someone at your lunch table" should be amplified by "for 3 turns." Turn taking with conversation is a more useful way to quantify the requirement than "for 2 minutes" since time elements require measurement and add an unnecessary artificial component to conversation. The child with word retrieval difficulties may initially require a topic suggestion, such as, "Talk about your new bike" or "Ask someone about sports." All conversation requirements should be rehearsed prior to the activity to avoid prompt dependency. Peer interactions should not be limited to situations requiring language use. Cooperative partner activities within the classroom can be designed for success and the social element emphasized and rewarded. Partner reading activities also lend themselves to enhancing socialization among school age children with autism.

Greetings

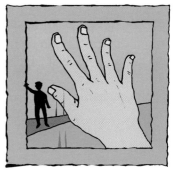

Children with autism may not initiate greetings, may not smile when they see a familiar face, and may not respond when greeted. Any or all of these issues make a person seem antisocial, discourteous, or rude. Simple greetings should be early targets on the school checklist.

Adults are often easier for the child to address since their body language, facial expressions, and verbal responses are more predictable. Saying "Hi" to the teacher, with eye contact, each day should be mandatory. Once the child has mastered greeting his own teacher, he should be encouraged to greet other adults at school. Familiarity with adults at the school broadens the base of support and protection for the child with autism. It also helps to decrease anxiety among those individuals who are less familiar with the child's abilities, as well as his vulnerability.

Children should be selected from the child's peer group for interaction based on familiarity and cooperation so that the child with autism experiences success. Children who appear uncomfortable around the child with autism will probably not help the child as much as those who "like" him or routinely approach him. Cooperative children can simply be told to "help him practice greeting others" or "help him to be more social." Peers should always be praised for such assistance, and encouraged to applaud the child for his efforts. Adding the requirement of greeting a peer (or several peers) to the target behavior checklist gives the child motivation to initiate and succeed at simple social interactions.

Self Defense

Impairments in socialization and language use make the child with autism vulnerable to physical and verbal abuse. Teasing, bullying, mocking and insults should be anticipated and defensive language use should be taught. Many books exist on teaching children how to handle these situations that are relatively common among school age children, with or without disabilities. School and public libraries are a good place to acquire materials to use in discussions with a child affected by autism.

Language responses that can limit or halt verbal abuse by other children should be taught. "Leave me alone," "Don't do that," and "You are bothering me" are standard responses made by all children who learn quickly the importance of defending themselves. Although the use of "please" is appropriate in many settings, it is rarely employed in provocative situations and the child may be ridiculed as a result. Thus, it is recommended to teach the child language responses that model those of his peers.

Role-play is a useful method to employ in the development of appropriate language responses. Practicing with a script and a sibling can offer a controlled environment free from the anxiety found in a real life scenario. Any number of situations can be created, but emphasis should be put on those that currently exist at school or are most likely to occur. It may be counterproductive to create too many scenarios that leave the child feeling overwhelmed or frightened.

Social stories are helpful for increasing understanding of social situations, so that language and skills are taught within a framework that makes sense to the child. Knowing why children tease other children can help the child understand the need to respond appropriately.

Defense skills that equip the child with autism to avoid or remove himself from problem situations should also be targeted. The ability to distinguish when a situation becomes problematic may be weak or absent. Thus, specific situations should be addressed and the appropriate action delineated.

Photography is a useful tool that can make abstract learning more concrete. Still photos can slow and isolate complex interactions, allowing the child  time and opportunity to process details. Facial expressions and body language can be identified and discussed. A digital camera allows daily events to be viewed immediately and problem solving strategies implemented prior to the next school day. Video cameras expand the child's learning from a static to a dynamic event with the benefit of rewinding, repetition, and pausing for instruction.

Behaviors that set the child apart from his typically functioning peers should be brought to his attention and targeted for change. Mannerisms, style of dress, language impairment, or poor eye contact may all contribute to provocation. Working with the child to help him blend in may minimize or eliminate some negative issues with peers.

Equipping the child with understanding, language, and skill to act appropriately in threatening situations contributes greatly to decreasing the level of anxiety associated with these encounters. Certainly, these skills are not a substitute for appropriate adult intervention. The child should understand when to seek help or report a situation to an adult. Similarly, the adults responsible for the care of the child with autism should be well aware of his vulnerability and maintain vigilance in supervising and disciplining social interactions.

Examples
Determining Expectations

Non-verbal targets
1. Line up
2. Parallel play such as swings, jump rope

Verbal targets
1. Child should respond when spoken to 90-100% first with familiar adults, then with classmates.
2. Child should greet his teacher every morning. Expand to greeting three other children or the classmates at his table.

3. Child should ask to join in whenever familiar peers are playing basketball at recess. Initial target is once a day.
4. Child should initiate one conversation per day, for 3-turns, starting at lunch and expanding to other opportunities within the classroom.

Designing a plan

The social plan should include immediate targets as well as how to expand to future targets.
1. Expand responses to include less familiar adults (substitute teachers included), 90-100% and less familiar children.
2. Expand greeting requirement from "Hi" to "Hi, how are you today?" (adults) or "Hi, how's it going?" (kids).
3. Increase requirement for joining a group to include soccer at recess.
4. Expand number of conversations initiated to three, without initially changing the number of turns taken.
5. Expand length of conversation to 4-5 turns.

Addressing language concerns

Success in the classroom will probably require some effort at home such as social stories, worksheets, rehearsal and role-play.

1. **Practice reciprocal comments and questions before school.**
   (P)=parent (A)=child with autism.
   a. The parent comments to initiate the conversation, allowing no more than 3 seconds to respond.
   b. If the child does not respond, give an informational "No." Repeat the identical comment.
   c. If the child responds with a reciprocal comment, say "Good" and continue the conversation. If he does not respond, prompt with "It's your turn."
   d. Prompted trials must always be followed by an unprompted trial to establish the necessary association between a stimulus, a response, and a reinforcement.
   (P) "I like to play tennis."
   (A) "I like to play basketball. Do you like to play basketball?"
   (P) "Sure, I like basketball, but I'm not very good at it. I never make any free throws."
   (A) "I like football more."
   (P) "Really? I don't like football very much because it's too hard to catch."
   (A) "But a touchdown is worth a lot of points. That's cool!"
   (P) "It's been nice talking to you. See you later."
   (A) "Bye."

2. Prepare a conversation cue card with a suggested topic and key words to be used as a prompt for 3-turn conversation at lunch.

Topic: favorite movies

Key words:

Shrek

Toy Story

No monster movies

3. Rehearse with and without the cue card prior to school.

4. Include a recall element on the checklist or for after school.

"I talked to _____ at lunch.

We talked about favorite movies. His favorite movie is _____."

Teaching useful social skills

Written cues may help to delineate the expectations associated with both verbal and non-verbal social targets. Written rules for social interaction also increase understanding of social expectations and behaviors. These should be discussed with the child prior to school or peer play. The rewards associated with these rules should also be outlined. For example:

"Rules for Talking with Friends":

Turn your body to face your friend.
Look at your friend's eyes some of the time.
Listen when your friend talks.
Answer when your friend asks you.
You can earn a (+) each time you do this.

"Rules for Working with a Partner":

Look at what your partner is doing.
Listen to what your partner says.
Make a comment about what you are doing.
Ask your partner to help you.
You will earn a (+) for each partner activity.

Photographs can be used for a variety of teaching activities. Pictures taken during successful social situations can be used as visual reminders of target behaviors achieved. For example, "Look, here is a picture of you talking to Ryan at recess. You got a (+) for that. That's great being social!"or "Here is a picture of you playing on the swings with Diana, because you asked her to play with you."

Social targets on the checklist

a. Response to peers: Prompt, "Answer (when someone asks you a question)."
   Checklist: (+) for each time child answers when spoken to.
b. Initiate play: Prompt, "Ask someone to play (on the monkey bars) with you."
   Checklist: (+) for initiating play.
c. Initiate conversation: Prompt, "Talk to Joey about sports."
   Checklist: (+) for on-topic, 3- turn conversation at lunch.

Chapter Summary

Teach socialization by:

Determining reasonable expectations

Designing a plan for success

Addressing language concerns

Teaching useful social skills

CHAPTER 8

DEVELOPING INDEPENDENCE
Teaching self-regulation and information-seeking

Introduction

The parents and educators of the school-aged child with autism should work cooperatively to plan and promote the child's independence. The child with autism typically enters school dependent on an aide. Even high-functioning children benefit greatly from the assistance of an aide who is knowledgeable about autism and behavioral practice. The use of an aide, however, must be decreased over time in a systematic fashion without compromising the child's success. Independence must be viewed as the long-term goal of the child's educational process. Independence develops, it does not occur. Each individual skill mastered adds to the overall level of independence, but efforts to develop information seeking skills and self-regulation should be priorities. Through the use of structure, visual cues, and accommodations, the child with autism learns to take responsibility for academic achievement rather than simply remaining prompt dependent into adulthood.

> *Independence must be viewed as the long-term goal of the child's educational process. Independence develops, it does not occur.*

Domain

1. Observational learning
2. Information seeking skills
3. Self-regulation
4. Fading the use of an aide

Approach

Observational learning

Observational learning refers to the acquisition of necessary information through observation, or simply "learning by watching." The general instruction for observational learning tasks is "Do what the other kids are doing." This approach is far superior to a direct prompt such as "clap your hands," which requires no independent effort from the child. From very early in the educational process, observational learning should be used to facilitate the development of independent action. People of all ages and abilities utilize observational learning to determine appropriate behavior in a variety of settings. Sporting activities, cooking, job skills, and peer interactions are just a few examples of common situations that require observational learning skills. A child learns more about the game of baseball by watching others play than by reading a book about it. Cooking skills are acquired through hands-on experience and observation rather than by reading an instruction manual. Most

> *From very early in the educational process, observational learning should be used to facilitate the development of independent action. People of all ages and abilities utilize observational learning to determine appropriate behavior in a variety of settings.*

job skills are learned through practical experiences, internships, or apprenticeships; no doctor, nurse, or pilot enters their profession equipped only with knowledge gained through exhaustive study. A teenager knows that no book can substitute for experience in the social setting. Clearly, observational learning is a useful skill across the entire spectrum of academic and social activities for the individual with autism. Group work and independent desk work in the elementary school years follow imitation of motor activities in the preschool setting. Specific target behaviors should be isolated, mastered, and expanded to produce generalization.

Imitation of motor activities should begin at home at a very young age and be continued in the preschool setting. For the school-aged child, this should be a well-developed skill that can then be applied to more difficult tasks. Learning to play a musical instrument, completing complex art projects, and participating in gym class or after-school sporting activities are all situations that require observational learning skills.

Pairing the child with autism and a peer who can be "assigned" to model behavior in certain settings is a useful intermediate step in the development of independence. In selecting an appropriate "buddy," care should be exercised to ensure that the peer is kind and patient toward the child with autism, as well as an adequate model of the target behavior. The child selected should be cooperative and willing to perform the assigned duties. In similar fashion, the child with autism should understand that his "buddy" will serve as the prompt for on-task behavior necessary to earn the desired reinforcement.

Group work is another situation in which observational learning skills are employed. The target behavior should be clearly defined so that the child begins to acquire information on his own through the use of observation. The child should understand that the target behavior is not simply task completion, but rather acquiring the necessary information that will equip him to work independent of the aide or teacher. Where previously he was instructed to "do what your friends are doing," now he is instructed to "watch your friends so you know what to do."

Independent desk work and related on-task behavior is learned through a combination of skills and instructions. Gathering necessary supplies and following through on classroom instructions may initially require the use of a visual cue or list. As the child utilizes observational skills to acquire information, visual cues can be faded out and replaced by the instruction "Look at what your friends are doing." However, the child should also understand that in certain situations, "watching your friends" is not allowed. Children are introduced to test taking in first and second grade. By third grade, most children begin taking standardized tests, so it is important to teach the child parameters for the inappropriate use of observation in the classroom.

Socialization skills can be promoted through observation of peers, siblings, or through role-play. For the adolescent or adult with autism, recognizing and interpreting social cues remains difficult, and reliance on observation is necessary to progress in the social arena. With this in mind, the school-aged child should develop strategies that include observation and imitation of play skills, determination of appropriate interpersonal space, and observation of facial expressions to interpret emotions.

Generalization of observational learning skills develops by incorporating the mastered skill into an information-seeking strategy. This concept is expanded in the following section. The prompt to watch his peers should be faded to a more general prompt such as "How can you find out what to do?"

Information seeking skills

A variety of strategies should be taught to enable the child with autism to acquire the information necessary to complete classroom activities on his own. Both the child and teacher benefit when these strategies are displayed in a written or visual fashion. In this way, the child knows what is expected of him and the teacher does not facilitate dependence by continual prompting.

Independent work completion should be isolated and targeted for prompt mastery. Since the child is more likely to follow through on information that is explicit, he can achieve a measure of independence quickly by carrying out clearly delineated, sequential instructions. Auditory group instructions that elude the child because of the transient nature of verbal information become manageable through the use of visual modifications. For example, a 10-minute classroom explanation in which children determine a topic within a given subject, conduct research, and present findings may leave the child with autism dumbfounded. He may be quite capable of accomplishing the given assignment if supportive accomodations are made. A simple, short list of key elements may be all that is needed to enable him to work independently:

> **Brainstorm:** list 3 types of climates.
> **Choose** one climate. This is your topic.
> **Research:** look in the encyclopedia and find this topic.
> **Findings:** write 5 things that you learn about this climate.
> **Report:** use these 5 things to write a paragraph about your topic.

This is an example of *accommodation* without *modification*. The opportunity to succeed is created through differential instruction rather than allowing inevitable failure or lowering expectations. Additional examples are presented in the following section.

Acquiring information

Once the child has demonstrated mastery of independent task completion in a specific setting, the target is expanded to include the acquisition of information that precedes it. This backward-chaining approach allows the child to succeed first with the easier, more concrete component before attempting the more difficult and abstract. Information is acquired in many different ways. This may be intuitive for the typical child, but for the child with autism, specific strategies must be targeted and reinforced. For instance, a simple formula presented on an index card can be displayed on the child's desk or work folder:

"Find out what to do":
> **Listen** to the teacher.
> **Look** at the board.
> **Look** at what your friends are doing.
> **Determine** what to do.
> **Ask** last.

Pairing the mastered skills of information acquisition with independent work completion is the final step toward independence in the classroom setting. Now the child who has mastered these two components in isolation is required to combine them into one target behavior such as "Find out what to do and do it by yourself." Reinforcement is given for the completion of the combined task, rather than for the individual components. It should be understood that the child is not required to perform flawlessly, only on-topic.

Self-regulation

Self-regulation refers to the ability of the child to manage his emotions, behaviors, and interactions with others. Self-regulation includes both ability and responsibility. Developing independence requires that the child gain the skills to complete tasks and assignments on his own, as well as the maturity to apply himself to his work without artificial reinforcement.

Ability to self-regulate emotions is developed by discrete targets, fostered by consistent follow-through,

> Ability to self-regulate emotions is developed by discrete targets, fostered by consistent follow-through, and encouraged through appropriate reinforcement.

and encouraged through appropriate reinforcement. The ability of the child to respond to new or different situations without negative behavior is referred to as frustration tolerance. For example, the school-aged child should be able to manage his anxiety in the event that a change in the daily routine occurs. Attending an assembly with his class should not provoke a tantrum or other unreasonable behavior. However, negative behavior is likely to occur unless appropriate positive behavior is taught and required. Frustration tolerance must be planned and developed using a behavioral approach, and is discussed in detail in Chapter 11. Continuity of intervention between educators and parents must exist so that the child's behavior is consistent across settings from home to school. Inconsistent follow-through may produce inadvertent reinforcement of negative behaviors.

Responsibility for on-task behavior must be transferred to the child if independence is to occur. Using language such as, "It's your job to finish your work, not mine" can cultivate a work ethic while artificial reinforcement remains in place to motivate the child. It is imperative that primary and secondary reinforcement be used in conjunction so that the emphasis on verbal praise can gradually replace the token economy. With achievement and mastery comes confidence, and artificial reinforcement can be faded out incrementally. Behaviors that previously earned a token are now praised and intrinsic rewards are emphasized. For example, "When you finish your math you can choose a board game to play with your partner," represents a naturally occurring reward within the context of the classroom. In addition, natural consequences now replace an artificial cost response, so that failure to perform the expected behavior results in the loss of a privilege. Thus, the child who procrastinates may suffer the loss of privilege that is afforded those who complete their work. Natural consequences can also extend beyond the classroom. For example, "If you don't get your writing assignment done before lunch you will have to finish it at home tonight," represents the loss of some measure of playtime after school. In this way, the child is required to complete assignments in the same fashion as his typically functioning peers. When implementing natural consequences, the educator should verify that

mastery has occurred. For example, "Anyone who is noisy during quiet reading will miss five minutes of recess" is a reasonable consequence if the child has demonstrated that he can comply with the required behavior. If not, he will be unjustly punished for a behavior he has not acquired.

Fading the use of an aide
Transfer of stimulus control to the teacher must occur so that the child's dependence on the classroom aide diminishes. Each specific target behavior mastered is systematically assigned to the control of the teacher and removed from the control of the aide. The child is informed that the teacher now requires the target behavior and will control token distribution or reinforcement. Once stimulus control has been transferred from the aide to the teacher, the aide should distance himself and eventually exit the room during mastered activities.

Activities rather than isolated behaviors are targeted by chaining together individual components that have been mastered. Activity blocks such as independent reading, journal writing, or math replace previous individual targets. For instance:
"Pick a new book from your book bucket."
"Write the title in your reading log."
"Read quietly until the timer goes off."
"Fill in your reading comprehension card."
are mastered in isolation and combined to become the single target activity, "Warm-up Reading." Now the teacher rewards the child for on-task behavior for the entire period, with the aide absent. The child must understand that he is required to complete all elements in order to receive reinforcement. Any omission results in failure to earn the reward. Some children will correct their behavior when they fail to earn reinforcement, but others may require a cost response to motivate them. The teacher may say something like this: "You did a great job picking a new book and reading quietly, and you remembered to write the title on your book log. But you did not answer your questions about the story, so no (+) today for Warm-up Reading. I hope that tomorrow you will remember to do all four things to earn your (+)." A statement like this reminds the child of several important facts:

1. There are four things to remember to do. This allows the child to make a mental checklist.
2. He is praised for what he did well.
3. There is no punishment for his failure.
4. He will have another opportunity tomorrow.

Problem solving within the classroom now becomes the teacher's responsibility. The aide should cultivate the teacher's ability to evaluate the effectiveness of behavioral intervention. In addition, the teacher should be able to make adjustments to requirements based on the child's actions. If, for example, the same element continues to be omitted from an established routine, there are several considerations:

1. The activity, or one of its components, is not mastered.
2. The child may be unable to remember the sequence of required components.
3. The child is insufficiently motivated.

If it is apparent to the teacher that the child has never clearly demonstrated mastery, then the behavior should be returned to acquisition status. The child cannot be required to accomplish behaviors for which he has not demonstrated mastery. If observation confirms that the activity is mastered, a visual cue or list of key words should be provided. If the behavior continues, a cost response can be instituted. Now the teacher may say, "You are doing a great job reading but you still are not answering the questions about the story. If this happens again tomorrow, I will have to take away a (+)."

Examples
Observational learning

Preschool. The target behavior is to sit on the rug for circle time. If the child fails to act on the auditory group instruction, "Everybody to the rug," then he is prompted to "Do what the other kids are doing." Other targets include:
1. Entrance routines such as hanging up a coat or backpack, finding and marking his name on an attendance list, moving a magnet on a chart, or saying "Hi" to the teacher.

2. Imitating hand or body motions.
3. Gathering supplies needed for a project.
4. Transitions, such as moving from group time at the rug to a worktable.
5. Lining up.
6. Exit routines such as checking a designated cubicle or mailbox, getting a coat or backpack, saying "Good-bye" to the teacher.

Kindergarten. At center time, the child is prompted to play parallel with the same instruction, "Do what the other kids are doing." Block play, puzzles, and manipulatives are good activities in which to introduce observational learning. Preschool activities not yet mastered should continue to be targeted and followed by kindergarten targets such as:
1. Drawing and writing tasks.
2. Looking at picture books.
3. Gym and recess.
4. Art projects, crafts, woodworking and science activities.
5. Lunch routines for children in full-day kindergarten.

First grade and up. More advanced observational learning is used when the child is seated at his table or desk for independent work. He now incorporates observational learning skills into an information-seeking strategy.
1. He observes that the other children are doing their math workbooks. He realizes that he should get out his math workbook and begin working.
2. He observes that the other children are getting out their scissors and markers to complete an art project. He realizes that he also needs to gather these supplies and begin working.
3. He observes that the other children are cutting and pasting according to a given model. He realizes that he also needs to work according to the given model.
4. He observes that the other children are getting out their chapter books and reading quietly. He realizes that he should get out his chapter book and read quietly with the class.
5. He observes that the other children are playing "Simon Says" and he joins in, observing and copying appropriately.

If the child fails to use observational cues to seek information and perform on-task, the teacher can simply remind him to "Use your strategies to find out what to do." If this prompt is insufficient to produce the desired behavior, he should be prompted more directly, "Look at what everyone else is doing and do it." As with all prompts, these must be faded out so that the child performs on-task behavior independently.

Information seeking skills

A written cue card is provided with the information-seeking strategies that the child should use:

Find out what to do:
Listen to the teacher.
Look at the board.
Look at what your friends are doing.
Determine what to do.
Ask if you still don't know what to do.

1. Listen to the teacher: The teacher explains to the class : "We are going to read a Dr. Seuss book and then we are going to write our own stories using the same style of writing as Dr. Seuss. So while we are reading, think about what types of characters, settings, and themes the author uses."
2. Look at the board: The child refers to any written instructions on the chalkboard/dry erase board that the teacher has provided for all of the children. Brainstorming by the class yields the following information:
   "Dr. Seuss writes using rhyming words."
   "Dr. Seuss uses imaginary characters."
   "Dr. Seuss uses silly characters."
   "Dr. Seuss writes about made-up places."
   "Dr. Seuss is funny."
3. Look at peers: The child looks at what the other kids are doing, observes that they are writing and illustrating.

4. Ask last: If the child has exhausted the above resources and still does not know what to do, he should be prompted to ask the teacher (or a reliable peer), "What should I do?"

At this point, the teacher should assist the child by providing a supporting accomodation that promotes independent work. A task sheet with a concise description of the required activity would give the child the necessary equipment to attempt the work independently.

1. **Brainstorm:** make up a character name.
2. **Rhyming words:** write 5 pairs of rhyming words.
3. **Write:** sentences ending in a rhyming word. 5 pairs = 10 sentences.
4. **Copy:** sentences to make a story.
5. **Illustrate:** Draw a picture to go with your story.

Once the child has adequate support he can be expected to pair information seeking skills with independent work effort. The child uses the information he has to complete the task, writing and illustrating according to the assignment.

Self-regulation

Target behavior #1: Promoting frustration tolerance with schedule changes.

"Today we are going to have an all-school assembly at 2:00, so we will miss gym today." Child responds to information without tantruming and comforts himself by saying, "It's OK." The child then asks the aide or teacher, "What do I need to do to get a (+) at the assembly?" He is told, "You need to sit still and sit quietly. Afterward you must tell me something about what you saw or heard. Then I will give you a (+)." The child is praised for "not getting upset about something different."

Target behavior #2: Decreasing negative response to receiving a (-).

"It's not OK to tantrum when you get a (-). You have to live with your choices. Next time you need to read slower so you understand what you read. Then you will be able to get 50% or higher on your card and you will get a (+)."

Target behavior #3: Promoting self-regulation of distractions.

"It's your job to pay attention. If you are looking around the room then you will miss out on the instructions and you won't know what to do. If you don't get your work done, I can't give you a (+)."

Target behavior #4: Using good manners.

"You need to be polite with your teacher and friends. That means saying please when you want something, thank you when you get it, and excuse me when someone is in your way." The teacher or aide keeps track of success with a chart that the child takes home to his parents. He is rewarded at home based on the number of successes at school.

Fading the use of an aide

Mastered activity #1: Entrance routine

The aide exits the room while the child hangs up his coat, backpack, and says "Hi" to the teacher. The teacher reinforces with a token.

Mastered activity #2: Job board

The aide exits the room while the child checks the job board and completes his job independently. The teacher reinforces with a token.

Mastered activity #3: Independent Reading

The aide exits the room while the child gets his book out and reads quietly for the entire reading period. The teacher reinforces success based on 50% or higher on a short, multiple choice card prepared in advance to evaluate comprehension:

1. The men wanted to be the first:
   a. Explorers to cross the Yukon.
   b. Explorers to cross Antarctica.
   c. Explorers to discover Antarctica.

2. This was a very dangerous trip because:
   a. They were chased by wild animals.
   b. The weather was severe.
   c. They were very lonely.
3. Some of the men became hypothermic. "Hypothermic" means:
   a. Suffering from severe hunger.
   b. Suffering from severe thirst.
   c. Suffering from severe cold.

Mastered activity #4: Lunch routine

The aide exits the lunchroom but the child remains supervised by the lunchroom staff. Reinforcement is faded out.

Mastered activity #5: Dismissal

The aide exits the room while the child checks his cubicle for papers to take home, gets his lunch bag, coat, and backpack, then lines up to wait for the bell. The teacher reinforces with praise.

Mastered activity #6: Group time

The aide sits at the back of the room while stimulus control is transferred to the teacher. The teacher praises the child for sitting appropriately and for paying attention to the story that is read. The teacher calls on the child in a select situation to participate by answering a question designed to promote success. "John, what mammal are you going to write about today?" is followed by an appropriate answer and reinforced with praise for "paying attention" and "participating." The teacher gives him a token.

When independence is viewed as the long-term goal, progress can be planned for and implemented by teaching global skills such as observational learning, information seeking, and self-regulation. Parents and educators should also recognize the need to systematically decrease the influence of the classroom aide while increasing the child's level of independent work.

Chapter Summary

Promote independence through:

- Observational learning skills: "Watch your friends so you know what to do."

- Information seeking skills: "Find out what to do."

- Self-regulation: "Now do it yourself."

- Fade the use of an aide: transfer stimulus control to the teacher

CHAPTER 9

READING COMPREHENSION STRATEGIES
Implications of learning style

Introduction

Many children with autism exhibit difficulties with reading comprehension. Abilities to decode written language may give the appearance of competency in the absence of understanding. Deficits may be isolated in nature, limited only to abstract concepts, or they may be panoramic in scope. Accurate intervention requires identification of specific and isolated comprehension deficits. Current literature and research acknowledge the challenges inherent in low reading comprehension and present a wide variety of interventions. It is beyond the scope of this book to address the numerous theories and applications available or their corresponding outcomes. Here we will offer specific strategies for school-aged children with autism that build on mastered concepts, promoting understanding and enjoyment through progressive achievement of isolated targets.

> *Abilities to decode written language may give the appearance of competency in the absence of understanding.*

Domain

1. Implications of learning style
2. Assessment
3. Useful strategies

Approach

Implications of learning style

Learning style is a function of cognitive processes in which an individual gathers information, processes it, and utilizes it to reason and problem solve. "Cognition and learning style are inextricably linked and any division of the two is artificial." (Gardner, p. 11). The unique learning style of an individual with autism may be better understood by considering the development of cognition as it applies to reading comprehension.

First-order representation refers to a child's ability to associate three-dimensional objects with purpose or function. Discrimination of objects and differentiation of function help the child learn the difference between a ball and an orange, recognizing that one is edible and the other is a toy (Gardner, p. 11).

Second-order representation refers to the association between objects and symbols. As cognition matures, the child understands that letters and words are ordered to represent objects and ideas. The normally developing child progresses from the concrete, first-order representation to the more abstract, second-order representation in the first few years of life. Impairment in the cognitive development of the child with autism may explain many of the characteristics that are commonly seen (Gardner, p. 11).

> "Research suggests that a cognitive deficit, which interferes with the ability to understand and use second-order representation, may account for the three key impairments associated with ASD (autism spectrum disorder). Imaginative play is difficult if the child can't understand or make second-order representation (imagine that a shelf is an oven in the home corner). The child will find complex communication with second-order representations very difficult ('hop to' actually means hurry, not hop). Finally, the child will have difficulty forming meaningful social relationships, as his inability to form second-order representations will inhibit his ability to understand the feelings and thoughts of his peers." (Gardner, p. 12).

The implications for reading difficulties should be obvious. The child whose cognition remains at the elementary level of first-order representations will likely struggle to understand what he reads. Decoding, which uses memorization of rules and patterns to decipher words, becomes the prevailing method of compensation for the child with autism. Although he may appear to be a competent reader based on vocabulary, comprehension often lags behind and must be properly assessed and addressed.

Assessment

To label a child deficient in reading comprehension is of little value in addressing the multitude of issues that compose such a fundamental academic skill. An accurate assessment identifying abilities and inabilities should be made.

Non-verbal evaluations must be used for the child with autism. Standardized testing is often language heavy and fails to accurately assess the needs of a child whose expressive language is weak. Receptive as well as expressive language skills must be utilized in the assessment of reading comprehension.

Accomodations of existing testing must be provided for the child who cannot be accurately assessed with language based evaluations. Unfortunately, we know of no existing test that eliminates the dependence on language for evaluation of comprehension. Thus, accommodations should be considered and provided for in the child's Individual Education Plan (IEP). Accommodations are supports that modify the task and allow the child an equal opportunity to succeed at the same level as typically functioning peers. Accommodations are not "cheating." Every child is entitled to a fair assessment of his abilities. "If we ignore the learning style of students with ASD (autism spectrum disorder) we are in fact denying them access to the curriculum and learning opportunities." (Gardner, p. 16). So, for example, multiple choice options should be provided in testing where open-ended or narrative responses are usually required.

Word Retrieval problems must also be eliminated in the evaluation process. Many children with autism lack the expressive language skills necessary to deliver their thoughts, and as such, determination of comprehension deficits may be impossible by standard methods. Multiple choice questions and a fill-in-the-blank format using a word list are much more appropriate assessment tools than open-ended or narrative questions.

Decoding, which uses memorization of rules and patterns to decipher words, becomes the prevailing method of compensation for the child with autism.

Useful strategies

Vocabulary is fundamental to understanding written language and can be expanded using synonyms, word pairs and worksheets using a word bank. Vocabulary is generally easy to acquire since word meanings are concrete. Teach Me Language (Freeman and Dake) as well as the SCORE! Educational Program are both excellent ways to teach and expand vocabulary.

Story elements that a child needs to recognize include characters, setting, and plot. The targets should be isolated and mastered individually, beginning with the character(s). Initially, the child can be required to identify the main character by listing it on his checklist, "Who is the story about?" and then receive positive reinforcement through his token economy. Visual cues are inherent in story books with pictures or illustrations so that a readily available prompt is to point to the character's picture and ask, "Who is this?" Prompted trials must be followed by returning to the target, which in this case is "Who is the character?" or "Who is the story about?" This may seem incidental and obvious, but the child must be deliberately instructed to associate the picture and name with the character and its place within the story. It should not be assumed that the child can make this association until it is observed. The setting can be targeted in a similar fashion. The "plot" is similar to the "main idea" and is addressed below.

Sentence comprehension expands on vocabulary by using the supporting context to enhance understanding. Multiple choice and fill-in type worksheets are useful for increasing sentence comprehension. A variety of workbooks are available commercially for this purpose. "Reading Milestones" is a series of stories and corresponding workbooks that teach and build, in a progressive fashion, on the acquisition of fundamental reading skills. Controlled vocabulary, use of visual cues, systematic and predictable presentation of material, and repetition of concepts make this an excellent choice of materials. "Reading Milestones" are available from Pro-Ed Publishers.

Passage comprehension requires more than simply understanding each isolated sentence in a passage. It requires that the child begin to chain thoughts together in a sequence, and analyze the association between the component sentences. Questions such as who, what, where, and when should be used to elicit evidence of comprehension from the reader. Teach Me Language, "Reading Milestones," and computer based instruction such as "SCORE!" are excellent methods of expanding the child's passage comprehension. All of these methods utilize intermediate tasks to bridge understanding and eliminate word retrieval issues in a variety of ways. Supplemental educational resources are addressed in chapter 20.

Sequencing story elements in a chronological fashion is a useful strategy to help the child begin to see the "big picture" rather than fixating on isolated details within the story. Visual representation of stories can be achieved using pictures, pictures with sentences, then sentences only. Commercially available sequencing cards, photographs or magazine clippings can be used. A corresponding story can be created if one is not already provided. The child should first discuss each picture by answering, "What is going on here?" Then he places the pictures in order to tell the story. He should use as much language as possible and use words that indicate time sequence, such as "First," "Next," and "Last." The trial can be advanced to incorporate both pictures and sentences. The story can be reproduced and cut up into component sentences, which the child matches to the corresponding picture. Finally, the pictures are faded out and the child organizes the sentences in chronological order. We highly recommend the Teach Me Language program for teaching a variety of sequencing tasks.

Main idea expands on the child's ability to identify story elements. Once he has mastered identification of characters and setting, the target can be advanced to "What happened?" Multiple choice should be used to avoid word retrieval difficulties. For example, "What happened to Sally-did she get lost or did she get hurt?" is a better way to evaluate the child's understanding than to simply ask, "What happened?" and have the child answer, "I don't know." Although "individuals

To Order Teach Me Language, telephone SKF Books, Inc., at
(604) 534-6956

with ASD (Autism Spectrum Disorder) may be good visual learners, they often have difficulty distilling discrete concepts from their visual experiences." (Gardner, p. 16). It cannot be assumed that what is obvious to the typically functioning child will be equally so to the child with autism. He may, in desperation, recall a salient detail rather than a comprehensive thought. As a concrete thinker, he may benefit from an equation such as "Who + What happened = Main Idea."

Summarizing is another task that may be difficult for the child with reading comprehension deficits. Key word extraction can help a child summarize global thoughts and avoid simple rote recall of words or phrases. Depending on the individual, initial instruction may warrant that key words are provided for the child in order to gain success. The child is then required to expand the thought by formulating a relevant sentence. For example,

"lost" becomes "Sally lost her key."

The target can be advanced to a multiple choice task:

Key words: Circle three	
Lost	Found
Hurt	Sick
Puppy	Key

Finally, the child can be required to extract his own key words from the written text. Key words are expanded into sentences and combined to form a meaningful story summary:

"lost" becomes "Sally lost her key."
"key" becomes "She needed her key to get into the house."
"found" becomes "She found her key in her backpack."

Summary: "Sally lost her key on the way to school. She needed her key to get into the house. She found her key in her backpack. She felt relieved."

Prediction is an abstract thought process that involves extrapolation based on analysis of information presented and previously accumulated knowledge. For example, predictions about a story based on the title, "Danny Goes to Camp" would consider other books about "Danny" that the reader is familiar with, as well as previous knowledge of "camp" experiences. Since there is often more than one possibility, there is also no "right answer." The child with autism will need assistance in learning to connect personal experiences with existing factual information. Brainstorming activities are useful to help the child expand his thoughts from "one correct answer" to "many possible answers." For example, the following conversation should be accompanied by written notes so that the child has a permanent visual resource for a transient auditory event.

Parent: "What do you know about Danny?"
Child: "Danny is silly."
Parent: "Good. What are some of the silly things he does?"
Child: "He likes to trick people. He likes to use made-up words."
Parent: "Right. Now what do you know about camp?"
Child: "Camp is outside. Camp is for kids."
Parent: "Good. When is camp?"
Child: "In the summer."
Parent: "Very good. What do kids do at camp?"
Child: "They swim and roast marshmallows."
Parent: "Excellent! So what do you think the book, 'Danny Goes to Camp' is going to be about?"
Child: "Danny is going to trick the other kids at camp."
Parent: "Wow! That's terrific! What could he do to trick them?"
Child: "I don't know."
Parent: "Could he trick them when they are roasting marshmallows?"
Child: "I don't know."

Parent: "Could he trick them by roasting something different?"

Child: "Yes. He could trick them by roasting a banana."

Parent: "That's a great thought! Danny is a silly guy, I bet he might do something silly like that. Let's read the book and find out."

Inference is an abstract thought process that often eludes the concrete thinker. Ideas that are not present in the text, yet are obvious to the typical reader, must be deliberately taught. The ability to "read between the lines" is not automatic for the child with autism. A worksheet designed to address inference is a useful strategy to differentiate the component thought processes in a concrete fashion. For example, the teacher reads a story to the class that begins like this:

"While we were walking to school, we saw a kangaroo."

She then stops and asks the children, "Where do you think the story takes place?"

The typical children will infer that the setting is Australia. The child with autism, finding nothing explicit in the text, may answer, "At school," since this is the only reasonable answer he can find for a "where" question. Using intermediate questions such as, "Where do kangaroos live?" or "If you saw a kangaroo, where could you be?" will help the child to make the transition from simple recall to inference.

Examples

Vocabulary

1. Worksheets can be created on a personal computer using a variety of formats. Matching synonyms or completing a sentence using a word list provided are two simple methods of introducing new vocabulary as well as reinforcing existing word use.

2. Games can be created using vocabulary cards and matching stimuli. Depending on the child's ability, matching stimuli can include pictures, synonyms, or definitions.

3. Oral games can also be created such as "What does not belong?" In this game, four words are given in which three are related and one is not. To use this game to teach vocabulary, choose words that are synonyms. For example, " happy, glad, disappointed, joyful" could be used to teach new vocabulary and encourage wider use of existing words.

4. Parents and educators who model vocabulary use should include an explanation of the word's meaning and use. For example, "Those flowers are lovely. Do you know what lovely means?"
Child answers "No."
"Lovely is another word for pretty or beautiful. So the flowers are lovely or pretty."

5. Asking questions to encourage word substitutions is another way to develop vocabulary. "What is another word for 'pretty'?" will help the child to learn that many different words may serve the same purpose but some words are more descriptive than others are. This is another example of the language rule that there may be more than one right answer.

Story elements

1. **Character:** ensure that question discrimination issues are mastered. The child should clearly understand that the character is a "who," not a "where" or a "what." If the child consistently answers "who" questions with locations, objects, settings, times, or labels, then question discrimination is not a mastered skill and should be addressed in isolation. Worksheets can be created that instruct and develop discrimination skills, and may include the following elements:

A *person* answers a *who* question.
A *place* answers a *where* question.
A *thing* answers a *what* question.
A *time* answers a *when* question.

This is then followed by multiple choice, matching, or fill-in-the-blank questions that expand upon these "rules."

Who went to the store?
cat   tree   Mom   ate

What did Mom buy?
Susie   groceries   yesterday   jumped

Where did Mom go?
Tomorrow   Billy   groceries   store

When did Mom go?
Yesterday   Dad   toys   bank

---

2. **Setting:** worksheets or brainstorming tasks can be created to help the child consolidate information related to setting. Specific vocabulary related to climate, vegetation, animal habitat, occupations and so forth are details that a reader uses to identify a setting. For example, a location that is described as "hot and dry" and where there are "camels and palm trees" directs us toward the conclusion that the setting is the desert. Such clues need to be presented in a systematic fashion that teaches these associations.

Sentence comprehension

1. Worksheets that inquire about details can be made or used. For example:

Read the sentence. Then write the correct answer.

"Katie bought a new red sweater."
What color was Katie's new sweater? _____

"Jonathon got a new pet golden retriever."
Who got a new pet? _____

"The baby was crying because he was hungry."
Why was the baby crying? _____

2. Use a dry erase board to play a game such as "Missing Word." Write a sentence leaving a blank. The child who comprehends the sentence should be able to complete it.

Passage comprehension

1. Reading with a partner who can stop occasionally and ask general questions can help the child to understand the broader meaning of the passage.
2. Creating questions that address the meaning of the passage can be utilized both at home and at school. Books should be read by an adult and index cards used to prepare multiple choice questions. The child can earn reinforcement based on his answers, which in turn reflect comprehension. For example:

"Stuart Little"
Stuart Little was a:
a. Boy who thought he was a mouse.
b. Mouse who thought he was a boy.

Stuart had a brother named:
a. George
b. Henry

Stuart saved the day by:
a. Winning the ballgame.
b. Winning the boat race.

Similar cards can be prepared for use with chapter books.

Sequencing

1. Short stories that contain discrete "beginning," "middle," and "end" phrases or sentences can be designed so that the child underlines each element in a different color. This broadens his sequencing skills beyond pictures and sentence fragments to paragraphs.
2. Sequencing common tasks and activities will help the child to recognize and utilize order and timing. Board games and chores lend themselves well to sequencing:

How to make a sandwich:

First I get everything I need: 2 slices of bread, 1 slice of turkey, mayonnaise, knife.
Next I spread a little mayonnaise on the 2 slices of bread.
Next I put the turkey on one slice of bread.
Next I put the other piece of bread on top of the turkey with the mayonnaise side down.
Last I put everything away.

How to play Scrabble®:

First I take 7 letters out of the bag.
Next I put them on my tray so no one else can see them.
Next I try to make a word with my letters and the letters on the board.
Next I put my word out on the board.
Last I add up my score.

How to make my bed:

Beginning I pull the sheet up and smooth it out.
Middle I pull the blanket up and smooth it out.
End I pull the comforter up and put my pillow on top.

Main idea

Worksheet example #1: Which answer tells you what the story was about?
 a. A boy who got a puppy for his birthday.
 b. A girl who got a cat for her birthday.
 c. A brother and sister who share the same birthday.

Worksheet example #2: Write the main idea using the key words provided.
 a. vacation
 b. sick
 c. operation
The story was about

_____

_____.

Worksheet example #3: Circle the words that you remember from the story. Then use them to find the main idea.

 School   Recess   Lake   Bully
 Principal   Circus   Clown   Fun

The main idea of the story: It was the first day of _____. The new kid at school was playing at _____ when a _____ hit him. A teacher saw what happened and the bully had to go to see the _____ because he was in trouble.

Summarizing

1. Make a "Book Report" sheet for each book or story that the child reads.

Title: _____
Author: _____
Characters: _____
Setting: _____

Key words or details:
1. First _____
2. Next_____
3. Last _____

Main Idea: Who + What happened.

_____

Summary: The story was about (who)

_____

(what happened first)

_____

(what happened next)

_____

(what happened last)

_____

Prediction

1. Make it a habit to address prediction before the child begins to read. Use the title and ask, "What do you think this story is going to be about?"
2. Use prediction in natural settings: "What kinds of animals do you think we will see on our hike in the woods?" "What fun activities do you think we will do on our trip to Florida?"
3. Make a worksheet that isolates prediction and encourages brainstorming:

Read each title. Then circle the correct answer.

"Has Anyone Ever Liked Lima Beans?" is a story about
a. Someone who really likes lima beans.
b. Someone who probably doesn't like lima beans.

"Today was a disaster!" is a book about
a. The Titanic.
b. A day when everything went wrong.

"The Tooth Fairy Goes on Strike" is a story about
a. The tooth fairy is tired of her job and quits.
b. The tooth fairy plays baseball.

Inference

1. Play guessing games to help develop inferential thinking: "I'm thinking of something that is cold and white unless the sun comes out. Then it disappears. What is it?"

2. Create worksheets that target inferential thinking: "You see waves and sand all around you. The air smells fishy and tastes salty. Where are you?"

"It is dark and quiet except for the brightness of the moon. When is it?"

"The man is yelling and shaking his fist. His face is bright red. How does he feel?"

"You are riding your bike when suddenly you hear a pop and your bike starts to wobble. What happened?"

Reading comprehension deficits among children of varying abilities is a popular topic of research, theory, and intervention. Many resources exist for those who wish to investigate in depth the issues as they relate to an individual. The key is to ensure that no child continues to struggle in a world dependent on language. The child with autism must receive the necessary support and accomodations to make reading comprehension accessible.

Suggested Reading Comprehension Resources

Teach Me Language, SKF Books, Inc., 1996-2003. To order telephone (604) 534-6596.

Reading Milestone Series, PRO-ED, Inc. 1992. To Order, telephone (800) 897-3202.

Spectrum Reading, McGraw-Hill Children's Publishing.

Basic Skills Series, McGraw-Hill Children's Publishing.

Homework Helpers, Frank Schaffer Publications.

Reading Comprehension, Learn on the Go Practice Books.

Reading Comprehension Homework Booklets, International Fair.

Comprehension and Critical Thinking, Teacher Created Materials, Inc.

Nonfiction Reading Comprehension, Teacher Created Materials, Inc.

Reading Comprehension and Skills, Kelley Wingate Publications, Inc.

Chapter Summary
Reading Comprehension Strategies:

- Determine learning style
- Utilize non-verbal assessments
- Eliminate word retrieval issues
- Incorporate useful strategies

CHAPTER 10

MANAGING NEGATIVE BEHAVIORS AND ADDRESSING DISCIPLINE ISSUES AT SCHOOL

Introduction

The child with autism often requires implementation of an "artificial" cost response system that provides meaningful negative reinforcement for undesirable behaviors. Over time, the artificial system can be integrated into a more natural system such as that which is used with typically functioning peers. Negative behaviors are identified and classified according to their purpose or function, rather than simply according to type. Behaviors unique to the diagnosis of autism must be differentiated from off-task behaviors or typical discipline issues. Self-stimulating or perseverative behaviors clearly must be managed differently from simple misbehaving, non-compliance, or failure to comprehend the required task. Understanding the function of a negative behavior is important to the successful management and eventual elimination of disruptive behaviors.

> *Understanding the function of a negative behavior is important to the successful management and eventual elimination of disruptive behaviors.*

Domain

1. **Negative or disruptive behaviors unique to autism**
2. **Off-task behavior**
3. **Advancing from artificial to typical discipline**

Approach

Negative or disruptive behaviors unique to autism

Self-stimulating behaviors should be extremely limited or non-existent in the school environment. Stereotypic behaviors include hand-flapping, jaw-clicking, spinning objects or self, picking at skin or objects, lining and stacking objects, eye movements and fixations, self-talk and echolalia to name but a few. These behaviors may be perceived as odd or frightening by the child's peers and may further alienate him. However, their ability to consume the child's energy and attention represents a greater problem than peer rejection. Self-stimulating behavior is far more enticing to the child than is generally recognized by typical educators. The function of the behavior should be identified whenever possible so that the antecedent stimulus is also addressed. If anxiety is the antecedent,

> *...a combined approach that addresses the source of the anxiety, teaches alternative behaviors for managing the anxiety and an extinction plan for eliminating the negative behavior is preferred.*

then merely extinguishing one particular behavior will be insufficient to alleviate the problem. Other behaviors will arise to replace the one that has been eliminated. Rather than simply targeting the behavior in isolation, a combined approach that addresses the source of the anxiety, teaches alternative behaviors for managing the anxiety and an extinction plan for eliminating the negative behavior is preferred. For example, if the child becomes anxious at 10:00 because the group activity has not ended on time, the target behavior should include:

1. Frustration Tolerance: "Sometimes things take longer. You don't need to worry about it. You will still get a (+) if you pay attention." Remove the child's watch or reposition him so that his back is to the clock.

2. Delayed gratification: "You are too worried about getting a (+). You never get your (+) until the activity is over." Appoint a specific time for the child to receive reinforcement. Encourage the child to keep his (+) "safe" in his memory until that time.

3. Elimination: "It is not OK to flap your hands at school. You will not earn a (+) if you flap your hands." Institute a cost response if the behavior continues in spite of the loss of reward.

4. Alternative behavior: "If you get nervous, you should sit on your hands to help keep them still. You will get an extra (+) if you make a good choice and manage it yourself." Prompt the child before he has the opportunity to fail.

5. Target behavior: "You will earn an extra (+) any time you manage your anxiety in a good way. You will lose a (+) any time you flap your hands."

Simply reprimanding the child will be inadequate to decrease the behavior. The child is drawn into and mesmerized by the comfort of routines, rituals and a

self-absorbed state. However, it is not helpful to allow the child to disconnect in this fashion and, if allowed, will only serve to solidify behaviors that will undermine function, socialization, and independence. Well meaning but ill informed teachers who attempt to discipline the child for stereotypic behaviors will usually fail to decrease the behavior as well. In fact,

Efforts to keep the child engaged in on-task behaviors are essential to the elimination of self-stimulation and disruption.

the behavior often escalates as the underlying anxiety increases. Parents and educators alike need to utilize appropriate methods of elimination when managing self-stimulating behaviors. The child must be occupied to the extent that no opportunity exists for the desired behavior. The child also must be more motivated for on-task behavior than he is for self-stimulating activities. Function and dysfunction are mutually exclusive. Efforts to keep the child engaged in on-task behaviors are essential to the elimination of self-stimulation and disruption. Redirection to on-task behavior must be constant, so that the child is afforded no opportunities for self-stimulation. The current reinforcement hierarchy should be evaluated for effectiveness to ensure that the child is highly motivated.

Perseverative behaviors often represent a subtle form of self-stimulating behavior, and therefore should be discouraged or targeted for elimination. For the purposes of this book, "perseverative behaviors" refers to an exaggerated interest in and attention to stimuli, which are otherwise considered within the realm of normal. For example, many individuals fidget with

...behavior that is relatively benign for the typical child can be disruptive and consuming for the child with autism, and subsequently erodes the level of function and attention that he has worked so hard to gain.

their clothing, pick at their skin, or bite their fingernails when anxious. The individual with autism, however, may become obsessed, absorbed, and distracted to the point of dysfunction. Obsessions with routines and rituals, verbal obsessions, and fascinations with a narrow subject should all be monitored for interference with on-task behavior. Herein lies the problem: behavior that is relatively benign for the typical child can be disruptive and consuming for the child with autism, and subsequently erodes the level of function and attention that he has worked so hard to gain. The degree of difficulty posed by exaggerated, "normal" appearing behavior is often underestimated. Teachers and parents alike may simply ignore the behavior with the assumption that the child will "grow out of it." However, identifying and addressing the underlying cause is important to proper management. In the same way that self-stimulating behaviors are addressed, perseverative behaviors require identification of an antecedent, instruction in alternative and appropriate behavior, and a plan for elimination. For example, the child who is absorbed in twirling a loose thread on his shirt is

unlikely to attend to group instructions, and the following approach can be used:

1. The target behavior may be "Quiet hands during group time."
2. Reward a positive behavior rather than consequating a negative one. The child is reinforced for what he doesn't do rather than scolded or disciplined for what he does do.
3. Outline a variety of behaviors that would violate the "quiet hands" rule:
   "No picking at your clothes."
   "No picking the rug."
   "No picking at your skin."
   "No twirling threads or shoestrings."
4. Reward the child according to the length of time he can succeed. Don't require him to maintain the target behavior for 5 minutes if he is only capable of 30 seconds. Use a frequency card to give immediate and incremental reinforcement, which represents accumulated earnings:

   "You will get a star for every 30 seconds that you sit with quiet hands. If you get 10 stars during group time you will earn an extra (+)."

5. Help the child understand that behaviors that distract him also prevent him from completing his assigned work. This, in turn, prevents him from earning his reward. If the child can make this connection, he will be more motivated to participate in the management of it. This is foundational to the development of self-regulation.

Disruptive behaviors must also be targeted for elimination. Ideally, these behaviors will have been addressed prior to the child's inclusion in the classroom. Self-abusive and aggressive behaviors are incompatible with successful education in an inclusion setting. Loud and unusual verbalizations can be extremely disturbing to the child's peers and should be eliminated. All self-stimulating and perseverative behaviors can be disruptive to the classroom environment and need to be aggressively managed. Disruptions caused by typically functioning children are generally perceived as belligerence, non-compliance, attention seeking, defiance, or rudeness. The child with autism may exhibit disruptive behaviors for very different reasons, and if this is not recognized, he is likely to gain a reputation for being difficult or belligerent. If the behavior is managed in a typical disciplinary fashion, it is more likely to escalate than diminish. Implementing a positive approach to the elimination of disruptive behaviors is essential for the child with autism who operates on a token economy of earned rewards. For example, the child who continually pushes other children because they are "in the way" needs instruction on an alternative and appropriate way to solve his problem. Simply punishing the child will do little to increase his understanding of what is, and what is not, socially acceptable behavior. A better approach would be to design a target behavior that reinforces positive behavior:

> "Say 'Excuse me' when someone is in your way. This is using good manners. It is not OK to push, just use your words. You will earn a star every time you use good manners."

Applauding the child's success is more likely to change the behavior than punishing it.

Off-task behaviors

Other behaviors that may interfere with acquisition of skills should also be addressed. The child with autism generally must work harder to stay on-task than his typically functioning peers. "Off-task" behaviors are simply activities that are irrelevant to the target behavior or assignment. Daydreaming, doodling, and fidgeting are examples of off-task behavior common to all children. Off-task behaviors are similar to perseverative behaviors in that they interfere with or prevent the child from accomplishing the required behavior. However, off-task behaviors are less likely to become compelling obsessions and are more likely to be ignored by the teacher. For example, frequent pencil sharpening is a common escape behavior for many children that is often reprimanded but rarely consequated. A teacher may set parameters to ensure that the children get their work done, but no one is "punished" for sharpening a pencil. Unless the children are given a better reason to get their work done, this behavior is likely to continue. For the child with autism, frequent pencil sharpening may be more than a simple escape from his work. This interruption may make it impossible for him to regain his focus and momentum. A simple reprimand may be sufficient for a typical child to discontinue the behavior, but a positive target or a cost response may be necessary for the child who is highly distracted. The aide or teacher should make it clear to the child that anything that interferes with getting his work done would also eliminate his reward. As always, a positive target behavior should be established before instituting a cost response. For example, allow the child to sharpen his pencil once before starting his work assignment. Then he is required to sit down and complete his work without interruption. Praise and reinforcement is given for "doing your work without leaving your activity." Bathroom breaks should also be managed in a pro-active way, outlining when they are allowed and when they are not. Breaks should generally be taken prior to the start of a work period, or after work completion, but not during work times. When a positive approach is inadequate, a cost response should be implemented: "It is not OK to leave your work area during writing. Sharpen your pencil before you get started. You will lose a (+) if you leave your activity."

Advancing from artificial to typical discipline

As the child with autism progresses, efforts should be made to fade artificial methods of discipline and introduce more typical methods, such as those that apply to his peers. The teacher must have established stimulus control in other areas before successfully making this transition. In addition, the child with autism must demonstrate an understanding of social anxiety, as well as a measure of desire to please others. "Social anxiety" refers to the appropriate concern that one's behavior will disappoint or provoke anger in a person with whom one has a meaningful relationship. The child with autism may lack social anxiety and may be dependent on artificial consequences, such as a loss of reward, while remaining oblivious to the emotions of others. Methods of discipline should always be accompanied by explanations that increase the child's understanding:

"I'm sorry that you lost a (+) but it's not OK to push someone who is in your way. You need to use nice words. Joey feels unhappy because you don't care about him. I feel mad because you did not make a good choice."

"I'm sorry that you made a bad choice to be loud while we were in the library. You will have to get your name on the board and miss out on 5 minutes of recess. I feel disappointed that you did not do your best."

Once negative behaviors are eliminated or under control, the child should be required to follow the behavioral expectations of the classroom. Typical discipline should be used as long as it is effective. If it creates undo distress or fails to change the behavior, alternatives should be considered.

Examples

Negative or disruptive behaviors
Self-stimulating behaviors
Target behavior #1: Spinning when anxious. "It's not OK to spin yourself around. That's weird, nobody does that. If you are nervous you should use your words. Then I can help you with your work."
Target behavior #2: Verbal obsession with loss of reward. "If you have any silly talk about numbers during group time you won't know what to do when you get to your desk. Silly talk will keep you from your work. I hope you make a good choice so you can earn a (+)."
Target behavior #3: Continued verbal obsession with cost response. "I am disappointed that you are still having silly talk at group time. This is not a good choice. You will lose a (+) if I hear number talk again."

Perseverative
Target behavior #1: Teaching appropriate opportunities for narrow interests. "It is not OK to talk about movies in the classroom. Since you love to talk about movies, you can talk to Sam at recess."
Target behavior #2: Fixation with time: "You need to stop looking at the clock. I know how much you like numbers, but looking at the clock is a distraction. You need to sit with your back to the clock at group time. I will give you an extra (+) if you face the teacher for all of group time but not if I see you turn around to look at the clock."
Target behavior #3: Breaking rituals: "You don't need to line up your markers. Just put them in your desk and get ready for lunch. Tomorrow you won't get your (+) for writing if you are goofing around with your markers."

Disruptive

Target behavior #1: Talking loud: "Your loud talking is bothering everyone. You can earn a check for every activity when you control your voice. If you have 10 checks at the end of the day you can earn a bonus prize of 30 minutes of computer time."

Target behavior #2: Banging on your desk: "It bothers the class if you are banging your books on your desk. I will not give you a (+) if you are noisy."

Target behavior #3: Throwing things: "It is never OK to throw pencils or other objects in the classroom. Someone could get hurt. You will be sent down to the office if you throw something. That's big trouble."

Off-task behaviors

Target behavior #1: Work throughout the assigned time period. "You need to keep busy to earn your (+) for writing. After you are done with your writing assignment, you can do the language worksheet in your folder."

Target behavior #2: Maintaining on-task behavior. "You need to find out what to do next. You can't keep busy unless you know what to do."

Target behavior #3: Preventing disruptions. "You need to stay at your activity. Leaving your desk will make it harder to get your work done. If you don't get your work done you won't earn a (+)."

Advancing from artificial to typical discipline

1. Earned reward for positive behavior (token). "Great job sitting quietly at group time! You earned a (+) for that."

2. No earnings for failure to perform target behavior (no token).
   "You were moving around and being noisy during group time. You can't earn a (+) like that. I hope you make a better choice tomorrow."

3. Cost response for failure to perform mastered behavior (loss of token). "Sitting quietly on the rug for group time is mastered. That means you need to do it. You were talking about the weather chart and bothering the whole group. You will lose a (+) for not being quiet."

4. Typical disciplinary measures (loss of classroom/recess privileges).

"Sitting quietly on the rug for group time is mastered. That means you need to do it. If you don't, then you will get your name on the board and lose 5 minutes of recess."

> **It is more important to identify and address the underlying cause of a behavior than it is to classify it as self-stimulating, perseverative, or disruptive.**

Many behaviors characteristic of autism can be successfully managed using a positive behavioral approach that rewards appropriate behavior. This appropriate behavior in turn will be repeated, replacing the undesirable behavior. Some children may require a cost response to provide motivation sufficient to produce appropriate behavioral choices. It is more important to identify and address the underlying cause of a behavior than it is to classify it as self-stimulating, perseverative, or disruptive. Overlap exists between classifications, and a behavior that is self-gratifying for one child may have little appeal for another. It is the individual child's response to a situation that must be identified and managed rather than a particular behavior. If anxiety is the antecedent, then anxiety needs to be addressed and alternative behaviors taught, rather than simply attempting to extinguish the problem behavior.

Chapter Summary

- Recognize self-stimulating and perseverative behavior
- Target disruptive behavior for elimination
- Address off-task behavior
- Advance from artificial to typical discipline

CHAPTER 11

TEACHING FRUSTRATION TOLERANCE
Enhancing emotional response and flexibility
Introduction

Children with autism often exhibit low frustration tolerance when presented with change, variety, or deviations from routine. They may display inappropriate or exaggerated emotions, which are erratic and unpredictable in nature. Emotional outbursts may be accompanied by extreme, negative behaviors such as violence or self-abuse. On any level, these responses will clearly and dramatically set the child apart from his typically functioning peers. Adults should recognize that the child is attempting to communicate his anxiety, fear, or dislike of the situation and promote more appropriate avenues of communication. Communication alone, however, is unlikely to eradicate the negative behavior. It is imperative that frustration tolerance be planned for and taught in a systematic behavioral fashion, reinforcing appropriate responses, until the child develops a measure of self-regulation across a variety of natural settings.

> **It is imperative that frustration tolerance be planned for and taught in a systematic behavioral fashion, reinforcing appropriate responses, until the child develops a measure of self-regulation across a variety of natural settings.**

Domain

1. **Strategies**
2. **Transitions**
3. **Routines**
4. **Enhancing understanding**

Approach and Examples

Strategies for teaching frustration tolerance

Identify reinforcement that the child will work for, and set it apart for exclusive use. Both primary reinforcement (tangible items such as a toy or food) and secondary reinforcement (verbal praise, "Thank you for not complaining about something new") should be employed. Inform the child that he will be rewarded with the desired item when he completes the target behavior. For example, "At 11:00 our play time will be over and it will be time to work. I will give you a star if you go to the desk without complaining or throwing a tantrum."

Clearly define the target behavior.

When targeting frustration tolerance, the target is the child's response to change rather than the demonstration of a task or skill. For example, if the child routinely tantrums when dinner is not served at exactly 6:00pm, then the target behavior is the elimination of outbursts related to the time that dinner is served. It should not be assumed that the child with autism will develop appropriate emotional responses without direct intervention. Nor should it be presumed that he will generalize them across settings without instruction and reinforcement.

Classify mastered activities according to the child's level of interest. Determine which activities are highly desirable (+), neutral (N), or not desirable (-). These activities will be used to present opportunities for the child to transition, which in turn will be used to teach the child appropriate responses through positive reinforcement of successes. Initial trials will present opportunities to transition from an undesirable activity to a highly desirable activity. This situation should easily produce success that can be rewarded. As the child develops an understanding that his appropriate response to change is directly and immediately rewarded, the target progresses systematically until the ultimate goal is attained, that is, appropriate responses to change from desirable to undesirable.

Example of a home activities classification:

(+)	(N)	(-)
computer	puzzle	peer play
swings	blocks	chores
TV	drawing	reading

Example of a school activities classification:

(+)	(N)	(-)
computer	centers	reading
math	job	chapter book
games	writing	spelling

These are examples only and should not be expected to apply to every child. Classifications must be individualized according to child's level of interest.

Establish frustration tolerance at home first, where variables are easier to control, then generalize to the school setting. Of course, naturally occurring opportunities in the classroom should always be utilized. However, some degree of frustration tolerance should be developed prior to enrolling the child in school. Transitions, schedule change, and unpredictable variation are inherent in the school setting, and the child who has been sheltered by a highly controlled home setting will be ill prepared to cope.

Set up for success. Trials can easily be set up at home that teach frustration tolerance in a systematic fashion. In addition, naturally occurring events within the home routine can be used to teach and reinforce desired responses. With acquisition and mastery of initial trials, the target is advanced to increase the degree of challenge presented. As the child masters a positive response to a transition from undesirable to desirable, the target then progresses to a trial from a neutral activity to a desirable one. Thus, the degree of challenge is slightly greater than it was when he had to transition from something he didn't like to something that he really did like.

Transitions

Transitioning between activities is a skill that is often difficult for children with autism. It may take an enormous amount of emotional energy to leave the comfort of the predictable and routine. As a result, the child may protest with tantrums or other outbursts that seem inappropriate to the demand or request made of him. Frustration tolerance for transitions should be specifically targeted in a behavioral fashion. The following formulas may be useful for creating discrete trials at home. Generalization of frustration tolerance can then be targeted in the school and public settings.

Using the classifications of (+), (N), and (-), set up the following situations:

- (-) to (+) undesirable to highly desirable
- (N) to (+) neutral to highly desirable
- (N) to(N) neutral to another neutral
- (N) to (-) neutral to undesirable
- (+) to (-) highly desirable to undesirable

Examples of home based activities that could be used:

- Chores (-) to Computer (+)
- Puzzle (N) to Swings (+)
- Puzzle (N) to Blocks (N)
- Puzzle (N) to Peer Play (-)
- TV (+) to Reading (-)

Examples of school based activities that could be used:

- Reading (-) to Computers(+)
- Writing (N) to Math (+)
- Centers (N) to Job (N)
- Job (N) to Spelling (-)
- Games (+) to Reading (-)

These classifications are examples and are not expected to apply to every child. (+), (N), (-) activities must be individualized based on the child's particular interests.

Shape the desired emotional or behavioral response by rewarding a decreasing resistance or negative response. It is unrealistic to expect the child to simply replace volatile behavior with an appropriate response. Frustration tolerance is a shaping procedure in which progressively better responses are rewarded. The child's best response becomes the standard of measure so that reinforcement is always applied to a more desired response.

> # Frustration tolerance is a shaping procedure in which progressively better responses are rewarded.

Teaching emotional skills can significantly improve the child's level of comfort and sense of control over situations that are otherwise frightening and overwhelming.

Teach appropriate responses such as, "It's OK if you don't like change. It's not OK to scream about it. You have to use your words." The child with autism may exhibit few positive emotions, often flat in affect until an event perceived as "out of order" provokes an extreme and negative emotional response. Targeting emotional responses rather than behaviors may seem problematic, since emotions are a normal and necessary part of human life. Parents and educators should recognize that this approach seeks not to eliminate emotions, but rather to teach appropriate responses to situations that are uniquely challenging to the child who experiences fear and anxiety in the face of change. Teaching emotional skills can significantly improve the child's level of comfort and sense of control over situations that are otherwise frightening and overwhelming. In addition, proper emotional responses are essential to developing socialization skills, as well as fostering a more stable family life. It is difficult, if not impossible, to enjoy public outings with a child who is volatile and unpredictable.

Don't give in to the child. Once a target behavior has been established, follow-through is essential. The parent or educator must stay ahead of the child in the "battle of wills." It is imperative that the adult maintain control of the setting and patiently require that the child display a progressively more appropriate response. The target should be developed to ensure the child's success and prompts should be sufficient to produce it. Efforts to remain neutral and ignore outbursts will help to avoid any inadvertent reinforcement of the negative behavior. Instead, energy should be focused on redirection to a more appropriate response. It is counterproductive for the adult to "back down" once the required behavior is presented; when this occurs, the child learns that he can escape from the situation by increasing the intensity or frequency of his negative response.

Routines

Frustration tolerance for time changes and activity changes should be targeted. Variations in what is going to occur or when are often sources of anxiety for the child with autism, and thus are also situations in which negative behaviors are likely to occur unless more appropriate responses are taught.

Time Changes. Children with autism often become very anxious when things do not happen "on time." They may rely on a watch or clock to establish an end point for an activity and may become frustrated when the activity exceeds the expected end point.

Approach: set up situations for the child to progressively accept time changes.

      (-) activity, delayed incrementally
      (N) activity, delayed incrementally
      (+) activity, delayed incrementally

Example: "Chores (-) will be at 10:00 today." Delay activity for 1-5 minutes, depending on the child's ability. Choose the longest amount of time that you think the child will be successful, starting small and incrementally increasing. The child must succeed, or there will not be anything to reinforce. Praise the child for "waiting without getting frustrated" or some similar comment. Progress to an (N) activity delay, such as "Lunch (N) will be at 12:00 today." After the child has demonstrated success, progress to delaying a desirable activity such as "Today we'll go to the playground at 3:00 instead of at 2:45." Isolate the two targets of increasing the delay time and changing the activity to a more challenging situation.

Activity Changes. The child may also become anxious or frustrated when an activity does not happen as predicted. For example, if recess is cancelled because of a school assembly, the child may exhibit negative behavior as a means of protest. Using the same classifications as they pertain to scheduled activities and subsequent change in predictable events, set up the following situations in writing or a visual format (such as a daily schedule):

    (N) to (-) becomes (+)
    (N) to (-) becomes (N)
    (N) to (N) becomes (N)
    (N) to (+) becomes (N)
    (N) to (+) becomes (-)

Examples of home based routines:

- "After lunch (N) instead of chores (-) let's go to the playground (+)."

- "After lunch (N) instead of chores (-) let's do a puzzle (N)."

- "After lunch (N) instead of puzzles (N) let's read stories (N)."

- "After lunch (N) instead of playing outside (+) we'll read stories (N)."

- "After lunch (N) instead of playing outside (+) we'll do chores (-)."

Examples of school based routines:

- "After writing (N) instead of chapter book (-) we'll have math (+)."

- "After writing (N) instead of chapter book (-) we'll have centers (N)."

- "After writing (N) instead of centers (N) we'll do our jobs (N)."

- "After writing (N) instead of math (+) we'll do our jobs (N)."

- "After writing (N) instead of math (+) we'll read our chapter book (-)."

Incorporating these transitions into the classroom may require flexibility in terms of the overall schedule of activities. The teacher may or may not be willing to alter the order of activities from time to time in order to facilitate the development of frustration tolerance. If not, selection should be based on choices within the classroom that are not directly related to the class schedule. For example, if all of the children are allowed to choose at center time, can the available choices be used to teach frustration tolerance? What existing choices can be used to facilitate transitions? Support should be provided for naturally occurring variations in routines to promote success through appropriate responses.

Enhancing Understanding

In addition to the above strategies, parents and educators should strive to increase the child's understanding of the demands of his environment.

> "Too often there is an inordinate emphasis on prompting children with autism to respond to situations appropriately, without the slightest regard for whether they have any understanding of the situation or event to which they are expected to respond. It should be apparent that it is virtually impossible to generate skilled, socially appropriate responses to situations that one finds inexplicable. At best, these responses will be situation specific and/or cue dependent…Consequently, it is vitally important to increase the child's understanding of environmental and behavioral information in order to provide a 'meaning link' between the behavior observed and the appropriate response to it" (Quill, p. 146-147).

Low frustration tolerance is rooted in the child's inability to interpret the demands of a dynamic and constantly changing environment.

> "Their [children with autism] comprehension of the demands in their environment is based more on piecing together gestural cues, other environmental cues, and expected routines than on understanding specific verbal messages. Their lack of cooperation or lack of independence may actually be the result of not understanding fully what is expected of them or what is going to happen. They may be interpreting only fragments of the communication message accurately" (Quill, p. 267).

The child with autism prefers the structure, order, and predictable nature of the world as he sees it. Disruptions in this order produce anxiety, which in turn produce coping strategies that may be dysfunctional at best, and harmful at worst. It is important that parents and educators recognize that the behaviors represent an underlying perspective that is different from our own:

> "Myopic, out-of-context treatment…occurs when symptoms of the disorder are viewed as discrete entities or, worse yet, as instances of willful behavior under the control of the child, rather than as manifestations of an underlying perspective and orientation that is different from our own and reflective of a system compromised by neurological impairment" (Quill, p. 134).

Empathy for the child, who must function in a world that is perplexing, coupled with strategies which bring order and understanding to bear on the challenges he must face, is a balanced and practical approach to managing frustration.

> **Low frustration tolerance is rooted in the child's inability to interpret the demands of a dynamic and constantly changing environment.**

Chapter Summary

- Identify reinforcement
- Define target behavior
- Classify mastered activities
- Establish frustration tolerance at home
- Set up for success
- Target transitions
- Teach appropriate responses
- Utilize routines
- Prepare for time and activity changes
- Enhance understanding

CHAPTER 12

EATING ISSUES
Expanding diet, decreasing frustration
Introduction

Individuals with autism tend to fear change, preferring the comfort of the routine and predictable. This underlying fear manifests itself in a variety of arenas, but may be particularly problematic when it comes to eating. It is not uncommon for children with autism to resist the introduction of new foods in extremely unpleasant, even violent fashion. Extreme behaviors may be exhibited early in life, and if not addressed, may be firmly established and resistant to intervention later on. In addition, hypersensitivity to tactile stimuli, oral motor weakness, and/or an over-reactive gag reflex can make mealtime very difficult. The child's insistence on routine often results in a narrow diet and poor nutrition. Rigid eating patterns may enslave both the individual with autism and those who care for him. Furthermore, the need for daily or occasional medication warrants flexibility and compliance to ensure the highest possible quality of life and health. Implementing a positive behavioral approach to introduce new foods and to applaud willing efforts will diminish anxiety, promote health, and encourage enjoyment of foods. By using the familiar structure of target behaviors, clearly defined expectations, and desirable rewards, the individual with autism can develop more normative eating habits, improve nutrition, and contribute to a more pleasant family environment.

> *Rigid eating patterns may enslave both the individual with autism and those who care for him.*

Domain

1. Sensory aberrations
2. Motor difficulties
3. Fear and rigidity

Approach

Sensory Aberrations

Discomfort caused by hypersensitivity to certain tactile sensations are common occurrences among individuals with autism. Temple Grandin, a well-known adult with autism, provides first hand perspective on this aspect of autism:

" From as far back as I can remember, I always hated to be hugged. I wanted to experience the good feeling of being hugged, but it was just too overwhelming. It was like a great, all-engulfing tidal wave of stimulation, and I reacted like a wild animal. Being touched triggered flight; it flipped my circuit breaker. I was overloaded and would have to escape, often by jerking away suddenly...

Overly sensitive skin can also be a big problem. Washing my hair and dressing to go to church were two things I hated as a child. A lot of kids hate Sunday clothes and taking baths. But shampooing actually hurt my scalp. It was as if the fingers rubbing my head had sewing thimbles on them. Scratchy petticoats were like sandpaper scraping away at raw nerve endings" (Grandin, p. 62-66).

Much has been written to address sensory issues in general; in this book we will address them only as they relate to eating disturbances. Eating and oral hygiene may be impeded by tactile hypersensitivity, as well as by a pronounced gag reflex. The child's aversion to particular textures may result in regurgitation or violent resistance. Sensitivity to temperature extremes may also influence the child's apprehension toward food. Careful evaluation of sensory aberrations must be made before an intervention plan can be designed and implemented. Data should be collected concerning what types of food cause the child to react and in what manner. Children with adequate expressive language can help by describing in detail what it is that troubles them. Other children may need assistance in expressing useful information. For example, a series of yes/no or multiple choice questions may be used to elicit information regarding temperature, texture and taste:

> "Is it too hot or OK?"
> "Is it too cold or OK?"
> "Is it too salty or OK?"
> "Is it too spicy—does it taste hot —- or OK?"
> "Is it yummy or yucky?"

In addition, comparing a new food experience with established favorites can also help with evaluation:

> "Which do you like better, hot dogs or BBQ chicken?"
> "Which do you like better, BBQ chicken or pizza?"

Even with observation and interrogation it may not be possible to identify the exact nature of the issue or issues that cause the child to react. Nonetheless, intervention should proceed according to a systematic and sound behavioral plan. As with all behavioral plans, success must be planned for and achieved in order to allow for positive reinforcement and repetition of the desired behavior. It is paramount that eating issues be under the control of the adult rather than the child. This does not, however, imply that a forceful approach be used. If eating becomes a battle, negative behavior will undoubtedly increase rather than decrease. Instead, the path to success should proceed from the least offensive experience to more challenging ones. Only when the child has succeeded

> **As with all behavioral plans, success must be planned for and achieved in order to allow for positive reinforcement and repetition of the desired behavior.**

with relatively benign alterations to his eating pattern can more dramatic changes be made. There are a few common sense principles to follow when introducing new foods:

Palatable or desirable food choices are always best for introducing a new food experience. Begin with foods that are considered palatable or desirable by most people. For example, most people enjoy both the texture and taste of a crisp apple, and children often  prefer it without the peel. This is a better choice to introduce initially than applesauce, which may present an offensive texture.

Always follow through on the task. Lack of follow through may be detrimental for several reasons. First, if the child succeeds in avoiding the task by exhibiting negative behaviors, his tantruming is inadvertently reinforced. Secondly, without task follow through, the child may be denied the opportunity to succeed, solidifying his adamant refusal to try new foods. Conversely, when negative behaviors are ignored or limited, and the child has a positive experience with a new food, he is reinforced both artificially (by the predetermined reward) and intrinsically (by the desirable new food).

Recognize that multiple exposures may be necessary before the child forms his opinion. One or two exposures to a new food are rarely adequate to determine like or dislike. Furthermore, numerous exposures may elevate the child's opinion from "tolerable" to "likeable" or "favorite."

Use highly desirable foods as reinforcement. Foods that the child enjoys may be offered as rewards for trying new foods. This is a reasonable and natural use of food as a reinforcement. However, if food reinforcement is reserved for higher priority targets such as language or comprehension, specific toys or privileges may also be used. The strong reinforcement required for priority targets should not be diverted for use with eating issues unless they are considered extreme and urgent.

Motor difficulties

Chewing and rotary tongue movements may be difficult, resulting in weak and ineffectual chewing. In addition to affecting eating patterns, the child may exhibit speech impediments or poor articulation. Careful observation should be made to determine the presence or absence of rotary tongue movements, bilateral chewing ability, and prominent gagging. The following questions may be helpful in evaluating motor difficulties:

1. Can the child stick out his tongue?
2. Can the child move his tongue in all directions?
3. Can the child chew comfortably on both sides of his mouth?
4. Does the child favor one side of his mouth for chewing?
5. Does the child seem unable to chew his food thoroughly?
6. Does the child seem to gag frequently when eating or brushing his teeth?
7. Does the child drool or spit out his food?
8. Has the child tolerated a thorough dental examination?
9. Does the child have any orthodontic problems such as malocclusion that would impair his ability to chew?
10. Does the child grind his teeth?

Weak facial muscles may also impair the child's ability to form common facial expressions. Imitation drills in front of a mirror can help to strengthen facial muscles as well as assist the child to recognize and utilize appropriate expressions.

Fear and rigidity

As noted noted frequently in this book, fear of the unknown or of new experiences can incapacitate and emotionally paralyze the individual with autism. It is highly recommended that the parent or caregiver first earn the child's trust and establish stimulus control in other areas prior to attempting behavioral intervention with eating issues. The child with autism who is presented with a new food may experience anxiety severe enough to elicit his worst behavior. A compassionate and understanding approach coupled with clearly defined expectations, unwavering follow through, and immediate reinforcement can be a highly successful method of managing this anxiety.

The common sense rules listed above with regard to sensory aberrations are equally important with regard to fear and rigidity. In addition, the following suggestions may help to alleviate the fears surrounding new food exposures:

- Make mealtime fun.
- Maintain a predictable setting.
- Demonstrate desirability.
- Clearly define the behavioral expectations.
- Reward the child's efforts.
- Gain the child's trust.
- Discuss comparisons.

Make mealtime fun. Create mealtime games that help the child to attend to the activity (eating) without being a substitute for the activity itself. In other words, games should improve the eating experience, not allow the child an escape from it. For example, language games such as "What does not belong?" are concrete enough for the child with autism to enjoy.

A: "What does not belong: triangle, trapezoid, nickel, rectangle?"

B: "Nickel."

A: "Right. Why does it not belong?"

B: "Because a nickel is a coin and the rest are shapes."

Educational place mats are another means of enjoyment for children at mealtime. Colorful place mats featuring math, geography, animals, flags, presidents, and many other themes can be purchased inexpensively or made to suit the interests of the child. For example, if a child has a particular interest in traffic signs, a unique place mat can be made using stickers or drawings and laminated for durability.

Maintain a predictable setting. Initially introduce new foods only at a predictable time. The child who lives in fear that he will encounter new foods at every meal is unlikely to succeed at all and certainly will feel apprehensive around mealtime. Perhaps once a week, "Every Saturday for dinner," for example, is all that the child can manage initially. With success, the frequency can be increased and a more informal approach can be used. The weekly event may then become "Tonight we are having something new for dinner." Final success may be the ability to be served a new food without advance warning and to try it without distress.

Demonstrate desirability. Showing the child that something new tastes good is a concrete visual tool that may help the child to muster up the courage or desire to try it himself.

Clearly define the behavioral expectations. The child who is already fearful may become terrified if he thinks he must eat a large serving or try several new foods in one sitting. Instead, the task should be clearly defined and an end point noted. For example:

"I want you to try one new food for dinner on Saturday. We are going to have steak. Steak is yummy. I want you to eat three small pieces. If you like it you can have more. If you don't like it, you can just eat the three pieces. Then you can have chocolate cake for dessert. But you can't just eat one piece and say that you are finished. No one can tell if they like a food with just one bite. So eating three pieces will help you decide if you really like it or not."

Be sure that the child understands that the target is trying a new food, not liking it. Also, instruct the child in advance that the behavioral target includes both effort and attitude:

"It is not OK to throw a tantrum when you try something new. Nobody does that. If you cry or scream you will not get any cake but you will still have to eat your steak."

Reward the child's efforts at trying new foods with both primary and secondary reinforcement. Praise the child for "trying something new" while reminding him that "New is good." Creating a colorful chart to display his efforts will help him to visualize gains and develop a sense of accomplishment. The new foods that he has tried can be listed along with the number of times he has tried them and his response to them. Accumulated rewards can be offered when several new foods have been successfully introduced. For example, the child may earn a trip to his favorite restaurant when he has three exposures for each of five new foods introduced.

Gain the child's trust before introducing less desirable foods. The child should experience many successes before attempting to introduce foods that are commonly less desirable to children, such as dark green vegetables. However, everyone has unique tastes, and children often surprise us with their likes and dislikes. A variety of new foods should be introduced, and vegetables are a necessary part of a healthy diet. Success is most likely to occur when new foods are introduced in a systematic fashion, beginning with those that are most likely to be desirable.

Multiple exposures are necessary to determine likes and dislikes. A new food should be presented numerous times to allow the child to form his own opinion about it.

Discuss comparisons to determine the relative hierarchy of food likes and dislikes. For example, "Which do you like better, donuts or waffles?" can help to determine which food would be a more powerful reinforcer.

Examples

Sensory aberrations
Tactile desensitization may be achieved by the use of an electric toothbrush. Before using it in the mouth, the child's fears may be diminished by allowing the child to use it on a less sensitive area of his body, such as on his arm.

Motor difficulties
Motor strength and awareness may improve with visualization of tongue movements in a mirror. Imitation drills are easy to perform. Simply stand next to the child and instruct him to copy your tongue movements and facial expressions.

Bilateral chewing may be improved simply by instructing the child to take turns chewing on the left, then the right side of his mouth. If the child cannot complete the task independently, have him start by inserting the food on the weaker side. Advance the task by coaching him to "Chew it once or twice before it moves to the other side." Continue to advance the task by increasing the number of times he chews on the targeted side.

Fear and rigidity
Make mealtime fun.

Creative food presentations such as drawing a happy face with syrup on pancakes, or making cookie cutter shaped omelets can contribute to a pleasant mealtime experience for the younger child.

Coloring activities, place mats and homemade menus may be enjoyable.

Playing "restaurant" on occasion can allow the child a measure of control over the food he eats.

Older children may enjoy word games or other mealtime privileges such as choosing to eat outdoors, selecting dinner music, or deciding on the vegetable to be served. The child who is highly interested in geography, animals, or math will likely enjoy a word game designed around his area of interest. For example: "Let's play a guessing game. I'm thinking of an animal that has tough skin and likes to swim. What is it?"

Theme nights such as "Mexican Fiesta Noche" in which ethnic food, music, and a game are present, enhance mealtime. A simple Spanish-English vocabulary game can be played while eating. "What is 'la vaca' in English?" followed by homemade flashcards, can be both fun and educational without disrupting the meal. Introducing a simple new food such as a quesadilla allows the child to fulfill the requirement of trying a new food while enjoying a time of family fun.

Chapter Summary

- Recognize and address sensorimotor issues
- Begin with desirable food choices
- Always follow through on task
- Present new food numerous times
- Use reinforcement (highly desirable food or other type)
- Alleviate fear of unknown food experiences
- Maintain predictable setting
- Clearly define behavioral expectations
- Reward child's efforts
- Gain child's trust

CHAPTER 13

SLEEP ISSUES
Setting limits, managing sleep disturbances
Introduction

Children with autism often have difficulty getting to sleep, nighttime awakening, early morning awakenings, or simply sleep less. Research reveals that "56% of all developmentally delayed individuals present with sleep-related issues. It has also been demonstrated that children with autism do not tend to 'grow out' of their sleeping difficulties" (Ward, p.1). A thorough evaluation should be made to determine the specific type of sleep disturbance that the child experiences. Observation and data collection will help to identify and define the problem so that appropriate intervention can be developed and implemented. There are many factors that influence a person's sleep patterns. Before developing a behavioral plan, environmental factors should be addressed and eliminated whenever possible. The following factors need to be considered:

1. Medications. Is the child on medications that adversely affect his sleep pattern? If so, are there alternatives or dosage changes that may improve sleep patterns?
2. Daytime sleeping or napping. Excessive or even moderate periods of daytime sleeping may disrupt the child's night time. Whenever possible, daytime sleep should be limited to enhance the nighttime routine.
3. Exercise. All children need adequate exercise to promote health and sound sleep. Inactivity may contribute to poor sleep.
4. Caffeine intake. Thorough evaluation of the child's diet for occult sources of caffeine intake should be conducted.

This chapter will address sleep issues not readily attributed to the above factors. Some sleep disturbances may require medical management. Here we will discuss a behavioral management approach, which can be implemented prior to or in conjunction with medical management.

> *"...children with autism do not tend to 'grow out' of their sleeping difficulties"*
>
> (Ward, p.1).

Domain

1. Difficulty getting to sleep

2. Night-time awakenings

3. Early morning awakenings

Approach

Difficulty getting to sleep
Success must be achieved. In order to do so, the parent should determine the child's ability to delay gratification. It may not be possible initially for the child to delay reinforcement until morning, although this is the goal to work towards. Immediate reinforcement may be necessary to establish stimulus control in a new environment. For example, the child may earn stickers that he can display on a chart next to his bed. Small intervals of 5 minutes or less in which the child stays in bed may be targeted initially.

Distractions in the room should be eliminated. Anything that may contribute to self-stimulation should be removed. It may be necessary to limit the amount of furniture, control access to lights, and prevent movement of doors. With progress and success, these controls can be decreased and a more normative environment established.

The time that the child goes to bed should be late enough to ensure that he would get to sleep within 30 minutes. Avoid putting the child to bed too early. It is difficult for anyone to stay in bed if they are unable to sleep. In extreme situations, the parent may need to introduce routines that gain the child's success. There must be success to reinforce. Often, parents will lie with the child until he falls asleep. This will certainly gain the success but there are problems associated with this approach. It is very difficult to fade out the parent's presence, and a systematic plan to do so should be developed from the very start. The child should understand that the parent will begin to spend less and less time in bed with him. He should be immediately rewarded for allowing the parent to exit without tantruming. Tokens or stickers can be given and displayed next to the bed, and a chart that records the child's success can be used to applaud his achievement.

Comfort items such as stuffed animals, soft music, or a favorite blanket may make staying in bed more desirable. The parent who lies down with the child can offer a comforting object as a substitute when he or she exits the room.

Boundaries for staying in bed should be established. The child should understand that he is expected to stay in bed, except for using the bathroom. Getting out of bed to play is not allowed. Define exactly what type of behavior is acceptable or not acceptable from the start. The child should understand that the target includes staying in bed quietly. If it is challenging to get the child to stay in bed, the targets may have to be isolated, so that the additional component of "quietly" is added once the child complies. This should be expanded as quickly as possible.

Reinforcement should be selected that produces success. The child that can delay gratification has more options than the child that must receive immediate reinforcement. Offering a favorite breakfast food as a reward for staying in bed is ideal. The child may lose this same privilege (the privilege of choice) if he does not comply. The child must then have a breakfast that the parent chooses, one that is less desirable but still palatable to the child (it is not a punishment). The parent should be prepared in the event that the child does not stay in bed, loses his reward, and then continues the behavior. Multiple violations must be expected if the reinforcement fails to adequately influence the child's behavior. This is an indication that the reinforcement is not powerful enough to produces the desired behavior and should be changed. See the Examples section for details.

Night-time awakenings

A behavioral plan must be in place so that the child understands the target behavior (staying in bed), as well as the reward for doing so. A cost response may also be used. As with all behavioral plans, follow through is essential. Night-time awakenings are disruptive to both the individual with autism and his family. The goal is to teach the child that once he goes to bed, he is expected to stay in bed until morning.

Boundaries should be established for staying in bed. Once the child goes to bed, he is expected to stay in bed until morning, or a designated time. It is not recommended that the child who awakens during the night be allowed to get out of bed to play. This will reinforce the behavior that the parent is trying to eliminate.

Reinforcement during the night should be delayed until morning. The child who earns immediate reinforcement at 3:00 am will likely continue the behavior rather than falling back to sleep. Instead, the child should be offered a reinforcement to be received after he gets up. For example, tell the child, "It's still night-time. It's still time to sleep. If you stay in bed quietly you can have 10 minutes of computer time."

Comfort items such as soft music may help a child get back to sleep. This should be presented as a privilege that requires his cooperation. "I will turn the music on if you stay in bed. If you get out of bed, I will have to turn it off."

Avoid lying down with the child during the night. The drowsy parent who is also awakened from sleep may find it fortuitous to simply lie down with the child until he falls back to sleep. This plan will likely backfire, as it will inadvertently reinforce the night-time awakenings, and is even more difficult to fade out than if the parent lies down with the child at bedtime.

Early morning awakenings

Establish an end point. Decide what is an acceptable time for the child to get out of bed. It should correlate with the time that he usually wakes up, if there is regularity to his sleep patterns. If not, notify him that he must stay in bed until a certain time. Be sure to display the time in his room, or ensure that he is made aware in some fashion. If the child cannot tell time, a digital clock can be used.

Quiet play in bed may be allowed for the child who wakens early from sleep. The play should be satisfying enough to keep him occupied without being so desirable as to encourage early awakening.

Picture books, headphones, cards, or manipulatives may be used for the child who lacks pretend play skills or interest in stuffed animals. This playtime should be considered a privilege that can be revoked if the behavioral parameters are not met.

A work requirement such as chores or extra worksheet may discourage the early riser from waking the rest of the family. For example, instruct the child that "If you get up before 7:00 you will have to put the clean dishes away before breakfast."

Examples

Getting to sleep. Positive reinforcement may include "If you stay in bed you can have your stuffed animals. If you get out of bed to play I will have to take them away." It is best if you can offer an immediate reinforcer and an additional morning reward for continuing the behavior. "You can get a happy face for every 5 minutes that you stay in bed. If you get out of bed to goof around you will get a sad face. If you have all happy faces in the morning you can watch a movie before school."

Night-time awakenings. In this situation, offer the child one reminder or warning regarding the rule, "It's night time. You need to stay in bed and sleep. If you  get out of bed to play, I will not be able to make pancakes for breakfast. You will have to have eggs." Of course, you need to be prepared for the child to violate the rule and require another one. "I'm sorry that you made a bad choice. You will have eggs for breakfast. If you get out of bed again you will lose playtime before school."

Early morning awakenings. Teach the child to use a clock or devise some other form of identifying an appropriate time to get out of bed. Reward him for staying in bed until the designated time. "Great job staying in bed until 7:00! You can have 15 minutes of computer time before breakfast."

In the event that a behavioral plan has been attempted without success, a consideration of medical management is in order. Many individuals with autism benefit from medication that promotes healthy sleep patterns without adversely affecting their waking hours. Treatment options include both prescription and non-prescription medications. Medical management should be discussed with the family's physician.

Chapter Summary

Achieve success:

- Eliminate distractions
- Create and utilize a behavioral plan
- Establish boundaries
- Reinforce desired behavior

CHAPTER 14

TEACHING PLAY SKILLS
Overcoming limitations

Introduction

Children with autism often have difficulty developing appropriate play skills. Their "play" may be endless hours of self-stimulation or repetitive behavior. Parents must recognize the urgent necessity of developing appropriate play skills, directing the child away from dysfunctional activities and toward useful play. Inadequate play skills will further isolate the child who is already socially impaired. Boredom ensues, and the child gravitates toward the comfort and predictability of ritualistic play. Adults who feel uncomfortable with the artificial nature of instructed play further complicate matters. Reluctance must be abandoned and an energetic approach to teaching appropriate play skills must be embraced. Play skills can be acquired in the same manner as academic skills, through clearly defined targets and positive reinforcement of desired behavior. The child must be prompted enough for success to be achieved. Only when the child is successful and reinforced will the play be repeated, intrinsically reinforcing, and "natural."

Play skills can be acquired in the same manner as academic skills, through clearly defined targets and positive reinforcement of desired behavior.

Domain

1. Independent play
2. Rewarding play
3. Social play

Approach

Independent play

Independent play is solitary play that the child can occupy himself with appropriately. It is desirable enough for the child to engage in it willingly, but not so desirable as to be consuming or reinforcing. Solitary play activities provide an avenue for the child to be occupied in appropriate play without constant supervision. It is exhausting for parents to maintain constant interaction with the affected child without compromising the family as a whole. Thankfully, as the child gains function, opportunities to expand independence occur and mastered activities can be used to engage the child in appropriate play. Opportunities for dysfunction must be eliminated by offering desirable alternatives. "Independent play" time should be both scheduled and readily accessible to the child during transitions or down time. Even short periods of time should not be left unstructured. Encouraging the child to choose an independent play activity "until dinner is ready" alleviates stress for both parent and child. The younger child can enjoy solitary play with blocks, manipulatives, or puzzles while in close proximity to a parent without requiring their undivided attention.

Rewarding play

Rewarding play refers to activities that are highly desirable and for which the child will perform on-task behaviors. Rewarding play is reinforcing, and as such, should be identified and set aside for exclusive use with target behaviors. These play activities must not be freely available to the child. Access to rewarding play must be controlled in order for reinforcement to be effective.

Social play

Social play refers to interactive play with other people. This type of play is usually the least desirable for children with autism because it is unpredictable, language dependent, and involves social cues that may elude them. The difficulties with socialization that are characteristic of autism have been addressed elsewhere in this book; here we will present strategies that facilitate acquisition of play skills.

Social play, or playing with others, is the most challenging type of play for the child with autism. This interactive play should first be targeted at home, then adapted to the school setting. As with all target behaviors, the amount of time spent on the activity should be less than what is the perceived limitation of the child's interest and cooperation. Thus, if the child is resistant to social play, initial periods should be very short and reinforcement highly desirable. To ensure success, use only mastered activities that the child is proficient with and which he enjoys. The child can be set up for interaction by controlling access to items so that he must request to share with his peer. For example, give him a coloring book, but give the crayons to his peer, so that an opportunity to ask is created. Reinforcement should be given accordingly. Board games also present opportunities for turn-taking and requesting. The behavioral expectations for peer play and the corresponding reward system should be clearly defined prior to the playtime. Inform the child that each person will get a turn to choose a game or activity and that he will also have to play what his friend chooses. Refusal to do so will result in forfeiting his turn to choose. Since imaginary and pretend play are difficult for most children with autism, but often favored by their peers, the play choices should be narrowed to exclude this type of play. Clearly, the peer chosen to participate should be cooperative and willing to abide by the parameters of the playtime. Otherwise, the play may be unsuccessful for the child with autism, further reinforcing his dislike of peer play. The choices available should include games and activities that are of high interest for both the affected child and for his typically functioning peer.

Parallel play, in which children play side by side at the same activity is a typical and age appropriate style of play for preschool and kindergarten aged children. Activities such as block play, coloring, manipulatives, and puzzles present opportunities for the child to be reinforced for "playing with a friend" in a predictable and non-threatening manner. Parallel play activities also offer opportunities to improve language skills by encouraging reciprocal statements without requiring complex language use. For example, "I'm building a rocket" is a statement that prompts the child with autism to respond following the same language pattern, "I'm building a tower." The parent or educator can prompt the peer in ways that promote corresponding language use by the child with autism.

Turn taking activities such as board games, cards, and simple ball play can be used to expand the child's play skills from parallel play to interactive play. Turn taking can be prompted with a visual cue such as a card that says "my turn" on one end and "your turn" on the other. The card is rotated with each turn to indicate the current player. Playing catch, shooting baskets, or kicking a soccer ball can also be used in a turn taking fashion.

Shared interests are activities or topics that the child with autism enjoys and which are also of mutual interest to a peer or peers. Shared interests allow the child with autism to be accepted into a peer group based on commonalities, rather than isolated due to his differences. Shared interests should be utilized whenever possible to promote socialization and play.

Interactive play includes sports and games with rules. This type of play requires a strong skill base to compensate for team dynamics. Common schoolyard games such as tag, "red light, green light" hide and seek, and four square are just a few activities that the child with autism may encounter. The child's ability to socialize often depends on his ability to participate in interactive games. Thus, the child should acquire and practice skills at home so that he is able to participate at school. A play requirement can be incorporated into his school checklist once he has demonstrated mastery at home. Sports that have an individual component should be mastered before attempting team play. Fundamental ball skills such as throwing, catching, and kicking are essential for school aged children and should be targeted for success.

Examples

Independent play

Preschool age children should be encouraged to engage in solitary play with activities that are mastered and enjoyable. Puzzles, coloring, manipulatives, blocks/building sets, and toys that are played appropriately should be readily available in areas of the house in which the parents spend time. Older children may occupy themselves with individual sports such as shooting baskets, card games such as Solitaire, reading, drawing/art, or other items of interest such as math games or flashcards.

Rewarding play

Examples of rewarding play have been mentioned throughout this book with reference to reinforcement. These may include computer time, listening to music, free playtime with electronic toys, or whatever games have been identified as highly desirable to the child. These activities are not otherwise available to the child. Do not allow him to practice self-stimulating behavior of any kind as a means of reinforcement. Inappropriate play such as playing with something that is not intended for use as a toy (garage door opener, telephone, remote control, light switches, etc.) should never be used as a reinforcer.

Social play

Parallel play can be made accessible in a variety of ways. One way that works well and maintains structure is to set up activity "centers" or play stations similar to center activities at school. Any activity that the child enjoys can be incorporated into a center. Some examples:

1. Legos, blocks, gears and other constructive toys.
2. Marble toys such as "Block and Roll®" or Discovery Toys "Marble Works®".
3. Interlocking puzzles or puzzle type activities.
4. Playdoh® and accessories.
5. Coloring or drawing activities, Spirograph®, cut and paste projects.

6. Pattern or matching games with cards or objects.
7. Manipulatives and educational games with pegs, tiles, interlocking pieces such as "Triominoes®", "Fractiles®" or "Super Mind®."
8. Math or geography activities.
9. Individual toys such as mazes or small pinball games.

Turn taking games include:
1. Bingo games can be purchased in a variety of themes such as addition, subtraction, multiplication, division, rhyming, time, money, colors and shapes and so forth. Additional games can easily be made at home to suit the interests of the child using pictures of animals, cars, license plates, traffic signs, sports, or other interesting stimuli.
2. Dominoes are also available in a variety of themes.
3. Educational board games come in a wide range of interesting themes.
4. Simple board games such as "Hi Ho Cherrio®," "Trouble®," "Candyland®," "Chutes and Ladders®" and many more can be used for simple turn taking play. Card games such as "Old Maid," "Go Fish," "Uno®," and "Crazy 8's" are also good choices.
5. CD-ROM versions of popular board games such as "Chutes and Ladders®," "Sorry®," and "Scrabble®" are also available and can be used for turn taking play.

Shared interests:
1. Playground activities such as swings, slides, monkey bars and tetherball.
2. Outings to the zoo, museum, hiking or exploring based on shared interests.
3. Hobbies and collections.

Interactive play:
1. Sports conducive to early social play include air hockey, rollerblading, ice skating, catch, soccer drills, bike riding, golf, tennis, basketball, batting, and gymnastic skills.
2. Scripted or rehearsed imaginary play for the child that is interested and proficient.

Peer play parameters should be established prior to the playtime:

"Today Andrew is coming over to play after school. You can have your free play first. Then you can play with Andrew from 4:00 to 5:00. You need to follow the

Rules for Playing with Friends:
Stay at your activity
Play what your friend picks
Share your toys and games
Take turns choosing what to play

You can earn 5 minutes of computer time for each game you play with Andrew. The activity choices are: board games, basketball, air hockey, or catch. Your friend always gets to pick first because that is nice and polite. Then you can pick next. You will not get your 5 minutes of computer time if you:
1. Complain about playing with your friend.
2. Leave your activity.
3. Act rude. Saying things like, "Are we done yet?" or "Is it time for Andrew to go home?" are rude.

Play can become an enjoyable part of life for the child with autism when a systematic and positive behavioral approach is used to teach fundamental skills and encourage participation.

Chapter Summary
Classify play for different purposes:
- Independent play
- Rewarding play
- Social play

Teach play skills with behavioral technique:
- Clearly define target behavior
- Prompt for success
- Reinforce success
- Establish mastery
- Advance target behavior

CHAPTER 15

DEVELOPING USEFUL INTERESTS
Broadening general interests, cultivating narrow interests

Introduction

If left to their own devices, children with autism naturally gravitate to the concrete and predictable, thus significantly narrowing their interests. A broad education should be used to diminish areas of weakness and encourage a variety of interests. In addition, areas of strength and interest should be channeled into useful activities with a long-term view toward developing vocational skills. Throughout this book we have offered strategies to help the individual with autism overcome deficits. Here we will take a different approach, encouraging educators and parents to utilize narrow interests for socialization, motivation, and vocational opportunities.

Domain

1. **Utilizing narrow interests.**
2. **Broadening general interests.**
3. **Cultivating narrow interests.**

Approach

Utilizing narrow interests.

Consider that preoccupations and unusual interests can be useful to motivate the child with autism. Rather than attempting to suppress these interests, they should be viewed as a useful tool among many to accomplish target behaviors. All reinforcement comes from interest and desire for an object, activity, or experience. Narrow interests expand reinforcement from tangible objects to valuable knowledge of a subject. So, for example, the child that was once motivated by earning small plastic zoo animals in the discrete trial setting can now expand this interest in animals to earning an opportunity to look at animal books in the classroom.

Utilize the child's narrow interests to promote success. Narrow interests can be useful as reinforcement for on-task behavior and as motivation to broaden general interests. Certainly, perseverative and self-absorbed behaviors need to be dealt with cautiously and should not be used as reinforcement. "Narrow interests" refers to typical interests that are taken to an extreme and to the exclusion of broad and varied interests found in the general population. So, for example, a child who is fascinated with numbers can be rewarded by the opportunity to formulate equations on his calculator once he has completed his writing assignment. This differs significantly from allowing a child to pace the room making odd noises. Although such a behavior may alleviate anxiety, it will likely alienate the child rather than endear him to his classmates, and is of little or no value as a useful "skill." Interest and expertise in math, on the other hand, is likely to be both admirable and useful. Simply sequencing material so that desirable activities follow undesirable ones can motivate the child to accomplish required assignments that he is otherwise unmotivated to complete.

$$31 \div X = 19$$
$$Y + 2\frac{1}{15} = ?$$
$$Y = 7$$
$$x + 21^{3} =$$

> " repeated failure fosters feelings of futility and frustration in fragile learners who lack self-confidence and may lack competencies for task-related problem solving" (Stewart, p1).

Broadening general interests

Exposure to a variety of subjects is necessary for any individual in order to determine areas of interest. Children with autism often resist exposure to new material, preferring the comfort and predictability of what they already know. The very thought of something "new" may be quite distressing. Since numerous subjects are required for the length of the educational process, it is inevitable that the high-functioning child with autism must learn about many subjects that he may dislike. However, until the child has had the opportunity to explore new subjects, he cannot know whether they will interest him or not. Exposure should be broad enough to allow for the potential development of additional and expanded interests.

Resistance to material outside of the child's interest must be targeted and diminished. Frustration tolerance, which is fundamental to the ability to expand beyond ritualistic and obsessive interests, is addressed in detail in chapter 11. Learning must be as enjoyable as possible when the child is resistant and efforts should be made to incorporate desirable activities related to areas of low interest. Situations that increase the child's frustration and anxiety should be noted, and modified or eliminated whenever possible. Once all possible antecedents are controlled, the child's frustration tolerance can be targeted directly and general interests expanded as the child earns positive reinforcement for appropriate responses to new events.

Anxiety related to the unfamiliar should be considered and addressed. Much of the child's resistance is based on anticipation of the unknown. To simply attempt to alter a behavior without addressing the underlying cause is unlikely to produce lasting change. Strategies should provide information in advance, a structured approach and visual cues to ensure success and decrease the anxiety and reticence related to new topics and tasks.

Motivation to increase the child's inclination to attempt something new is critical. A positive and enthusiastic approach that reinforces the child's

willingness and effort over the actual accomplishment will promote a cycle of success. Desirable reinforcement must accompany progressive willingness by the child to overcome his fears and expand his narrow interests.

Success must be achieved and failure avoided. Only through success will the child with autism learn that "new is OK," and perhaps even enjoyable.

> "In general, tasks and activities which learners associate with past success tend to stimulate interest. Success begets success! Challenges which trigger memories of past anxieties and failures tend to stimulate avoidance reactions and self-preservation responses. Although occasional failure is often seen as a challenge by learners who are highly motivated to learn through problem solving, repeated failure fosters feelings of futility and frustration in fragile learners who lack self-confidence and may lack competencies for task-related problem solving.
> When diligently applied, proactive strategies often prove successful in eventually eliciting positive, productive responses and pride in personal accomplishment."
> (Stewart, p. 1).

Eccentric or unusual behaviours are much more likely to be accepted in individuals who are able to demonstrate exceptional skills in certain areas, than they are in those who have no such redeeming features.

(Howlin, p26)

Cultivating narrow interests

Consider the following, often overlooked perspective regarding the narrow interest of the child with autism:

"There are a number of factors related to early development that appear to be significantly associated with later outcome. The presence of at least simple communicative language by the age of 5 or 6 years is one of the most important prognostic indicators, as is the ability to score within the mildly retarded range or above on non-verbal tests of ability…However, the presence of relatively good cognitive and communication skills alone does not necessarily guarantee a successful outcome. This is far more readily achieved if individuals possess additional skills or interests (such as specialised knowledge in particular areas or competence in mathematics, music, or computing) which allow them to find their own special 'niche' in life, and which enable them to be more easily integrated into society. Eccentric or unusual behaviours are much more likely to be accepted in individuals who are able to demonstrate exceptional skills in certain areas, than they are in those who have no such redeeming features. Thus, as Kanner, Eisenberg, and Rutter all proposed many years ago, adequate educational opportunities, and encouragement to develop skills that may lead to later acceptance, are crucial. Moreover, particularly for those who are more able, it would seem more profitable in the long term for educational programmes to concentrate on those areas in which the person with autism already demonstrates potential competence, rather than focusing on areas of deficit" (Howlin, p. 26).

Promote expertise in his area of particular interest. The child who is perceived by his peers as one who "knows everything about geography" is more likely to be respected and befriended. For the socially impaired child, this advantage cannot be underestimated. The desire to be proficient is a universal human experience, and most individuals value and are valued for their achievement, knowledge, and expertise of a particular subject. For the child with autism it is even more important to cultivate expertise in a subject, both for self-esteem and for future vocational opportunity. His narrow interest should be used to challenge him to excel and to achieve.

The child who is perceived by his peers as one who "knows everything about geography" is more likely to be respected and befriended. For the socially impaired child, this advantage cannot be underestimated.

Examples

Example #1: A child who loves numbers.

1. **Explore your community by observing and noting numbers. Help the child to see that numbers are a useful and necessary part of our community.**
   a. "Let's go to the grocery store and see what they use numbers for."
   b. "What's another place that uses numbers? How about the bank?"
   c. "Let's play a number game with house addresses. Let's add up all the numbers that we find on our street and see what the total is. How high do you think it's going to be?"
   d. "Let's brainstorm. Can you think of 10 places in our community that uses numbers?"

2. **Teach the scientific method by designing a project that uses measurements.**
   a. Formulate a hypothesis: "Things that are larger are also heavier."
   b. Data collection using measurements of objects for weight and size.
   c. Analyze the data collected according to objects that support the hypothesis and objects that do not. "70% of objects that were larger were also heavier. 30% of objects that were larger were not heavier."
   d. Summarize conclusions: "Usually objects that are larger are also heavier."

3. **Stimulate pretend play by making a number line and "pretend these are wild numbers and they are out of their cage! Call the 'Number Keeper!'"**

4. **Encourage abstract thinking by writing a fictitious story about numbers that are alive.**
   a. "What can you tell us about the number 7? Where does he live? What does he like to do?"
   b. "Does number 7 have any pets?"
   c. "Does he have any brothers or sisters? What numbers are they?"

5. **Teach money and time concepts.**
   a. "Let's take $3.00 and go to McDonalds to see what our money can buy. Do you think you will have enough to buy your lunch? Do you think you will have any money left?"
   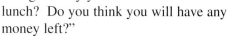
   b. "I put a special clock in your room. It has two clocks, one with hands and one with numbers. It will help you to learn to tell time."

6. **Create social opportunities with number games.**
   a. "Let's invite Mark over to play Bingo with you."
   b. "Since your class is learning the numbers from 1 to 1000, let's invite Jessica over to help us write a number line. Then you can take it to school and show your class."
   c. "Since you have an odometer on your bike, let's invite Steve to go for a ride with us. We can see how far it is to Washington Park. You could each make a guess before we go. Whoever is closest can choose where we stop for lunch."

Example #2: A child who loves animals.

1. **Motivate and teach reading skills, such as phonics, by using the names of favorite or exotic animals.**

2. **Enhance abstract thinking and writing using his interest in animals: "Let's think of a silly story about monkeys who think they are zebras."**
   a. "What do you think they would eat?"
   b. "What do you think they would look like?"
   c. "What kinds of activities would they like?"
   d. "Would they make a good pet? Why or why not?"

3. **Promote expertise by encouraging further learning and research.**
   a. Explore books and movies at the public library.
   b. Teach computer skills through an on-line research.
   c. Purchase or create animal information cards.

4. **Encourage social opportunities.**
   a. "Let's invite Sam over to play 'Safari.' We can hide all of your zoo animal figures and then turn the lights out and look for them with flashlights."
   b. "Let's plan our own field trip. Let's invite one or two friends to go to the zoo on Saturday. I am going to quiz you and your friends about the animals. I will give everyone a dime for each correct answer. At the end we can go to the gift shop and you can buy a new animal for your collection if you have enough money."

Example #3: A child who loves shapes

1. **Motivate and teach drawing skills by breaking the task down into component shapes, such as a rocket (a triangle on top of a vertical rectangle on top of a trapezoid).**

2. **Stimulate exploration by looking for shapes in multiple environments such as around the school, park, or in books.**
   a. "Let's walk around our community and look for shapes. We can make a list of all the kinds that we see."
   b. "Since you love shapes, let's play a game around the house that will help you learn to find things. Go upstairs and find something round and bring it to me."

3. **Foster brainstorming skills through shapes.**
   a. "Make a list of all the shapes that you can think of."
   b. "Now write how many sides each shape has."
   c. "Now list all the shapes that have parallel sides. 'Parallel' means that two sides look like the number 11, they are side by side and they don't cross."
   d. "Now you can put them into two categories."

4. **Encourage ownership and self-worth through collections.**
   a. "Here is a round tin that you can use for your shapes collection. I started it for you with a triangular button."
   b. "Every time you finish your chores you can make a shape at the art table. Then you can hang it on your bedroom wall in a pattern. Your collection shows everyone how much you help out the family."

Narrow interests can be applied to a variety of tasks to motivate the child to succeed as well as to encourage and expand interests in other subjects.

Chapter Summary

Broaden general interests:

- Provide exposure to variety
- Target resistance
- Reduce anxiety
- Increase motivation
- Achieve and reward success

Cultivate narrow interests:

- Identify particular interest
- Utilize it to promote success
- Encourage expertise

CHAPTER 16

STRUCTURING THE HOME ENVIRONMENT
Maintaining continuity between home and school

Introduction

Continuity between the home and school environment is critical to the long term and optimal success of the child with autism. The need for predictability and structure are not location specific. Elements of routine and clearly defined behaviors must be established so that the child does not operate under two different sets of rules and expectations. The same visual learning style implemented at school should also be incorporated into the home. In all settings, success must be planned for, and positive reinforcement made available.

Domain

1. **Schedules and routines**
2. **Play**
3. **Homework**
4. **Responsibilities**

The need for predictability and structure are not location specific.

Approach and Examples

Schedules and routines
Daily events should be displayed in a visual format until the child internalizes the daily routine. School days should have predictable elements distinct from weekends. Specific time periods should be included initially with a plan to fade them out. Once the child demonstrates mastery of the morning routine and is ready for school on time, the detailed parameters can be eliminated. For example, the morning routine on a school day might look like this:

7:00-7:30 Eat breakfast
7:30-7:40 Clean up breakfast
7:40-7:50 Get dressed
7:50-7:55 Brush teeth
7:55-8:00 Make bed
8:00-8:30 Do homework

Over time, the structure is decreased to look like this:

- Breakfast and clean up
- Get yourself ready for school
- Do 30 minutes of homework
- Play until it's time to go

Lastly, the visual cues are faded out when the child has demonstrated mastery of the routine. Reinforcement specific to the home targets should be used and faded out once mastery is achieved. Play time before school can replace artificial reinforcement.

Weekly schedules that offer predictable events for after school and evening hours can help the child learn to delay gratification. Accumulated earnings at school such as a weekend outing can be noted on the calendar when the conditions are met. For example:

After school:

Monday: SCORE!
Tuesday: Play with a friend
Wednesday: Bowling
Thursday: Sports practice
Friday: Bike riding
Saturday: School Prize!
Sunday: Church and outside play

After Dinner:

Puzzle Night
Chapter Book
Eat out with Dad
Library Night
Kid's Choice
Family Game Night
Movie Night

Monthly calendar displays offer long-term perspective and predictability, helping the child to self-regulate anxiety related to upcoming events and activities. Displaying a calendar for the month also helps the child to understand abstract time concepts such as yesterday, today and tomorrow. Achievement and mastery of skills can be recorded for the entire family to applaud, building self-esteem and a sense of pride in accomplishment.

Routines should be established for mealtimes, getting ready for school, after school and bedtime. Acquisition of target behaviors should continue until the routines are integrated into the child's memory and behavioral patterns. Established routines provide the necessary framework for the child with autism to fulfill expectations and decrease anxiety at home. For example:

Getting Ready for School

1. Get dressed. Check the thermometer before you decide what to wear.
2. Breakfast:
   Set the table.
   Get your juice and fruit.
   Take your medicines.
   Clean up after you are finished.
3. Pack your lunch.
4. Brush your teeth and comb your hair.
5. Check your homework folder.
   If you have anything left on the "To do" side, work on it until 8:30.
   If you are finished, read a book until 8:30.
6. Play from 8:30-8:50
7. Go to school at 8:50.

A variety of details can be incorporated according to the child's individual needs. For example:

Get dressed. Check the thermometer before you decide what to wear.

1. If the temperature is above 60 degrees, you should wear: Shorts and a short sleeve shirt
2. If the temperature is below 60 degrees, you should wear: pants and a long sleeve shirt. You should wear or take a sweatshirt to school.
3. If the temperature is below 40 degrees, you should also wear a coat, hat, and gloves.

These details are initially presented in a visual format and faded out when the child has demonstrated mastery of the task and can make appropriate decisions. Other details such as "How to pack your lunch" or "How to make a sandwich" should be explicit enough to develop independence.

A checklist for target behaviors in the home environment is developed in the same fashion as a checklist for school. Each activity should have no more than one or two priority targets at a time. Acquisition and mastery are achieved by positive reinforcement of target behaviors. Behaviors must be sufficiently prompted to achieve success, and prompts must be faded quickly. Existing written routines can be converted to a checklist simply by highlighting the target behavior(s) and delineating the reinforcement schedule. Several examples are shown below.

Mealtime

1. Set the table with Susie. *Your part is to set out the place mats and napkins.* You will get a star on your chart if you do this by yourself.
2. Take your shoes off before you come to the table so you won't play with them.
3. Sit on your bottom for mealtime.

4. Eat everything on your plate if you want to have dessert. Tell me if you don't like something and we can talk about it.
5. Help clean up the table after dinner. *Your part is to put the place mats and napkins in the laundry basket.* You will get a star on your chart if you do this by yourself.

Each star is worth 5 minutes of computer time after mealtime.

After school

1. Empty out your backpack and hang it up on your hook.
2. Clean out your lunch bag.
3. Show Mom your notes from school.
4. Tell Mom 3 things you did at school. You will get to choose your own snack if you can do this. Otherwise, Mom chooses the snack.

Bedtime

1. Get a snack if you are hungry.
2 Get ready for shower. Bring your pajamas.
3. Brush your teeth.
4. Read quietly until 8:30. You will get to listen to music from 8:30-9:00 if you read quietly.

Play

Play times should be
incorporated into the daily routine
and noted in the home schedule.
The child who earns his playtime
may become anxious if he does
not know when he is allowed to
enjoy it. As the child progresses,
increments of earned playtime
can be faded out to a more natural schedule in which
play follows work or responsibilities without the use of
a token economy. The child who has mastered
routines and responsibilities at home no longer needs
direct reinforcement for on-task behavior, and can
assume a more natural approach to work and play: "All
kids play and they earn it by doing their work first. So
after you finish your work, you can play until dinner."

Peer play may be challenging and of little interest to
the child with autism. He may prefer to play alone
and may resist efforts to play with peers. Positive
reinforcement is necessary to motivate the child in a
variety of behaviors, including appropriate play with
other children. This may be particularly
uncomfortable for adults who do not appreciate the
social impairment characteristic of autism. It is
difficult enough to teach endless academic tasks, but to
utilize artificial methods to teach play skills is
particularly disheartening. What is so "natural" for
typically functioning children may be completely
foreign to the child with autism. However, when
behavioral principles are applied to the development of
interactive play, the child learns to associate
appropriate behaviors with desirable rewards,
enhancing his social skills and increasing the
likelihood that elements of social interaction are
reinforcing in and of themselves. Initial efforts to
engage the child with peers should be scheduled to
decrease the anxiety created by unknown or open-
ended experiences. Assuring the child that the
playtime is occasional and limited, with clearly
defined behavioral expectations and reinforcement,
will offer him the best opportunity for success.
Further discussion regarding play skills is found in
chapter 15.

Expectations for peer play
sessions should be clearly
delineated for the benefit of the
child with autism, his peer, and
the adults involved. An index
card with simple instructions can
be made for the child to take with
him when playing at a friend's
house. Inform the parent that
they can use the card to guide the child's behavior and
that you will use it to reward his efforts after he
returns home. For example,

> ## Rules for Playing with Friends:
> 1. Stay at your activity.
> 2. Take turns choosing. Play what your friend
>   chooses if you want to choose the next activity.
> 3. Don't goof around with electronics or computers.
>
> You can earn a checkmark for each game you play
> with Thomas. Then you can have 5 minutes of free play
> for each check when you get home.

Rewards for peer play should be offered to
correspond with the behavioral expectations. Loss of
rewards or a cost response should be included to
maintain acceptable behavior. Once the child has
demonstrated the ability to engage in play activities
with a friend, incremental reinforcement through a
token economy can be eliminated and replaced with
privileges of a general nature.

Homework

When homework should be done may be a source of anxiety for the child with autism. Designating a specific time to complete required work each day will provide the child with predictability in the home setting. Observations should be made regarding the time of day that the child is most cooperative and productive. Immediately after school will not work if the child is eager to play after a long day at school; nor will late at night if the child is tired or inattentive. Completing most or all of weekly homework on the weekend is another option. Regardless of the time that is selected, establishing a routine with homework is helpful for decreasing anxiety and non-compliance.

How much homework the child is required to complete at any given time should be identified to alleviate anxiety associated with an open-ended task. An endpoint should be clearly delineated, at which point his work is evaluated for completion and adequacy. Once the work is completed satisfactorily, the child should be free to choose the activity that follows so that natural reinforcement is incorporated into the long-term plan for independent work at home.

What work the child is required to do should be broken down into component tasks, when necessary to support independent task completion. A checklist designed for the child to monitor himself should be provided, incorporating expanded instructions that address deficits in the child's understanding of the required work.

An example may look like this:

Homework for the week of April 2, 2003: Give yourself a checkmark after you finish each item.

1. Wednesday: Warm-up Reading
   Read the story first.
   Write the question.
   Answer the question.

2. Thursday: Spelling
   Read the instructions at the top of the page.
   Answer the questions on both sides of the page.

3. Friday: Pronunciation
   Fill in the answers on the worksheet in your folder.

4. Saturday: Writing
   Choose a topic:
   Favorite Sport   My Family   My Pets
   Brainstorm: write 5 things about your topic.
   Sentences: write long sentences using each of your 5 ideas.
   Edit: work with an adult to find any mistakes and correct them.
   Final Draft: copy your finished story onto a new page.

5: Sunday: Math
   Fill in the answers on both sides of your pages.

6. Monday: School Newspaper
   Read it first.
   Answer the questions on the last page.

You can earn 5 minutes of playtime for each checkmark. When you finish today's assignment, you can play.

Rewards specifically for homework assignments should be designated. If homework is done in the morning, allowing earned playtime immediately after homework and before going to school is a reasonable reward. Specific privileges distinct from reinforcement earned at school should be used. A separate token economy may need to be developed for home use and faded out to incorporate more natural reinforcement. Rewards should be delineated in the home checklist to ensure on-task behavior and motivation.

Responsibilities

The child with autism, like the typically functioning child, should participate in family life, making contributions through responsibilities as well as enjoying the associated benefits. Efforts to teach responsibility at an early age are essential to adult independence.

Chores that the child can learn through sequenced instruction can be introduced in the preschool or kindergarten years. Partnership activities with a sibling make acquisition of skills a joint effort and prepare the child for the many cooperative activities that lie ahead. Organization of the play area is important to facilitate clean up. Bins or storage areas should be labeled with pictures and/or words so that the child can put things away independently. Chores should be incorporated into the daily and weekly schedules and reinforced until they are integrated into the child's routine. Visual instructions should be posted until the child can complete the task on his own. For example:

Daily Chores:
1. Clean up your room.
2. Set the table at dinner.
3. Clear the table after dinner.
4. Clean up the playroom.

Specific task sheets can be made as needed and displayed in the appropriate room:

Clean up your room:
1. Make your bed in the morning before school.
2. Put all of your clean clothes away. Everything must be on a hanger or in a drawer.
3. Put books back on the bookshelf.
4. Put trash in the trash can.
5. Put toys back in the toy box.

Set the table for dinner:
1. Put out a place mat and napkin for each person.
2. Put a towel on each child's chair to help keep it clean.
3. Put the dishes out: plate, glass, and knife, fork and spoon. Follow the pattern on the drawing.

Clear the table after dinner:
1. Put your dirty dishes in the dishwasher.
2. Put your dirty napkin and place mat in the laundry basket.
3. Put your towel back in the drawer unless it is dirty. Then put it in the laundry basket.

Clean up the playroom:
1. Put all of the toys back in the correct bin.
2. Bring any dishes back to the kitchen. Put them in the dishwasher.
3. Put any cans in the recycling bin.
4. Put any trash in the trashcan.

Weekly Chores: *These are partner chores. Work with your sister.*

1. Empty the small trashcans. One person empties and the other person holds the bag.
2. Sweep the front porch. One person sweeps with the broom and the other person holds the dustpan.
3. Help put the recycling bins out in the alley. Each person holds one end of the bin and together you can carry it.

Daily living responsibilities such as tooth brushing, hand washing, dressing, and bathing are opportunities to teach responsibility. Routines can be acquired and rewarded using charts that display and applaud accomplishments. Sequenced task sheets should be displayed until the child incorporates the elements of the routine. For example:

Washing your hands:

1. Turn the water on. Hot + Cold = Warm.
2. Get your hands wet.
3. Get a little soap on your hands.
4. Rub the soap all over your hands.
5. Rinse the soap off under the running water.
6. Turn the water off. Turn off both handles.
7. Dry your hands on the towel.

Brushing your teeth:

1. Find your toothbrush and put it on the handle.
2. Get your toothbrush wet. Then turn the water off.
3. Put a small glob of toothpaste on your brush.
4. Push the green button on the handle to turn it on. *Don't turn it on until it is in your mouth or it will spray everywhere!*
5. Hold the brush in each place and count to ten in your head.

On the bottom left.
On the bottom right.
On the bottom in the front.
On the top left.
On the top right.
On the top in the front.

6. Turn the brush off and spit out the toothpaste. *Don't swallow it.*
7. Put some water in the glass and rinse your mouth. Spit out the water, don't swallow it.
8. Rinse off your brush and put it back on the shelf. Put the handle in the charger.

Taking a shower:

1. Turn the water on. The handle should be at "11:00" to start.
2. Get undressed while you wait for the water to warm up.
3. Test the water with your hand to make sure it is the right temperature. If it is too hot, turn the dial to "12:00." If it is too cold, turn it toward "10:00."
4. Stand under the shower to get your hair wet first. Then rub shampoo into your hair.
5. Put some body soap on the washcloth and wash your body.
6. Stand under the shower to rinse. Rinse your hair and body.
7. Turn the shower off.
8. Get out and dry yourself with the towel.
9. Last, get dressed.

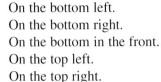

Family responsibilities may include social activities such as playing games or sports together, going to church, helping to unload groceries, and so forth. Since the child with autism prefers structure and predictability, family life may be more pleasant and successful if structure is extended to social and recreational activities. It is within the "safe" environment of the family that the child learns about the needs and interests of others. Isolated, self-absorbed activities cannot be allowed without limits or parameters. The child with autism must be assisted in understanding the social nature of the world he lives in. Participation in family life is a reasonable place to start. Time and effort should be spent to develop skills that increase the child's ability to participate in family outings. Motivation and reinforcement should be included to ensure cooperation and enjoyment. For example, a family bike ride can be motivated by stopping for a soda or snack along the way, or by visiting a desirable location such as a playground. The child can also earn rewards at home after the outing by participating "without complaining." Family activities should be selected fairly so that the typically functioning siblings are not merely "dragged along" based on the interests of the child with autism, or vice versa. Accommodations should also be made to keep the child with autism functionally occupied while his siblings play. For example, if his brother has a soccer game that the entire family wants to watch, a strategy for rewarding "watching" can be developed prior to the game. For example, the child may earn a dime for each 2-minute period that he stays at the sidelines and watches the game. At the end he can use his money to buy something at the concessions stand. Another accommodation may be to reward on-task behavior with play privileges. For example, for each 5-minute period that he stays at the sidelines he is allowed 5 minutes to play with his handheld electronic game upon returning home. This strategy promotes the child's involvement in family activities instead of simply attempting to control negative behaviors.

> *The child with autism must be assisted in understanding the social nature of the world he lives in. Participation in family life is a reasonable place to start.*

Structuring the home environment is beneficial for both the child with autism and for his family. Every opportunity should be used to promote function, skills, and socialization. The hours spent at home should be purposeful and the environment structured and predictable. The lifelong gains necessary for adult independence are rooted in continuity between the home and school environments, and through constant, planned intervention.

Chapter Summary

- Create and utilize schedules and routines
- Structure play time
- Incorporate and reward peer play
- Facilitate homework with structure
- Define responsibilities
- Reward success

CHAPTER 17

VACATION STRATEGIES
How to pack for success

Introduction

Just as a diabetic does not leave his condition behind, nor travel without insulin, so a person with autism does not leave his need for structure behind. However, many exhausted and frustrated parents dream of having a "normal" vacation, that is, one that is free of the constant and emotionally draining routine and rigidity that can feel oppressive at times; after all, the entire family does not have autism, yet the influence of autism is felt by all. In failing to accept the continuous need for structure, they may set themselves up for great disappointment or a miserable experience. On the other hand, the parent that approaches vacation realistically and incorporates behavioral strategies into the vacation plan can expect to enjoy a return on his investment of time and foresight. This plan for success includes anticipating problems, teaching specific skills prior to departure, incorporating rewards, as well as planning schedules that provide predictability. All of these strategies help to decrease the child's anxiety and frustration related to variation and fear of the unknown.

Domain

1. **Choosing a destination**
2. **Anticipation**
3. **Preparation**
4. **Getting there**
5. **Daily/Trip schedules**
6. **Earning rewards**
7. **Public settings**

Approach

Choosing a destination
Whenever possible, careful selection of a vacation destination that offers bountiful opportunities for the individual with autism to succeed should be made. The following considerations can help make the vacation a success.

...many exhausted and frustrated parents dream of having a **"normal" vacation,** that is, one that is free of the constant and emotionally draining routine and rigidity that can feel oppressive at times...

1. What activities will there be that the child will enjoy or work for? When indoor, what activities will occupy the child? What activities will he attend to independently and/or supervised?
2. What supplemental activities will you need to bring to ensure on-task activity?
3. How will you get there? Can the child be occupied en route, or is "getting there" a matter of survival?
4. If weather does not allow outside activity, will there be enough things to do inside?
5. What type of sleeping arrangement is needed? If the child with autism does not sleep, neither will anyone else.
6. Where will meals be served? Can the child eat at a restaurant?
7. What accommodations can be made? Will the child have to stand in line for activities or can he bypass them? For example, Disneyland and Disney World offer privileges for the disabled that allow the entire family or group to bypass the line.
8. Will the family be able to stay together for activities, or will you have to split up? If you split up, will you carry walkie-talkies or cell phones? Will you have a back up plan if it does not go well?

Anticipation

Visual materials can be prepared that create anticipation for the child and reduce anxiety. Verbal explanations alone may be inadequate for a visual learner and may do little to alleviate anxiety or promote interest. Instead, offer written information and pictures of the destination and the activities the family might partake in. Beginning a week or two in

advance, follow the newspaper or on-line forecast to prepare the child for what the weather will be like. Discuss what types of clothing he will need to bring, and what types of activities he might enjoy. Visit web sites or obtain travel brochures that depict the area and its activities, modeling enthusiasm for the trip that will help the child with autism to see that it will be "fun." Show the child on a map where you are going and what route you will travel to reach your destination. Discuss with the family, including the child with autism, what they want to do while on vacation, so that the child understands that it is a family vacation.

Include the child with autism in family discussions and planning. It is helpful to explain that everyone in the family "sometimes likes to do the things you like, but sometimes we like to do other things too. Everyone will get their turn to choose, because that is what's fair." Perhaps everyone in the family can make a list of the things that they would like to do, comparing what they have in common as well as their differences. In this way, the child with autism can be assured that he will get to do the things he wants to do. This is also an opportunity to inform the child that certain activities can be earned or require his cooperation with other family activities. For example, "You can earn a trip to play miniature golf if you don't complain about what your sister chooses when it's her turn." Outline the various target behaviors and the rewards that he can earn during the vacation so that anxiety can be replaced with interest and enthusiasm.

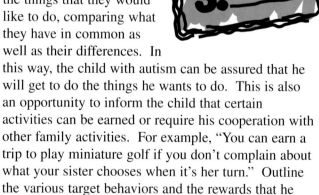

Anticipation of problems that may arise is an important part of preparation for a vacation. New and novel events are rarely successful without anticipating the anxiety and fears that they may provoke and designing a plan for the child to succeed. Public settings may be particularly problematic for the child who experiences sensory overload in noisy or crowded conditions. Individuals with autism may also fear the unpredictable tactile stimulation they encounter when in close proximity to other people. Only after the child has conquered the auditory, visual, and tactile threats of the public arena can his behavior be predictable and polite. Manners are of little concern to a child who is overwhelmed by unwanted sensory stimulation. Once these concerns are addressed and alleviated, the child can learn the socially acceptable behaviors that allow him to blend in and operate comfortably in public settings.

Sensory issues that may adversely affect the child should be evaluated before traveling. The child's tolerance or intolerance of motion, air pressure changes, and unexpected delays may significantly impact the mode of travel selected. Travel sickness can be managed with medication but it is a miserable situation to encounter unprepared. Many individuals find air travel challenging, and the child with sensory aberrations may find it intolerable. Chewing gum, yawning, and nose blowing are several tricks for managing the changes in air pressure experienced while flying. The child who requires a rigid schedule will need assistance in the event of unexpected delays. Parents should be prepared to manage the child's anxieties and offer reinforcement for positive behavior. For example, explain to the child well before going to the airport that "sometimes planes are late, but that's OK. If it is late we can play cards while we wait or go and get a snack. The airline will tell us the new time that we are going to leave."

Preparation
Involve the child with autism in the preparation phase of the trip. After thoughtful selection of a vacation destination and anticipation of difficulties, parents can help their child to "pack for success." Offer the child the opportunity to be involved in the preparation by packing his own suitcase and activities. Work with the child to create a packing list, which he can then

use independently, taking advantage of the natural opportunity to teach. For example, "We are going to the beach. Think about what we will do there and what we will wear. What will you need to pack?" Discuss with the child the time and method of travel so that he will know how best to keep himself occupied.

Develop a behavioral plan specifically for the travel day that will provide the structure and predictability necessary for the child to decrease anxiety and promote positive behaviors. Take the child shopping to select a few new activities as well as new reinforcers for use on the trip. Set these aside for exclusive vacation use, explaining to the child that he will be able to earn them while traveling. Clearly define the behaviors that are required to earn its use. For example, "If you earn 10 stars on the plane for keeping busy with your workbook, then you can have your new game as soon as we get to the hotel."

For longer travel days, evaluate the child's ability to sleep while traveling. When traveling to a different time zone, consider the use of a sleep aid. Packing appropriate snacks and, if traveling by air, notifying the airline, are recommended accommodations for the child with dietary limitations or concerns.

Address anxieties and frustration tolerance.
Identifying in advance situations that provoke anxiety or negative behaviors allow the parents to address these situations prior to encountering them in a public setting. Practice drills, social stories, and role-playing are useful methods of preparing the child for new and unpredictable situations.

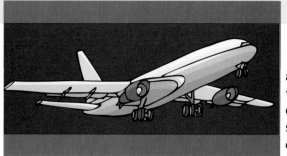

Getting there

Anticipation and preparation will help to make the travel day more tolerable for the child, and hopefully even enjoyable. Determine how much direction or freedom the child should be given with his activities. Children who become anxious without a schedule should be given one for the travel day (see examples at the end of the chapter). Children who are more flexible may be able to keep themselves occupied with their activities independently. Regardless of the child's level of dependence or independence, the goal of the travel day is to "get there." Ultimately, the time and effort spent on anticipation and preparation will be rewarded with compliance, on-task behavior, and enjoyment for the child and his family.

Daily/Trip schedules

It may be useful to take along a blank outline for each day and fill it in once the day's activities are known. If activities and outings are planned in advance, make a schedule of the entire trip. The level of structure and use of schedules can always be decreased if the child seems comfortable without them. Several examples are presented in the following section.

Earning rewards

Using the same familiar method of behavioral intervention, delineate in writing how the child will earn rewards, what the rewards are, and the cost response. As always, the target behavior should be manageable. If the child cannot achieve success, there is nothing to reward. So, for example, if the child has not demonstrated the ability to stand in line in familiar settings such as at school, do not expect him to be able to do so at an amusement park. Parents should be aware of and take advantage of desirable activities and rewards that are inherent in the vacation setting. For example, if a child prefers a certain meal at a restaurant, on-task behavior can be gained by requiring him to "earn" it. The child will require some frustration tolerance to make this work. He must be able to choose a different meal if he fails to

accomplish the target behavior without ruining the family outing. If he is not able to do so because of tantruming or other negative behavior, this would not be a successful situation and the reinforcement should be changed. Some activities may be difficult for the child with autism if they are open-ended, abstract, or unfamiliar. For example, "Today we are going to ride bikes" can be extremely anxiety producing for the child who requires predictability. "How far are we going to ride? How long will it take? Will it be hard? Will we miss lunch?" are all questions that may torment the child unless he is given more information and motivation. Whenever possible, designate an endpoint to the activity, either a time or a destination. In addition, be prepared to develop "on-the-spot" rewards during the activity that help the child to maintain on-task behavior for an extended period of time. Thus, the family bike ride may be more successful if the child is given a token reinforcement for every 10 minutes he rides without complaining, or knows that every 15 minutes he can stop for a break.

If the child cannot achieve success, there is nothing to reward.

Public settings

Before traveling, be sure that the child understands the behavioral expectations for public settings, and identify what those settings are. Develop a plan for making wait periods successful, both the expected and the unexpected. Brief, unexpected wait periods can be the most difficult when not anticipated and planned for. If the parent knows that there will be a 30-minute wait for a train, the child can be kept occupied with a walk or a game of cards. However, if the parent discovers that the hotel room is "not quite ready" and there is nothing to do, those five or ten minutes can be challenging. It is helpful to be organized so that an activity is always readily available.

Examples

Anticipation:

Example #1: "We are going to the beach." Create interest and desire using pictures or movies. Practice building sand structures at the playground.

Example #2: "We are going to Disney World." Visit the web site, order travel brochures. Visit a small local amusement park to determine the child's interest and tolerance of various rides.

Example #3: "We are going camping." Set up a play campsite with a tent, flashlight, and sleeping bag. Have the child sleep there, first inside, and then outside. Serve a "camping" meal at home. Practice playing cards by lantern light.

Example #4: "We are going to Grandma's house." Practice the sleeping arrangement if it is different from what the child is accustomed to. Play games that the child can bring with him. Look at photo albums to familiarize the child with relatives. Label unfamiliar relatives to help the child learn to recognize them.

Preparation:

Example #1: Practice drills for travel time. How long will the child need to sit and remain occupied? Set up a simulated situation at home or in the car, with travel activities and determine the longest amount of time that he can sit, rewarding this time interval. To produce success you must be ahead of the time interval and reward success before the child has a chance to fail.

Example #2: Practice outings to public places. Reward the child for time spent in a noisy place without negative behavior. Identify sensory overload and target tolerance. Target behavior may be 5 minutes at a busy store, reinforcing the absence of negative behavior. Gradually increase the time interval. If one particular setting is too challenging, start with a quieter/less crowded public place (perhaps the grocery store is more tolerable than a department store). If quiet outings are planned, such as a trip to a museum, practice this as well, rewarding use of an appropriate voice and attention to the activity. The public library is a convenient place to practice quiet behaviors.

Example #3: Practice eating at a restaurant. If the child has difficulty sitting in a restaurant environment, start with "fast food" and progress to ordering from a menu. If the child is selective with food choices, practice ordering "something different" and reward it. As in many other situations, determine the child's limit and ensure success by rewarding shorter intervals of on-task behavior.

Example #4: Practice waiting in line. Reinforce the child for progressively longer wait times. Identify and provide activities that can be used to keep the child on task. If the child is fidgety, provide a visual marker such as an "X" for him to stand on that defines his space. With success, the marker can be faded out and the child can draw an imaginary "X" on the ground with his finger, eventually fading the "X" out completely.

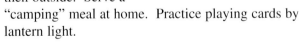

Getting There

The following is an example of a travel day schedule:

7:00   Get up and have breakfast.

7:45   Leave for the airport.

8:15   Arrive at the airport.
We will have to stand in line. You can listen to your headphones.

9:30   Get on the plane.
If our plane is late we can play cards while we wait.
On the plane you can play with the games in your backpack.

11:40   Get off the plane in Denver. We have to get on another plane.

12:30   Get on the plane. We will have lunch on the plane.

3:00   Arrive at the airport in San Diego.
You will have to wait while we get our luggage and car.
You can listen to your headphones while waiting.

4:00   (or a little later) Arrive at our hotel.
You have to wait for us to unpack before you can go to the pool.
You can play on the computer while you wait.

5:00   Pool

6:30   Dinner

8:00   Playtime

9:00   Bedtime

Daily/Trip Schedules

The following is an example of a highly structured daily schedule.

7:00   Stay in bed until 7:00.

7:00-7:30   Play until breakfast.

7:30-8:00   Breakfast

8:00-8:30   Play with your sister = 30 minutes of computer time.

8:30-8:45   Computer time. Save the rest for later.

9:00-10:30   Ride bikes.

10:30-11:00   Play catch with Dad = 30 minutes of computer time.

11:00-11:30   Beach.

11:30-12:00   Computer time.

12:00-12:30   Lunch.

12:30-5:00   Sea World. You can earn a trip to mini golf.

5:00-6:00   Play mini golf.

6:00-7:00   Dinner

7:00-8:00   Remaining computer time and family games.

8:00   Kid's choice: puzzle, movie, or pool.

9:00   Shower and bedtime

The following example represents a less structured daily schedule.

Morning	Wake up and play quietly.
	Breakfast
	Bike ride
	Kid's choice: beach or pool
Lunch	
Afternoon	Sea World
	Mini golf
	Dinner
	Kid's choice: movie, ice cream, or pool
	Games
Bedtime	Shower and quiet reading until 9:00

Earning Rewards

Example #1: Delineate activities or behaviors that will be rewarded:
"You can earn a (+) for every 5 minutes you wait in line."
"You can earn a star for each workbook page that you do while waiting for us to unpack."
"You can earn a star each time you try something new without complaining. You can earn a trip for ice cream if you earn 5 stars."

Example #2: Take advantage of intrinsic rewards:
"I see that you really like going to the beach. You can go to the beach again after dinner when you sit well at the restaurant."
"It seems like you had fun playing at the fountain. We can go back to the fountain tomorrow when you stay in bed quietly tonight."
"I didn't know that you liked roller skating so much! That's great! You can skate around on the sidewalk with your brother when you finish your reading."

Example #3: Develop on the spot rewards: The child who is speaking too loudly during a trip to the museum can be motivated to use and maintain a quiet voice: "You can earn points every time you use your quiet indoor voice. If you earn 10 points you can watch TV after dinner. You will lose a point every time you shout."

Public Settings
The following is an example of behavioral expectations for dining at a restaurant.

Rules for Eating at a Restaurant

Sit Well	Keep your shoes on. Sit on your bottom, not on your knees.
	Face the table, don't turn around.
Wait Nicely	Keep busy while you wait for your meal.
	Keep busy while you wait for everyone to finish eating.
	Keep busy while you wait for us to pay the bill.
Be Polite	Never shout in a restaurant. Use a nice indoor voice.
	Look at the server when you order your meal.
	Say "Please" when you want something.
	Say "Thank you" after you get it.

Similar behavioral plans can be designed for each new or novel activity. For example:

Rules for the Amusement Park

Stay with your family	Never go somewhere by yourself in a crowd. Always wear your ID tag.
Wait Nicely	Wait in line until it is your turn.
	Take turns choosing rides.
	Ride what your brothers and sisters pick, not just what you pick.
What to do if you get lost	Look for someone wearing a yellow hat and a yellow nametag.
	Show them your ID tag. They will call us.
	Then stay with them until we find you.

Vacations need not be frustrating or exhausting for the families of children with autism. Recognizing and respecting the ongoing need for structure and predictability is the first step in planning a successful family vacation. Thoughtful consideration of the abilities and limitations of the individual with autism, in conjunction with anticipation and preparation, are valuable for all members of the family.

Chapter Summary

- Consider destination choice
- Promote interest and enthusiasm
- Involve child in preparation
- Plan for successful travel day
- Prepare a behavioral plan with rewards
- Anticipate problems prior to journey

CHAPTER 18
SIBLING INTERACTIONS
Making the most of inherent socialization
Introduction

Children with autism need cooperative and willing peers to help them learn socialization skills. Cooperation, play, and language use are best introduced in a predictable setting with a familiar peer. Siblings are the natural choice for initial success because they are readily available, familiar, knowledgeable of the child's strengths and weaknesses, and usually willing to participate. However, the needs of the typically functioning sibling must be considered carefully and an effort made to ensure that the child's efforts are rewarded. A plan for providing motivation, positive reinforcement, and appreciation for the cooperative sibling must be included. It is relatively easy for parents to expect too much from the typically functioning sibling. They may expect him to understand and accept the characteristics of autism with a maturity that is beyond his years. Exhausted parents, who lack the energy to monitor interaction with siblings, may inadvertently expect the unaffected child to willingly participate in cooperative "play" in the absence of any external reinforcement. If this "play" is difficult or unpleasant, any cooperation that exists will be quickly extinguished. Parents who are emotionally spent by the rigors of constant behavioral intervention may erroneously think, or in desperation hope, that play and socialization will come naturally within the familiar setting of home and family. Behavioral expectations, predictable structure, and positive reinforcement, all fundamental to the success of the child with autism, should not be overlooked or discarded within the family setting.

> *Behavioral expectations, predictable structure, and positive reinforcement, all fundamental to the success of the child with autism, should not be overlooked or discarded within the family setting.*

Domain

1. Educating siblings on characteristics of autism
2. Cooperation and socialization strategies
3. Reinforcement of sibling's efforts

Approach

Educating siblings on characteristics of autism

Young siblings need information that is relevant to their world. Information regarding social impairment, cognitive function, and lifelong disability are irrelevant to the young child. He simply wants to know "why John threw the book" and what to do about it. As siblings grow, more information can be made available to them. Parents should be proactive in providing information, as well as adept at taking advantage of naturally occurring opportunities. Parents must decide when and how they will present information, but maintaining an open and comfortable approach to discussion should be part of the family atmosphere.

All members of the family should be valued and their contributions acknowledged. Here are a few examples of explanations parents may choose:

1. "Everyone is special in their own way. You are special and Julie is special. That's what makes our family unique."

2. "People learn in different ways. There is no 'right' way to learn, and no 'wrong' way to learn. Lisa learns in a different way than you do."

3. "It is hard for Mark to talk. Sometimes he just can't find the right words to tell you what he wants. Thank you for being patient with him. We can help him by asking him in 'yes' or 'no' questions."

4. "Tim has a hard time understanding feelings. He doesn't know that you are mad at him unless you tell him. It is good for all of us to learn how to communicate better."

5. "Your brother does not have a good imagination like you do. I think that you would have more fun playing with him if you choose a game that has rules. Then he will know what he is supposed to do."

6. "It is hard for your sister to look at you when she is talking. It may be because she sees lots of little tiny movements of your eyes that we don't notice, and it feels uncomfortable, just like it would for you if you watched cars whizzing by on the highway. We can help her by prompting her to look at us when she is talking, and you can always give her a penny for the jelly bean machine when she does it. If she remembers to do it without a prompt, make a big deal out of it and give her two pennies."

7. "Your brother has autism. That means that he sees the world differently than we do. It doesn't mean that he is dumb, he is actually very smart. He just learns in a different way. In some ways we can help him, and in some ways we can learn from him."

Behaviors exhibited by the individual with autism will directly affect his siblings, sometimes in negative ways. Siblings need help understanding why these behaviors occur, as well as how to respond to them. Explanations should be direct and useful. "We are helping John to use his words when he is angry, but he is still learning. Whenever he throws something, you just come and tell me. I will take care of it."

Language difficulties may be frustrating for the typically functioning sibling. Repetitive or echolalic speech patterns are annoying to most people, and the child who is constantly exposed to it is not immune. The sibling needs help understanding language impairments and how to respond appropriately. A family label, such as "silly talk," may be helpful to empower the sibling. For example, "When your brother keeps talking about movies or computer games, we call that 'silly talk.' You can tell him that it is not OK to have silly talk when he is playing with you. If he keeps doing it, you can come and tell me about it so I can handle it."

Narrow interests may also be frustrating or poorly tolerated by siblings. They will quickly tire of endless play with the same objects or games. Both the child with autism and his sibling can benefit from rules that define and regulate interactions. Instructing both children in turn taking, sharing, and other elements of cooperative play should receive priority.

Cooperation and socialization strategies

The child with autism may lack initiative, demonstrate weak play skills, and prefer isolation to sibling interaction. Cooperative play and socialization may need to be encouraged and developed through target behaviors in the same fashion as academic skills. A checklist or other visual aid can be used to delineate the behavioral expectations and associated reinforcement. Reinforcement for the typically functioning sibling is discussed in the following section.

Imitation is a fundamental social skill that is easy to teach in the home environment. Many play activities incorporate imitation skills and are simple enough for a sibling to direct. Games such as "Follow the Leader" and "Simon Says" are excellent tools for promoting social interaction and play between the child with autism and his typically functioning peer or sibling. Imitation skills developed at home can be generalized to the school setting and will serve the child well in a variety of social, academic, and vocational situations later in life.

Sharing can be promoted by setting up situations that require the child with autism to use language or cooperation. For example, cut and paste activities in which only one scissors is available can be set up and the child prompted to "share." Initial activities should be set up using neutral items such as scissors, crayons, or other supplies, rather than items that may be highly desirable and more difficult to share. Once the child has demonstrated some success, more desirable items such as toys or candy should be targeted.

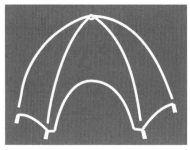

Turn-taking skills can initially be taught using board games. Predictability and visual cues are inherent to board games, and existing rules define the activity. Turn-taking skills can be generalized to "choices," such as which game to play, what park to go to, or whose turn it is to enjoy a certain privilege or outing. A variety of family activities and routines can also be used to promote turn-taking skills and the corresponding concept of "fair." For example, "Yesterday, your sister set the table by herself so today it is your turn."

Socialization skills can be fostered in a number of ways within the home environment. Sharing a room can be a healthy opportunity for children to interact in a casual fashion, as long as they are both agreeable to the arrangement. Making a "fort" or "camping" on the floor may be imaginary activities that both children can enjoy. Partnership activities, such as simple chores, can be designed for successful socialization and cooperation. Emptying small trashcans, putting away clean dishes, or maintaining a clean room are cooperative activities that can be used to foster interaction between siblings. As always, rewards or reinforcement should be offered, especially for less desirable activities and responsibilities. Verbal praise should always accompany any efforts at cooperation and socialization. Using a phrase such as "being social is good" can offer the sibling a tool to motivate on-task behavior from the affected child.

Joint attention can also be targeted with a sibling. Joint attention refers to "the child's ability to draw other people's attention to the things that he finds interesting or important" (Freeman, p. 43). The child with autism lacks the perspective that other people experience independent thought ("mindblindness") and as a result he may lack joint attentions skills. Simple games can be created that encourage reciprocity between the children, such as "Look, here is my new stuffed animal. Show me yours." The well-known classroom experience of "Show-and-Tell" can be practiced at home to teach joint attention skills.

Play efforts should be supported and applauded. Parents should recognize whenever the sibling yields to the play choice of the child with autism and praise him immediately. Parallel play activities should be widely available and reinforced as the first step toward "playing together." Once success is achieved in parallel activities, more interactive

choices can be made. Designated play times for interactive play can help both the child with autism and his sibling enjoy successful play. Open-ended play can be anxiety provoking for both children and should be avoided. Scheduling desirable activities immediately following the interactive playtime can serve as reinforcement for both children. For example: "I would like you to play one game of 'Sorry' with your sister. Then we can go out for ice cream."

Language use can be fostered in the comfortable environment of familiar family members. A variety of language skills can be developed and should be addressed in a systematic way, from "easiest" to "hardest." Responding when spoken to, initiating language, and conversational skills all vary in their level of difficulty for the child with autism. Simply directing the child to "Answer" every time he is spoken to can prompt response skills. As always, reinforcement should be offered and prompts faded quickly. The cooperative sibling should be encouraged to ask simple questions in an effort to promote the affected child's response. For example, "Ask your brother if he will play pinball with you" or "Please find out if he wants to go to the park" are ways that the sibling can evoke a verbal response, which in turn can be rewarded. Desirable stimuli should always be used for targets on acquisition. Thus, prompting the child to gain a response related to a desirable activity (a trip to the park) should be used before an undesirable choice ("Ask your brother if he wants peas or beans.") Initiating language begins with the child's wants and needs. Language should be required whenever possible. Well-intended, caring parents often get in

> *Naturally occurring opportunities for language use should always be capitalized upon.*

the habit of anticipating their child's wants and needs and acting on his behalf, without any verbal exchange. Naturally occurring opportunities for language use should always be capitalized upon.

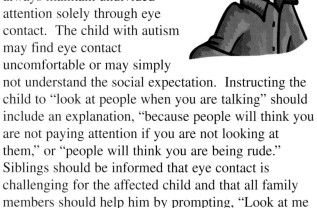

Eye contact can be encouraged in the home environment, taking advantage of the familiarity of siblings. Eye contact should not be required in an absolute fashion, as typically functioning individuals do not always maintain undivided attention solely through eye contact. The child with autism may find eye contact uncomfortable or may simply not understand the social expectation. Instructing the child to "look at people when you are talking" should include an explanation, "because people will think you are not paying attention if you are not looking at them," or "people will think you are being rude." Siblings should be informed that eye contact is challenging for the affected child and that all family members should help him by prompting, "Look at me when you are talking," as well as to praise him verbally and offer reinforcement according to the designated schedule. Siblings can feel empowered and useful, for example, if they are given the "authority" to give tokens for appropriate behaviors.

Social entry skills such as greetings, joining existing games, and inviting someone to play are all skills that can be practiced and acquired at home with a sibling. Greetings can be taught in a playful fashion, such as allowing the children to dress up and ring the doorbell, play "mailman" or other interesting adaptations that incorporate the target of greeting each other. The child with autism can be prompted to approach his

sibling and ask to join in, "Can I play cars with you?" Similar imaginative play can be created to practice initiation of play so that the child with autism invites his sibling to join him. Typically functioning siblings, who may feel denied the opportunities for imaginative play with the affected child because of his deficits in this arena, often welcome the chance to play with him in this fashion. This may be highly rewarding for the sibling and offer balance to the otherwise highly structured play at home.

Reinforcement of sibling's efforts

The target activity must be a positive experience for both children. Positive reinforcement, an essential component of behavioral change for the child with autism, is also a powerful tool for motivating the typically functioning sibling. Parents who mistakenly assume that the "normal" child will naturally interact and "play" with the affected child may be

> The social impairment, narrow interests, and language deficits of the child with autism may make it unpleasant for the sibling to interact without corresponding reinforcement.

disappointed. The social impairment, narrow interests, and language deficits of the child with autism may make it unpleasant for the sibling to interact without corresponding reinforcement. Over time, as success and acquisition of skills occur on the part of both participants, this interaction can become intrinsically rewarding.

Behavioral expectations for the sibling should be clearly delineated. The quantity and quality of the interaction should be described in detail. For example, "I would like you to play with Conner for 10 minutes while I finish getting dinner ready. Since he likes games with rules, please choose a board game that you both like." The sibling should not be expected or required to keep the affected child occupied in an unlimited fashion. Offering choice and rewards will

make the initial efforts more pleasant. Recognizing the challenging nature of the interaction can help to alleviate any anxiety that the sibling may have: "I know that sometimes it is hard to play with Eric, and I really appreciate it when you do. It might be more fun for you if you let him pick the game. I know that you don't like to play air hockey as much as he does, but he will stay with the game better that way. After that, you can watch a movie if you'd like."

Rewards should also be clearly defined. Younger children may be motivated by having their own checklist or sticker chart similar to that which is used by the affected sibling. Others may cooperate for increased privileges or special events. For example, "Every time you ask your brother to play a game with you, I will give you a dime. When you have enough money, we'll go to the store and you can buy a candy bar."

Attention is an important issue to recognize in the family dynamics. The child with autism often demands an enormous amount of attention from the parents. The higher functioning child may receive attention related to his unique strengths, unusual interests or hard-earned accomplishments. The typically functioning child must also be applauded for his attributes and accomplishments in an equal fashion to avoid resentment. Special activities designed to reward the child should be balanced with attention that does not need to be "earned." The child should know that he, too, is of great importance to the parents and is entitled to desirable experiences simply because he is a member of the family.

Examples

Cooperation and socialization

Sharing with neutral items

Example #1: Prompt the child with autism: "Ask Haley to share her crayons" or "Can I use the scissors when you are done?" Prompt the sibling: "Wait for Carter to ask you for supplies he needs." Reinforce the child with autism for 'good asking' and the sibling for 'helping him learn to share.'

Example #2: Prompt the child with autism: "Please share the blocks with your brother." Or set up the activity so that the child must request them, "Can I have some of your blocks?" Reinforce the child with autism for 'sharing' and the sibling for 'helping.'

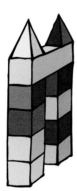

Example #3: Prompt sibling to request items from the affected child: "Can I have a turn with the Frisbee?" Reinforce the child with autism for 'being social' and the sibling for 'helping him to be social.'

Sharing with desirable items

1st sibling shares: "Nathan, you can have a turn riding my scooter." Reinforce the sibling for 'helping him to learn about sharing.'

2nd even trade: "If you share your Skittles with Sally she will share her M&M's with you." Reinforce both children for 'sharing.'

3rd affected child shares: Prompt "Sharing is nice. Please share your stuffed animals with your brother." Reinforce the child with autism for 'nice sharing.'

Cooperation

Example #1: "Work with your brother to empty the small trash cans. One person holds the bag while the other one dumps the trash in." Reinforce and praise both children for 'working together.' "Great job! You can both have an extra quarter for being such good partners and working together."

Example #2: "Can you both please get the baseball equipment from the garage? One of you can get the bat and ball, the other can get the gloves." Reinforce both children for working together.

Turn-taking

Example #1: Any Bingo game, especially if the child has a unique interest such as shapes (Colors and Shapes Bingo) or numbers (Addition, Subtraction, Multiplication and Division Bingo) can be used to acquire turn-taking skills. It is easy and inexpensive to make a Bingo style game based on a child's particular interests: license plates, traffic signs, sports teams, animals, family members, and so forth. Narrow interests can be utilized to promote and achieve turn-taking skills.

Example #2: "Candyland®," "Chutes and Ladders®," "Hi Ho Cherry O®," or other simple board games are excellent for teaching turn-taking.

Example #3: "SORRY®," "Monopoly®," "Parcheesi®," "Scrabble®" or other advanced board games may be used. It may be necessary to modify some of the rules or criteria for winning as the child may lose interest if it takes too long.

Example #4: Simple card games such as "Old Maid," "Go Fish," "Crazy Eights" are also useful for teaching turn taking. Once simple turn-taking is mastered with concrete situations, advance to the more abstract task of making choices:

1st give the child with autism the choice: "You can pick the first game that we play. Then you have to play what Laura picks." Or "You can pick which playground we go to. Laura will get to pick our snack."

2nd give the sibling the choice: "Laura is going to pick the first game. After you play what she picks, then you can choose what game we will play."

Play

Example #1: Block play. Prompt the sibling to initiate: "Ask your brother to play Legos® with you. Since you are very creative, maybe you can build a city, and he can be in charge of building the towers."

Example #2: Coloring. Prompt the child with autism to initiate: "Ask Hannah to color with you. You will get 20 minutes of computer time for playing together and sharing the crayons."

Example #3: Cut and paste. "I have a fun art project for you two. Here are some magazine pages with pictures of animals. You can cut out the animals and make a poster. Then we will hang it up in your room."

Example #4: Making a fort. Prompt the child with autism to initiate, "Will you build a fort with me?" Offer a variety of supplies that are interesting to both children such as flashlights, walkie-talkies, and stuffed animals.

Example #5: Doing a puzzle. If the sibling can begin a puzzle, the child with autism can ask to join in.

Language

Example #1: Quiz time. The sibling can use cards or questions to quiz the child with autism on favorite subjects and interests. Tokens, pennies, or playing chips can be offered for correct answers and the child applauded for knowledge and language use. Flashcards and game cards can be purchased or created to accommodate the child's special interests.

Example #2: The WH game (Teach Me Language, p. 197-204). A board game can be made that incorporates question discrimination for who, what, where, and when questions. A variety of question cards are made that identify topics of interest to the child. A spinner or dice can be used to indicate which question category the player must use. For example, a card that says "baseball" and a spinner that points to "who" means that the child needs to think of a question such as "Who likes to play baseball?"

Example #3: Finding out about someone (Teach Me Language, p. 39-41). Create a board or card game that incorporates simple inquiries such as "What is your favorite color?" or "What is your favorite sport?" The game can be played with family members and peers.

Example #4: The Name Game. A card or board game can be made in which participants are required to "Name something…" A card that states, "with four legs" means that the child would need to name something in that category. The child's interest in animals, shapes, geography, and so on can be utilized and knowledge can be expanded as well.

To Order Teach Me Language, telephone SKF Books, Inc., at (604) 534-6956

Reinforcement of sibling efforts

Example #1: "I need you to help me teach John to play with other kids. I know that playing with John is hard but it will get easier as we help him. Thank you for being a good sport about this. Let's teach him how to play basketball. Then you can play with Ryan until dinner."

Example #2: "Let's make a chart. Every time you help me teach John to play you'll get a star. For 5 stars you can earn a trip to the mall. Would you like to teach him how to play 'Red light, Green light' now?"

Example #3: "Everyone needs to learn to share. We can help John learn to share. Then he will be more fun for you to play with. Can you think of something you have that you could trade for something of his, just for a few minutes? Then you can help me make cupcakes."

Example #4: "Every time you share your toys with him you can earn a dime. When you have enough money, we can go out for ice cream. Could you share your cars with him, just for 5 minutes?"

Siblings can be a wonderful source of enjoyment and learning for the child with autism. Parents must take care to recognize and address the unique needs of these children also, while providing the structure and predictability necessary for the affected child. The family environment can be enriched by parental efforts to educate and reward the sibling's involvement in the life of the child with autism.

Chapter Summary

- Educate siblings on the characteristics of autism
- Increase their understanding of negative behaviors
- Equip siblings for language and play limitations
- Reward siblings' efforts

CHAPTER 19
MANAGING NEGATIVE BEHAVIORS AND ADDRESSING DISCIPLINE ISSUES AT HOME
Balancing compassion and consequences

Introduction

Although there are many similarities between management of negative behaviors at school and at home, there are additional strategies available at home that are not conducive to the classroom setting. The theoretical foundation of practice is the same for both environments. Positive reinforcement of desired behaviors in conjunction with the elimination of problem behaviors through negative reinforcement, or cost response, is the approach in both settings. Specific strategies for addressing discipline issues in the classroom are found in chapter 10. Here we will deal specifically with negative behaviors in the home environment.

Individuals with autism often lack, or are deficient in, developing social anxiety and theory of mind. "Social anxiety" is the recognition that one's behaviors negatively affect another person, and as a result one feels regret, remorse, or discomfort for causing disappointment, sadness, or anger. "Theory of mind" is the understanding that people are distinct from inanimate objects and from each other, possessing unique beliefs, thoughts and emotions. The term "mindblindness" has been coined to provide perspective on this cognitive deficit and it's ramifications.

"Mindblindness" suggests that the individual with autism "can't see" with regard to the thoughts, beliefs, and emotions of others. Furthermore, the normal development of theory of mind is impaired in individuals diagnosed along the autism spectrum. As a result, "Children with ASD (Autism Spectrum Disorder) often can't conceptualise the feelings or predict the behaviour of other people." (Gardner, p. 13). This "mindblindness" has profound implications for social interactions. The individual with autism is often unable to interpret body language, facial expressions, voice inflection, and other displays of emotion. This is important to the implementation of discipline for several reasons. First, the escalating anger of an adult who does not directly identify the source of his anger will fail to change the behavior of the child. The cues that usually indicate a need to stop or change behavior such as a raised voice or an angry look may be completely meaningless to the child with autism. Secondly, the child with autism lacks the interpersonal motivation to follow social norms, choosing instead the utilitarian approach to life. Without social anxiety, he does not realize that his behavior has a negative impact on others. Without theory of mind, he does not realize that others experience frustration, disappointment, and anger as a result of his behavior. He is "blind" and must be helped, not punished. Successful discipline for a child with autism should include reinforcement of desirable alternatives, clearly defined consequences meaningful to the individual, and instruction regarding the emotional violations that he does not understand.

Domain

1. **Definition of behavioral expectations**
2. **Implementing consequences**
3. **Teaching understanding of emotions**

Approach

Definition of behavioral expectations

Desired behavior should be presented in a positive fashion. More important than knowing what *not* to do is knowing what *to* do. Parents should not presume that if the child is well informed regarding negative behavior that he will automatically understand what positive behavior is required. For example, the child

More important than knowing what not to do is knowing what to do.

who throws his food when he wants attention must learn that to throw his food is unacceptable. But he must also understand that the appropriate way to get someone's attention is to "use your words." The child who lacks inferential thinking skills will not "read between the lines" and must be specifically taught what is considered appropriate and desirable behavior.

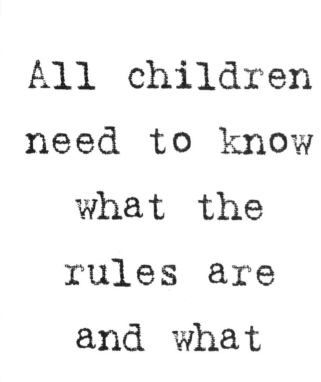

All children need to know what the rules are and what happens if they break them.

Violations of existing rules must be clearly defined. All children need to know what the rules are and what happens if they break them. Children with autism benefit from detailed rules in writing or other visual form. The rules should specify exactly what is considered a violation and what corresponding consequence will result. If there is a frequency component, such as "every time," this should be included, not assumed. For example, "It is never OK to lie. You need to tell the truth all the time. If you lie to me again by saying 'I already did brush my teeth' when you did not, I will take away your dessert privileges for 3 days. If you won't brush your teeth, I can't let you have any sweets."

Natural consequences should be utilized whenever possible. Lost privileges that directly relate to the violation should be enforced, as in the above example. Natural consequences make use of environmental factors that contribute to the child's motivation and change in subsequent behavior. In addition, they are generally unobtrusive and parents feel comfortable applying them in public settings.

Artificial consequences related to the child's token economy should be used when natural consequences are insufficient to produce the desired behavior. Loss of earned rewards or earning opportunities are reasonable cost responses for inappropriate behavior. For example, the child who has accumulated 30 minutes of movie time may lose some or all the reward. In another case, a child may lose the opportunity to earn an anticipated reward, such as "I will not let you earn money for doing your chores today because you were not willing to clean up your mess in the kitchen. You will just have to put the dishes away and you won't earn any money for it."

Implementing consequences

Warning the child prior to instituting a consequence is generally perceived as "fair."

He should be given one warning, after which continued violation must be followed by the stated consequence. Failure to follow through on the delivery of a consequence will invariably prove to be counterproductive. The child will learn quickly that his behavior achieved what he desired and he is reinforced to repeat it. Permissive parents who vacillate will likely encounter the negative behavior again, as well as other behaviors that the child may now think he can "get away with." Behavioral boundaries must be firm and implementation of consequences guaranteed. Warnings can and should be faded out once the child has demonstrated mastery and compliance, at which point the behavior is routinely expected and the child is required to regulate the behavior himself.

Time out is a popular disciplinary approach among typically functioning children. It is convenient to apply in the school and public setting. However, this common method of discipline must be evaluated for its effectiveness with each individual child. The reasoning behind a "time out" includes removal of attention and negative social anxiety that directly results from the child's behavior. A period of "time out" isolates the child so that he suffers a social "loss of privilege." For the child who lacks social anxiety, this may be meaningless and ineffective. The loss must be something that the child strongly desires in order to achieve a change in behavior. In addition, strict rules of behavior must apply to the "time out" condition. If "time out" is truly a loss of privilege, then the child should be required to sit quietly for the duration. Any violation during the "time out" means the time period starts over again. Explain to the child that "You are in 'time out' for 5 minutes because you kept writing on the table even though I told you to stop. 'Time out' means you must sit on the step quietly for 5 minutes or I will have to start the timer over again. It's your choice." All interaction and eye contact must be avoided during that time.

Careful consideration should be made for the child with self-stimulating behaviors. If the child is allowed an opportunity to engage in this behavior, it will invalidate the disciplinary effect, and worse, may even encourage repetition of the antecedent because of inadvertent reinforcement. "Time out" must be monitored so that it is not merely an opportunity to escape into dysfunction.

Children who have developed some measure of social anxiety may benefit from "time out." The generally accepted rule is one minute per age in years. In this way, the negative reinforcement increases with age and discourages the child from continued violation. However, if the child is frequently put in "time out," this may be an indication that it is a weak or ineffective strategy for this particular child. All disciplinary approaches can be evaluated for effectiveness based on the simple observation of behavioral change. Effective discipline results in a decrease or elimination of the antecedent behavior.

Loss of privilege

The child with autism may respond better to the more mathematical approach of earnings and losses. Good choices have positive results (earning desirable things) and bad choices have negative results (loss of desirable things). As with all disciplinary methods, the loss must be valuable enough to the child that he is willing to change his behavior to regain it or to prevent future loss. The family atmosphere should include vocabulary such as "privilege," "responsibility," and "consequence." The child should be able to distinguish between activities and conditions that are permanent and those that are variable. Breakfast, lunch, and 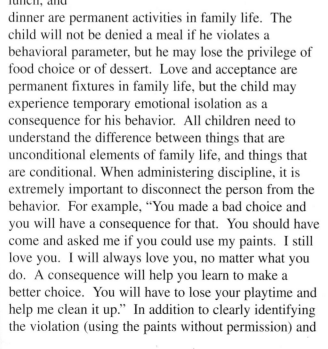 dinner are permanent activities in family life. The child will not be denied a meal if he violates a behavioral parameter, but he may lose the privilege of food choice or of dessert. Love and acceptance are permanent fixtures in family life, but the child may experience temporary emotional isolation as a consequence for his behavior. All children need to understand the difference between things that are unconditional elements of family life, and things that are conditional. When administering discipline, it is extremely important to disconnect the person from the behavior. For example, "You made a bad choice and you will have a consequence for that. You should have come and asked me if you could use my paints. I still love you. I will always love you, no matter what you do. A consequence will help you learn to make a better choice. You will have to lose your playtime and help me clean it up." In addition to clearly identifying the violation (using the paints without permission) and

the corresponding natural consequence (loss of playtime), this statement also directs the child to appropriate behavior ("You should have asked me") and separates the person from the behavior ("bad choice" rather than "bad boy"). This is quite distinct from, "You bad boy! What a mess you made! You know you shouldn't use my paints!" These situations are excellent opportunities to expand the child's understanding of responsibilities and privileges. A phrase that identifies chores and other responsibilities as required aspects of family life can be helpful to the child with autism: "Everybody has to do work. It is just part of being in the family." This helps the child to cooperate with activities that he may otherwise perceive as punishment.

Added work can be a useful and creative approach to discipline. The child may be motivated to comply with behavioral rules so that he is not required to substitute work for playtime. Added work should be just that, added. It is not simply insisting that the child perform routinely required tasks such as homework. He already has to do his homework. Added work would be in addition to his homework, such as an extra reading or writing assignment in place of play. The work should not be challenging to the extent that it requires adult assistance. This, then, becomes a punishment for the parent! Instead, a mundane task such as copying or writing sentences that reinforces an understanding of appropriate behavior is sufficient. For example, the child who perseverates by pushing buttons on the remote can be required to write, "The remote is not a toy." The number of sentences should be age appropriate as well, such as "10 for 1st grade, 20 for 2nd, 30 for 3rd" and so on. The work should be clearly defined in terms of the amount required and the quality expected. Additional chores can also be used as a consequence. As with all negative reinforcement, the child must understand the connection between the antecedent (his behavioral violation) and the consequence. He may be confused unless this is clearly explained, thinking only in concrete terms that "now I have to do more chores."

Parents should take advantage of every opportunity to establish a sense of security based on unconditional love while clearly identifying unacceptable behavior.

Teaching understanding of emotions

Natural opportunities to teach social anxiety should be utilized. As previously mentioned, social anxiety is the recognition that one's behaviors negatively affect others. As a result of weak or absent social anxiety, parents may need to directly instruct the child in the differentiation of common emotions. Anger, frustration, and disappointment may need to be dramatized using exaggerated facial expressions and explicit language. Rather than simply yelling or screaming, a parent should attempt to convey anger by lowering his voice, putting his hands on his hips, and scowling while stating "I am angry because you made a lot of noise and woke me up. I would feel happy if you stayed in bed quietly until 7:00." The need to separate the behavior from the person cannot be overstated. Parents should take advantage of every opportunity to establish a sense of security based on unconditional love while clearly identifying unacceptable behavior. "I still love you, but if you keep making noise, you will lose your playtime before school."

Scripts are a useful method for expanding the child's understanding of emotions. A script is a written tool that explicitly identifies common elements of a specific emotion. For example:

Feeling Sad

When I am SAD, I FEEL BAD.
When I am SAD, I DON'T FEEL HAPPY.

There are MANY THINGS THAT CAN MAKE ME SAD.
  I get SAD when I LOSE MY FAVORITE DOLL.
  I get SAD when I GET HURT.
  I get SAD when MOM OR DAD YELLS AT ME.
  I get SAD when I CAN'T FIND MY MOM.

When I am SAD, sometimes I CRY.
When I am SAD and I CRY, a hug from Mom or Dad MAKES ME FEEL BETTER.

When I AM SAD, it is IMPORTANT that I let Mom or Dad know why I am SAD.
I need to TELL THEM OR SHOW THEM WHY I AM SAD.

WHEN I TELL MOM AND DAD WHY I AM SAD, THEY CAN HELP ME FEEL BETTER.

Feeling Sad Equation

FEELING SAD = FEELING BAD = NOT FEELING HAPPY

(Teach Me Language, p. 57)

To Order Teach Me Language, telephone SKF Books, Inc., at **(604) 534-6956**

As the above example shows, Teach Me Language (Freeman and Dake) offers excellent, reproducible scripts that teach a variety of emotions. Worksheets are included that allow the parent or educator to incorporate personal experiences that are relevant to the child. Scripts and worksheets should show the cause and effect relationship between the antecedent behavior and the corresponding emotional response. For example, "When I scream in the store (cause) it makes Mom mad (effect) and I loss my computer privileges (consequence)."

Social stories are designed to increase the child's understanding of difficult social situations and to teach appropriate responses. Visual components, such as photographs depicting the anticipated event or situation, can be used to enhance the text. The story is read with the child to familiarize him with the situation, so that he can anticipate and discuss his anxiety prior to the experience. In addition, behavioral expectations are presented in context, so that the child's understanding is developed to support his behavioral choices. Examples of situations that can benefit from social stories are going to the doctor/dentist, riding on the bus, attending a birthday party, responding to a bully, and so forth. When creating a social story, include a title that identifies the content of the story, such as "Visiting the Doctor when you are not sick." Include as much specific information as possible, keeping in mind that the goal is to help the child prepare for the situation and anticipate anxiety-provoking elements so that he can better manage his response. The story should address and answer any questions that the child may have, and should assume the child's perspective ("I am going to the doctor on Tuesday"). Desired behaviors should be presented in a positive fashion, such as "If I feel nervous, I can say so," rather than a negative fashion, "I can't scream if I am nervous." The formula for a social story as developed by Carol Gray (Gray, 1999) includes four suggested types of sentences:

Descriptive sentences are statements of fact and opinion-free, and usually answer 'wh' questions ('My name is Tom' or 'I am in 4th grade').

Perspective sentences refer to the internal states of other people, including knowledge ('My teacher knows about math'), opinions ('Many children like hot dogs for lunch'), beliefs ('Some people believe in Santa') or physical conditions ('Sometimes people feel sick when they eat too much').

Affirmative sentences reassure or stress a point, and usually follow one of the other types of sentences. The italicised sentences below are the affirmative sentences: 'The toilet makes a sound when it flushes. *This is okay*.', which is reassuring or 'Most people drink water on hot days. *This is a good idea*.', which stresses an important point.

Directive sentences describe a suggested response to a situation to gently direct the student's behavior. Directive sentences often use softeners to avoid the student thinking it always has to be this way. Examples include 'I will try to stay in my chair' ('will try to stay' is softer than 'will stay') or 'I may play on the swings' ('may' softens the sentence). (Gardner, p. 59).

In addition to these story elements, the specific reinforcement plan should be included to encourage success. The following is an example of a social story:

Visiting the doctor when you are not sick

Sometimes I visit the doctor when I am not sick. This is OK.
Everyone visits the doctor sometimes when they are healthy.
Some things that might happen at the doctor's office are:

I might get my height and weight checked. This is fun!
I might get my ears and throat looked at. This doesn't hurt.
I might get my tummy examined. That means the doctor will feel my tummy. This might tickle but it doesn't hurt.

When I am healthy and I visit the doctor, I usually don't need any medicine.

Sometimes even if I am healthy, the doctor will give me medicine to keep me healthy.

Sometimes I may get a shot to keep me healthy. A shot does hurt a little, just for a second. It is OK to cry when I get a shot.

Dr. Karen will always tell me what she is going to do before she does it.
I will try to use my words if I am nervous or scared.
I will try to sit still when Dr. Karen needs me to.

I will earn a (+) every time I use my words.
I will earn a (+) every time I sit still for Dr. Karen.

I can trade my (+)'s for quarters when I get home.

Empathy for the child who struggles to understand the complex world of social interactions is invaluable. For the higher-functioning child with autism, his capabilities in other arenas may mislead others to assume that he is equally capable in the social realm. Unfortunately, this may unjustly penalize the child. He may be punished for behavior that is misunderstood and attributed to malice or willful disobedience, rather than to impairment characteristic of his condition. Many individuals with autism are

> *For the higher-functioning child with autism, his capabilities in other arenas may mislead others to assume that he is equally capable in the social realm.*

incapable of malice, deceit, or dishonesty. Sadly, however, children with autism may be unfairly characterized by adults who fail to recognize the social deficits characteristic of autism. Any approach to discipline needs to be compassionate and knowledgeable of the child's disability, incorporating the necessary elements of instruction in appropriate behavior, and assurance of individual worth.

Examples

Define behavioral expectations

Rules for lunch:
- You need to stay at your activity. It is time for lunch.
- At lunch you need to stay in your chair.
- You need to sit well. Sitting well is sitting on your bottom, not on your knees.
- You need to eat with your fork. It is not OK to eat macaroni and cheese with your fingers.
- If you sit well for lunch you can have 10 minutes of computer time after lunch.
- If you eat with your fork you can have a cookie when you are finished.
- If you get out of your chair to goof around you will have to eat beans for lunch.

Conditions for each target behavior should vary to maintain motivation for each one. The reason for eating with a fork is to earn a cookie; the reason for sitting properly is to earn 10 minutes of computer time. Individual behaviors must be shaped. For example, if "sitting well" is violated after the first 5 minutes, what will be done to motivate the child to comply for the duration of the activity? In this case, short time intervals of the desired behavior must be targeted for success and reinforced. Incremental reinforcement with checks, pennies, or a punch card can be used so that an accumulation of 10 is worth a token.

Warnings and Loss of Privileges

Example #1: "It is never OK to bite another person. Joey is crying because you hurt him. You need to tell him right now that you are sorry. If you ever do that again, you will have to give me all of your electronic toys for 3 days."

Example #2: "I'm disappointed that you made a bad choice to eat all those cookies. You should ask before you eat cookies. Eating sweets is a privilege. Next time you will lose your sweets for a week."

Example #3: "It is never OK to pour your milk on the floor. That is wasteful and messy. You will have to help me clean it up before you go to play. If you do that again you will lose all of your playtime for the rest of the day."

Example #4: "Running is not allowed in the library. If you do that again you will not be allowed to check out a movie."

Example #5: "It is time to do your homework. If you don't do it now, then you will have to do it after school before you have a snack or any playtime."

Warnings and added work

Example #1: "It is not OK to pull your sister's hair. She is crying because you hurt her. If you do that again, you will have to write 'I am sorry for hurting you' 30 times instead of playing."

Example #2: "I am sorry that you decided to put your clean clothes back in the laundry basket instead of hanging them up in your closet. That is lazy, and if you choose to be lazy then I will choose to give you more work. Now you will have to hang up your brother's clothes also."

Example #3: "It is not OK to just sit here when it is time to do your homework. If you don't finish by 4:00, then you will also owe me 10 minutes of extra reading after dinner."

Chapter Summary

- Present desirable behavior in a positive fashion
- Clearly define violations
- Utilize natural consequences
- Institute artificial consequences
- Employ consistent follow through
- Increase understanding of emotions

CHAPTER 20
EDUCATIONAL RESOURCES
Introduction

It is important for parents and educators to realize that a high functioning child with autism may blend into the general education classroom yet lack motivation or comprehension. Compliance and on-task behavior may divert attention away from cognitive deficits. The child with autism may benefit from educational resources that enrich his understanding and enhance his acquisition of skills. The following resources represent a sample of educational supplements that have been found to be helpful. It is not an exhaustive list.

> The child with autism may benefit from educational resources that enrich his understanding and enhance his acquisition of skills.

TEACCH

The Treatment and Education of Autistic and Communication-Handicapped Children program, or TEACCH, was developed in the early 1970's in North Carolina. The program uses a highly structured approach that focuses on the person with autism and the development of skills and interests.

"The program was developed in light of research reporting positive outcomes when structured educational programs were used with students with ASD (autism spectrum disorder). The highly-structured TEACCH system uses the student's strengths (rote tasks, insistence on routines) to learn new skills in an adapted environment designed to address the specific deficits associated with ASD. The TEACCH system is a framework for teaching any content; it is not a curriculum" (Gardner, p. 22).

Physical organization, the use of schedules, the use of work systems and task organization make up the components of structured teaching that have made the TEACCH program successful. The perspective that focuses on the individual rather than on any particular methodology means that strengths and interests are cultivated and become the basis of successful adult functioning (Mesibov, p. 2). "TEACCH cannot be reduced to a technique, not even to a set of techniques, not even to a method. It is a complete program of services for autistic people which makes use of several techniques, of several methods in various combination depending upon the individual

person's needs and emerging capabilities" (Trehin, p. 2). Nonetheless, the TEACCH program has been used around the world as a model for comprehensive service delivery for individuals with autism.

Teach Me Language

This language manual and workbook of companion exercise forms are a wealth of practical information, drills, and activities for promoting language use and development. It is designed for use by parents, speech therapists, and those who implement therapy programs in which language difficulties are addressed.

"Teach Me Language was written because we saw the need for a book to provide specific language activities designed for children with autism, Asperger's syndrome, and other related pervasive developmental disorders. There are many books advocating one therapy method over another, as well as books chronicling a child's unexpected recovery from autism. A few of these books provide information on setting up therapy in the home; however, no books that we could find give hands-on, explicit instructions for working on the language needs specific to these children, despite the fact that delayed language is one of the most common and limiting symptoms of children with developmental disorders. This book is designed to do just that. Teach Me Language introduces exercises and drills which attack language weaknesses common to children with pervasive developmental disorders" (Freeman, p. 2).

Reproducible exercise forms make the manual convenient and easy to implement. In order for the book to be useful, the child must be a visual learner, "table-ready" and able to communicate, either verbally or non-verbally. Clearly delineated drills are presented that encompass a wide range of social language, general knowledge, syntax and grammar.

To Order <u>Teach Me Language</u>, telephone SKF Books, Inc., at **(604) 534-6956**

SCORE! Educational Centers

SCORE! Educational Centers are computer based, learning enrichment centers designed to improve academic achievement and student confidence. The program utilizes a strong behavioral approach in motivating students to develop a "love of learning." There are many reasons for enrollement in the SCORE! program, including:

1. Bright students that need more challenge than they are afforded in their current educational environment.
2. Unmotivated students.
3. Students who lack confidence in their ability to achieve.
4. Students with reading comprehension difficulties.
5. Students with math comprehension difficulties.
6. Students who wish to improve their test taking abilities.
7. Students who wish to learn how to set goals and achieve them.

SCORE! uses a curriculum that was designed for, and has been implemented, in school systems. It was established as a private business endeavor in 1992. All interested students may try the program without obligation for one month. An initial placement evaluation allows the staff to begin the curriculum at a level approximately 6 months behind the child's current ability to ensure success. The curriculum advances systematically according to the child's response. Both the pattern of response and the percentage of correct answers are used to determine comprehension and success. For example, if the answer pattern alternates between correct and incorrect, the computer interprets this as insufficient comprehension or "guessing." If, however, the answer pattern is a series of incorrect answers that convert to a series of correct answers, then the computer interprets this as evidence that the child has acquired the concept and can advance.

There are several things to consider for any child interested in trying the SCORE! enrichment program:

1. Audio and visual stimuli are paired. This is the primary reason that a high-functioning child with autism may be able to take advantage of the program. Visual learners often excel under these conditions.
2. The format circumvents word retrieval problems. By using multiple choice questions and word lists for fill-in-the-blank, children with word retrieval problems can display more accurately their level of understanding.
3. Concepts that are missed are repeated. The computer interprets incorrect answers as an indicator that the material should appear again systematically until success is achieved.
4. The curriculum is divided into math and reading lessons. Within these two divisions, isolated components are addressed. For example, math skills are further divided into computation drills and math applications. Examples of computation include addition, subtraction, multiplication, division, decimals, and fractions. Math applications include math word problems, speed games, conversions, and geometry. Reading programs isolate vocabulary, interpretive skills, sentence and passage comprehension, inference, prediction, and main

idea. The computer records data for each curricular strand so that specific areas of difficulty can be readily identified and addressed. The concepts which are difficult for the child are targeted for achievement while mastered material appears frequently to maintain success and promote confidence. Thus, overall balance throughout the reading or math program is achieved.

5. Success is ensured according to percentage of responses that are correct. The goal is to maintain a 70% response rate. When percentages fall consistently below this level, the curriculum can be backed down to present easier material, thus boosting both the scores and the child's confidence.

6. The established reward system follows the behavioral model. Students are rewarded with "SCORE! cards for achievements, which can then be redeemed at the "store" for a variety of prizes on display. If a child is not interested in the available prizes, it is easy enough to make the cards valuable in whatever way is meaningful to the child. The child can earn playtime or tokens that he can cash in on privileges at home.

7. Both primary and secondary reinforcers are used. In addition to the SCORE! cards, children are continually praised by staff members who supervise and interact with students. Students are greeted enthusiastically by coaches who are committed to promoting individual achievement and self-confidence.

8. Staff members, or coaches circulate throughout the center to assist students and to make notations to discuss with parents. Concepts and isolated tasks that are difficult for a child are noted and discussed when the session is completed. Parents are kept informed of curriculum content as well as statistical success or failure. Parental involvement is expected and conferences are scheduled routinely to discuss the child's progress and parental satisfaction. Coaches and parents work together to maximize the learning experience.

9. Coaches also instruct through indirect prompting. Students are instructed to raise their hands when they have a question or need assistance. The coaches will discuss and prompt a child but will allow him to choose an incorrect answer rather than simply answering for him. Thus, teaching occurs through computerized instruction and human interaction.

The SCORE! Educational Center has much to offer both the typically functioning child as well as the higher functioning child with autism. However, it should be noted that this program was not designed specifically for children with autism or profound learning disabilities. In order to make SCORE! a successful experience the following skills should be well established:

a. The ability to sit for 50 minutes with short breaks at 10-minute intervals.
b. The ability to follow verbal instructions from coaches.
c. The ability to work in an environment that has multiple distractions.

For the child who can succeed in this learning environment, the SCORE! Educational Center provides a differential educational approach that can significantly improve comprehension, self-confidence, test-taking skills, and overall attitude toward education. For more information visit the web site at www.escore.com.

Reading Milestones

Reading Milestones is a linguistically-controlled reading series. It has been extensively used for a variety of students who have reading levels lower than those of typical students of similar ages, including those with language delays and developmental disabilities. Each level includes ten readers and corresponding workbooks that incorporate a variety of exercises to aid the developing reader. Elements of linguistic competence are controlled to directly enhance comprehension:

"Several factors of linguistic competence are directly related to comprehension. One factor is the number of difficult words, or the number of words in the text with which the reader is not familiar. A second factor is the length of the sentences. Especially at the beginning reading levels, student will have more difficulty with text that contains longer sentences than with a text with similar content containing shorter sentences. A third factor that affects comprehension is syntax. Young readers will have more difficulty with text that contains complex syntax than they will have with text in which the sentences are generally made up of basic syntactic structures (Ekwall, 1986). The use of figurative language is another factor of major importance. All of these factors are controllable in specially constructed texts but not in trade books or classical literature" (Quigley, p. vi).

Cognitive processes such as inference, prediction, and sequencing are taught through the predictable structure of the workbooks. Story elements such as character, setting, and main idea are addressed. New vocabulary is introduced and implemented. Each series includes a teacher's guide. "Reading Milestones" are available from PRO-ED, 8700 Shoal Creek Boulevard, Austin, TX 78757.

"Fast Forword"

"Fast Forword" and "Step Forword" are computer-based language programs designed to increase language use and auditory discrimination. A language assessment test is administered before and after the program to quantify language gains. Verification of auditory processing deficits indicates that the child will likely benefit from the programs. The instructional material

is presented in a series of games using repetition and motivational graphics. Performance data is downloaded over the Internet to Scientific Learning Corporation, which is then analyzed and available for interpretation by a licensed provider (speech and language pathologist). Isolation, identification, and discrimination of phonemes, which are the building blocks of language, can result in improved expressive and receptive language skills in many participants. For further information, visit the web site at **www.ScientificLearning.com.**

Note about Web Sites

There are many excellent sources of information available on-line. We have chosen not to list any particular web sites for two reasons: first, information is readily accessible through a word search and second, we cannot guarantee the reliability or accuracy of any information presented in this fashion. Users should exercise common sense, caution, and critical thinking when obtaining and implementing information via the Internet.

Appendix A: Classroom Strategies

1. Motivate on-task behavior.

"You can do your work at school or you can do it at home."
Use a daily report card to encourage and reward efforts. For example:

Daily Report Card for Monday, Sept. 23, 2003

Science (G)   Social Studies (G)   Math (U)

Reading (P)   Writing (R)   Spelling (G)

Penmanship (G)   Working with a partner (G)

Nice job on your plant observations with your partner!
I like your map of Africa too. Congratulations, you scored 100% on your spelling! You had nice, neat penmanship today.

You need to finish your math page at home. You scored 65% on your reading comprehension worksheet. You did not do your writing at school so you will have to do it at home.

70% or higher	G = Good Work!
50%-69%	P = Practice after you play
less than 50%	R = Re-do before you play
Unfinished	U= finish at home after you play
Disruption	D = lose play privileges

2. Quantify tasks whenever possible.

Create worksheets to supplement in-class instruction so that knowledge acquisition and comprehension can be assessed and rewarded using a percent score. For example, an introductory science lecture on plant life could be supplemented with the following multiple choice worksheet.

1. What part of the plant draws nutrients from the soil?
   a. the leaves   b. the roots   c. the stem
2. What is photosynthesis?
   a. Using sunlight to grow.
   b. Using photographs of plants.
   c. Using oxygen to produce carbon dioxide.

3. What is chlorophyll?
   a. The chemical that turns dying plants yellow.
   b. The chemical that turns living plants green.
   c. The chemical that turns leaves orange in the fall.

3. Require independence with information-seeking strategies.

"How can you find out what to do?"

"If you can't find out what to do, you won't get your work done. If you don't get your work done at school, you will have to do it at home, which means less play time." This may be included on the daily report card as a specific target behavior or may be incorporated into the expectations for each subject. Using the above example:

Finding out what to do (G)
Listen, look, ask last

> Great job looking at the directions on the board! You wrote a nice story about ants.

4. Require independent work for mastered activities.

Mastered tasks can be quantified using a task sheet that delineates required elements. For example:

Independent Reading Checklist:

Name _____ Date _____

Before I read:
Book Title _____

What do I already know about this subject? _____

Prediction: I think _____

Now I can read. After I read:
Something new I learned: _____

5. Create and use task cards for routine activities.

(See examples in the following section.) Routine activities are opportunities for success and can be supported using an index card file or spiral. Any frequent or daily activity can be listed on a card and the expectations delineated. Some typical routine activities include, but are certainly not limited to:

Bathroom Rules	Using the Library
Worksheet Strategies	Rules for Social Play
Keeping Busy	Reading Strategies
Finding out what to do	Writing Strategies
Using a Story Map	Penmanship
Lunch	Dismissal

6. Allow time for processing instructions and independent action.

Removal from the group setting may be helpful when auditory instructions become overwhelming. Allowing the child to complete a worksheet at his desk may result in more significant knowledge gains than passive participation in a group setting.

7. Prompt enough for success without promoting prompt dependency.

Adequate support should be provided to allow task completion, followed by fading of prompts to allow the development of independence. Written cue cards are an excellent means of transferring responsibility to the child.

Appendix B: General Instructions for Creating Worksheets

1. **Instruct** with a story or paragraph. Include immediate fill-in-the-blank questions in conjunction with instructive text. For example:

   Baseball is a sport. There are nine players on a baseball team. Players use a bat to swing and hit a ball that is pitched to them. Then they run around the bases to score runs. Whenever a player crosses home plate, one run is scored.

   How many players are on a baseball team? _____

2. **Multiple choice** questions eliminate word retrieval issues and give a better indication of knowledge acquisition than fill-in-the-blank questions, in the absence of an instructive text. Multiple choice questions can be used to determine knowledge acquisition when instruction is given in an auditory fashion. For example:

   True or False?

   1. Air that is heated expands.   T   F
   2. Air that is cooled expands.   T   F
   3. Air has no pressure.   T   F

   Choose the correct answer.

   1. What does "hemisphere" mean?
       a. A continent divided in half by mountains.
       b. One half of the globe.
       c. A map that shows physical features.
   2. What is the name of the line that divides the northern and southern hemispheres?
       a. The Greenwich Median
       b. The continental divide
       c. The equator
   3. Which continents are entirely in the southern hemisphere?
       a. South America and Africa
       b. South America and Asia
       c. Antartica and Australia

3. **Fill in** questions, in isolation from the instructive text, should follow up multiple choice to evaluate knowledge acquisition and retention. Initially a word bank may need to be provided. For example:
   1. The _____ is a pump that circulates blood throughout the body.
   2. The _____ are like balloons that expand when you breathe.
   3. The _____ is the control center of the body.
   4. The skeleton is made up of _____.

word bank:	
lungs	bones
heart	brain

4. **Recall,** such as generating a sentence or paragraph, requires the greatest effort. This should be done after the previous steps have been completed successfully. For example:
   1. Name the four things plants need to grow.
   2. What might happen to a plant that is put in a dark room?
   3. What does the word "drought" mean?

Appendix C: Task Cards for Routine Activities

Reading Strategies
1. Make a prediction in your Reading Journal.
2. Read the story first.
3. Write the date and title in your Reading Journal.
4. Reread to look for key words.
5. Write the key words in your Reading Journal.
6. Write the main idea in your Reading Journal.

Example:
1. "I think the story will be about a pet that gets lost."
2. I read the story "Sam's Canine Adventure."
3. Today is 9/23/03. Title: "Sam's Canine Adventure."
4. Key words: thin ice, rescue, hero.
5. "Sam the dog was a hero because he rescued the boy on the thin ice."

Strategies for Worksheets
1. Read the directions first.
2. Circle the action words that tell you what to do.
3. Do them in order.
4. Raise your hand if you need help.

Writing Strategies
1. Always write long sentences.
2. Use details to make it interesting.
3. Use your best, neat handwriting.
4. Use punctuation.

Writing with a Story Map
1. Fill in the middle circle with your story idea.
2. Fill in the outer circles with details.
3. Use the story idea for your title.
4. Write a sentence for each detail.

How to Find Out What to Do

Listen to the teacher's instructions.

Look at the instructions written on the board.
Look at what your friends are doing.

Ask a friend what you should do.
Ask the teacher if you still don't know what to do.

Penmanship
1. Watch the teacher demonstrate.
2. Practice writing neatly in your penmanship book.
3. When you are finished, show a friend.

Keeping Busy
1. Read from your book bag.
2. Write a letter to a friend.
3. Draw using your drawing book.

Dismiss
1. Quietly get your backpack.
2. Get everything out of your cubby.
3. Get your daily report card from the teacher.
4. Line up.

Finding a good library book
1. Think of a topic you like.
2. Find that section of books.
3. Choose a book. Mark the spot with your card.
4. Look inside the book:
    Too hard: put it back
    Too easy: put it back
    Just right: check it out!

Bathroom Rules
1. Only one morning break.
2. Only one afternoon break.
3. Only when you are at your desk, not during group times.
4. Only when there is a boy's pass available.
5. *Always* at lunch or recess.

Lunch
1. Stand in line to buy your milk.
2. Find a friend to sit next to.
3. Enjoy your lunch!
4. Today I'm going to talk to my friends about _____.

References

Freeman, S. & Lorelei, D. (1996-2003). Teach me language (2nd ed.). Langley, B.C: SKF Books, Inc.

Grandin, T. (1995). *Thinking in pictures.* NY:Vintage Books.

Gray, C. (1999). From both sides now: teaching social understanding with social stories and comic strip conversations. Council For Exceptional Children. 36(2), 14-19.

Howlin, O. (1997). Autism: preparing for adulthood. Andover: Routledge.

Maurice, C. (1996). *Behavioral interventions for young children with autism.* Austin: pro-ed.

Mesibov, G.B. (n.d.). *What is TEACCH?* Retrieved February 23, 2003, from http://www.teacch.com

Quirley S.P., McAnally, P.L., King, C.M., Rose, S. (1992). *Reading milestones teacher's guide.* Austin: pro-ed.

Quill, K.A. (1995). *Teaching children with autism: strategies to enhance communication and socialization.* NY: Delmar Publishers.

Safran, S.P. & Oswald, K. (2003). Positive behavior supports: can schools reshape disciplinary practices? *Exceptional Children*, 69(3), 361-373.

Stewart, R. (n.d.). Motivating students who have autism spectrum disorders: Indiana Resource Center for Autism Articles. Retrieved March 3, 2003, from http://www.iidc.indiana.edu/irca/education/motivate.html

Trehin, P. (n.d) Some basic information about TEACCH. Retrieved March 30, 2003, from http://www.autism-resources.com/papers/TEACCHN.htm

Ward, K. (updated 2001). Parent skill building series. Retrieved December 11, 2002, from http://www.autism.ca/sleep.htm

NOTES

NOTES

NOTES

NOTES

NOTES